"*Pious Ambitions* is a judicious, readable, and ⟨...⟩
pleasure to meet a latter-day heroine whose faith and heady portion of ambition
left a legacy for a university and a region."

—*Edwin G. Wilson, Wake Forest*
provost emeritus and professor of English

"From a riveting New England conversion-tale to a harrowing and hopeful
backwoods North Carolina journey, *Pious Ambitions* stands among the handful
of works that bring the early nineteenth century US vividly to life. Replete with
fascinating details about Sally Merriam Wait's world—her and surrounding
figures' passions, torments, sorrows, and joys—this beautifully crafted study is
an instant classic in the fields of historiography and gender studies alike."

—*Rogan Kersh, Provost and Professor of Politics &*
International Affairs, Wake Forest University

"The story of Sally Merriam Wait provides a productive prism to unpack the
cultural pressures, political developments, and religious piety of a fracturing
evangelical movement in nineteenth century America. *Pious Ambitions* captures
the complex contours of this hyper-gendered and racially stratified world that
continues to shape our contemporary context."

—*Jonathan Lee Walton, Dean of the School of Divinity and Presidential*
Chair in Religion & Society, Wake Forest University

"*Pious Ambitions* is a vivid and valuable study of Baptist culture in the Early
Republic. The story does a wonderful job of capturing the balancing of
submission and ambition among evangelical women."

—*Christine Heyrman, Robert W. and*
Shirley P. Grimble Professor of American History

"In this elegantly written and engaging cultural biography, we learn how young
Sally Merriam Wait's evangelical conversion in New England sent her on a
southbound search for more voice and opportunity at the end of the Early
Republic. This beguiling Baptist minister's wife who once dreamed of serving
as a missionary in Burma, fought against gendered inequalities and constraints,
but too often to no avail, serving instead as exemplary helpmeet to her
husband's quest for opportunity and status. Tribble handles the complexities
and disappointments of Wait's transformation into a slaveholding North
Carolinian with clarity and honesty."

—*Michele Gillespie, Presidential Endowed Chair*
of Southern History, Wake Forest University

"Ambition can propel us to achieve our highest aspirations. It can also blind us to injustices in our society and world. With deft insight and critical compassion Mary Tribble's *Pious Ambitions: Sally Merriam Wait's Mission South, 1813–1831* troubles the smooth texture of Sally Wait's writings in revealing the complex and, at times, competing aims at work in her life and world.

—*Corey D. B. Walker, Wake Forest Professor of the Humanities, Wake Forest University*

"Mary Tribble's fascinating study of Sally Merriam Wait gives voice to a remarkable nineteenth century woman as she encountered her times. Using journals and correspondence not previously studied, Tribble demonstrates how Wait becomes a case study in the way in which one Baptist woman appropriated and advocated for revivalistic spirituality, missionary imperatives, and the need for educational institutions in the American South. Sally Wait's long neglected story needed to be told."

—*Bill Leonard, Dunn Professor of Baptist Studies and Church History Emeritus, Wake Forest University*

PIOUS AMBITIONS

Sally Merriam's

Journal

Continued.

"Soon fades the flower,
Soon [...] the reaper breath,
In midst of life,
we tread the verge of death."

Pious Ambitions

Sally Merriam Wait's Mission South, 1813–1831

MARY TRIBBLE

AMERICA'S BAPTISTS
Keith Harper, *Series Editor*

THE UNIVERSITY OF TENNESSEE PRESS
Knoxville

To Jan & Dave,
Fellow deacons!
I hope you enjoy
Sally's story — a
little bit of WF
history!
All the
Best!
Mary

The America's Baptists series will bring broader understanding of the places Baptists have occupied in American life. Many of these works will be historical monographs, but the series will embrace different types of primary and secondary works, including but not limited to annotated collections of diaries, letters, and personal reflections as well as biographies and essay collections.

Frontispiece: The title page of Sally's journal, 1815–1817, reads "Sally Merriam's Journal Continued," indicating an earlier version existed. Unfortunately, it has been lost or destroyed. © Special Collections & University Archives/Wake Forest University; photo by Ken Bennett.

LIBRARY OF CONGRESS CATALOGING-IN-PUBLICATION DATA
Names: Tribble, Mary, author.
Title: Pious ambitions : Sally Merriam Wait's mission south, 1813–1831 /
  Mary Tribble.
Description: First edition. | Knoxville : The University of Tennessee Press, 2021.
Series: America's Baptists | Includes bibliographical references and index. |
Summary: "Mary Tribble mines a journal and a trove of letters from the Special Collections and Archives of Z. Smith Reynolds Library at Wake Forest University to introduce
  a significant figure in North Carolina and Baptist history. The writings of Sally Merriam
  Wait reveal a northernborn woman with antislavery leanings engaging with an unfamiliar
  environment in the slaveholding South. Her ambitions lead her from young convert in
  revival-swept New England to devoted wife of Reverend Samuel Wait, the first president
  and founder of Wake Forest University. Her decisions are shaped by a surging evangelical
  movement, changes in the American economy, the rise of women's social agency, fracturing political traditions, and the moral conflicts inherent in a slave economy. Tribble's study
  provides a rare glimpse into the spiritual and worldly education of a young woman of faith
  at the dawn of market capitalism in Jacksonian America"— Provided by publisher.
Identifiers: LCCN 2021031086 (print) | LCCN 2021031087 (ebook) |
  ISBN 9781621906834 (hardcover) | ISBN 9781621906841 (pdf) |
  ISBN 9781621906858 (kindle edition)
Subjects: LCSH: Wait, Sarah Merriam, 1794–1871. | Spouses of clergy—North Carolina—
  Biography. | Baptists—North Carolina—Biography. | Baptists—Missions—North
  Carolina. | North Carolina—Church history—19th century.
Classification: LCC BX6495.W275 T75 2021 (print) | LCC BX6495.W275 (ebook) |
  DDC 286/.1092 [B]—dc23

LC record available at https://lccn.loc.gov/2021031086
LC ebook record available at https://lccn.loc.gov/2021031087

TO THE WOMEN WHO
PRESERVED THE ARCHIVES

Sarah
Sally
Ann Eliza
Sally
K.T.
Lib
Byrd

CONTENTS

FIGURES

FOREWORD
Keith Harper

Ambition. It sets a trajectory for motivated people to follow. It fuels accomplishment. But the Bible teaches that Christ's followers are to be meek and lowly, servants to the needy. Is it possible to be a dedicated Christian *and* ambitious? Mary Tribble points to Sally Merriam Wait as an example.

What separates "pious ambitions" from other ambitions? Is it the opportunities one encounters? Is it the choices one makes? Or is it what undergirds those ambitions that really sets them apart in some way? As a young woman in the Early Republic, Wait did not lack opportunities. The nation was expanding westward at a phenomenal pace. Moreover, the revivalism and the mission movement occupied the thoughts of many Christian youth. While there is extensive scholarship on men who experienced the Second Great Awakening colliding with the Market Revolution, the experiences of women in this time are sparsely documented. Because Sally's journals, letters, and other documents have been preserved, Tribble is able to draw upon them to create a rare, nuanced view of how one woman navigated her religious calling and her worldly pursuits. Her diaries and correspondence reveal that Sally absorbed stories of Ann Hasseltine Judson and Harriet Atwood Newell, heroic missionaries to exotic lands, and she longed to be like them. When she met Samuel Wait it appeared that Providence had smiled upon her. They would marry, raise a family, and serve fulfilling lives together. In a fairy tale, one might read "and they lived happily ever after." But this is no fairy tale.

Sally's marriage to Samuel was not the end of her story. Rather, it is more like the beginning. In marriage, Sally learned that ambition did not necessarily follow the path that she might have charted for herself. Throughout her life of service she found herself separated from her husband for extended periods of time. Neither did her life of service lead her to an exotic, far-away land. Rather, she left her native Vermont and ultimately settled in Wake Forest, North Carolina. Samuel was a fund raiser and administrator at the institution that would become Wake Forest College, not the pastor of a prestigious church on the town square. Perhaps most surprising for someone who had grown up in Vermont, Sally embraced slavery in her service with her husband at the fledgling college, much to the consternation of her antislavery family.

The life that Sally Merriam Wait dreamed of as a young girl was not the life she lived as a mature woman. Over time she learned that "pious ambitions" involved the sacrifice not only of where she might prefer to live, but the type of service she would offer to God. In the end maybe ambition is not about what you want to accomplish, but rather what you are willing to surrender in pursuit of a higher goal or calling. For Sally, that meant being a helpmeet and doing what she believed to be her duty. Mary Tribble tells her story with graceful clarity, and the University of Tennessee Press is pleased to present it.

KEITH HARPER
Southeastern Baptist Theological Seminary

ACKNOWLEDGMENTS

Jake Ruddiman guided me on every step of this journey. He challenged my thinking, answered my late-night emails, and reassured me when I cried in the archives. Bill Leonard shared his deep knowledge of Baptist history, which helped me understand Sally and Samuel's world. Michele Gillespie inspired me to dig deep for Sally's truth. Thank you. The future of the past is safe in your hands. I learned from, and was encouraged by, many faculty members, students, alumni, and administrators at Wake Forest University. The Liberal Studies Department and the Slavery, Race and Memory Project gave me the context I needed to interpret Sally's story. I am grateful to Andrew Canady, who was a resource and sounding board along the way. The archivists and experts at Z. Smith Reynolds Library spent many hours assisting me in my research. The historians and scholars who connected me to the sites where Sally lived have been generous with their time and knowledge, especially Ed Morris and his team at the Wake Forest Historical Museum. A special thanks goes to Faith Claussens, who invited me into the Brandon Baptist Church archives when I showed up one Sunday morning. Jill Santuccio, Lyn Tribble, Katie Hall, and Audrey Mayville provided editing and moral support, and Michelle Guiliano provided excellent indexing skills. I am appreciative of Scot Danforth and Keith Harper of the University of Tennessee Press, who believed in this project from the minute I brought it to them. Thanks to my friends and colleagues in Alumni Hall who supported me and gave me grace along the way. When I returned to Wake Forest University after three decades, it was my mother, Byrd Barnette Tribble, who reconnected me to its past. It has been an honor and delight to continue the research she began more than twenty years ago. She, my sister Lyn, my brother Lewis, and the rest of my family have given me inspiration and support.

INTRODUCTION

This would be the seventh burial in as many weeks.

Mr. McGregore and his wife. Mr. Meachem and his three-year-old son. Deacon Barr, then Marcy Hale.[1] The epidemic had settled onto Brandon, a quiet town nestled between the green mountains of Vermont and Lake Champlain on the border of upstate New York. Sally pulled on her wool pelisse to guard against the gloomy spring morning. She had become used to the sight of bedside vigils, the smell of disease, the sound of a death rattle. But Nabby's death was different. To Sally, it became something much more. Abigail Farrington—no one called her that, they all knew her as Nabby—had been "cut off from her prime and usefulness," as the *Rutland Herald* reported.[2] Nabby was not popular because of her father's distinguished service in the current war with the British, nor her family's place of respect at the Brandon Baptist Church, although both were important predictors of virtue. Judging from the newspaper report, Nabby had won the town's heart with her Christian goodness.

News of Nabby's death probably brought nineteen-year-old Sally Merriam to her knees in a "feast of tears," as she called her solitary explorations into regret and redemption. She gave herself over to these liberations freely; in fact, she conjured them up. Some Sundays, she stayed behind while the family went to church meeting. In these rare moments away from others, Sally paced the house, wrote in her journal, cried, and prayed aloud.[3] To one unfamiliar with the dynamics of the world around her, Sally's "feasts" might seem to cross the blurry border between religious reverie and madness. To a young woman facing the uncertainty of the times, they were anything but extraordinary. The year 1812 had been a frightening one for citizens of the emerging American republic. Typhoid and spotted fever swept through New England. War and weather had brought horrors and hardship. In the South, a terrifying fire in a Richmond theater killed hundreds, fueling fears of insurrection, even after the rumors of an enslaved arsonist proved untrue. Farther afield but no less talked about, thousands had perished in an earthquake in South America that was felt all the way to the Ohio Valley. Perhaps these were the harbingers of end times that Elder Young preached about from his pulpit and Uncle John warned of over supper. Now sixteen-year-old Nabby Farrington had succumbed to typhoid and was to be buried that very morning. Sally was shaken. Surely it was time to save her soul.

We do not know the exact details of Sally's conversion that day. From a poem written by William McKinney, a friend of Nabby's, perhaps Sally was among the "six fond mates [who] did kindly drop a tear, and marched in woe to grave the funeral bier."[4] However it unfolded, Sally emerged that afternoon a transformed woman, later writing, "How bright and resplendent shone the sun . . . Jesus said to me daughter be of good cheer thy sins are forgiven thee." The clouds had parted and the "enormous load of sin and guilt" was lifted.[5] Two months later, Sally waded into the chilly Neshobe River to experience the Baptist ritual of cleansing and rebirth.[6] But it was not her baptism she commemorated every year; it was the third of April—the day of Nabby's funeral—that defined her life.

Sally grew up in a time of religious fervor, when revivals swept the New England landscape like a series of barely controlled brush fires. Evangelical Protestant preachers staged camp meetings that lasted for days and drew sometimes thousands of the curious and the contrite. While individual denominations conducted revivals, Congregationalists, Presbyterians, Methodists, Baptists, and others presented a united front in the burgeoning evangelical movement, forming national societies to further their mission. Conversion represented a key moment in their coming of age for young people, even if, like Sally, they had been raised in an evangelical church. Conversion marked a graduation into adulthood that signified the transition from childish frivolities to pious living, moving from relative carelessness to responsibility. Most religious memoirs of the day recount a recursive experience of conversion characterized by a shaken faith alternating with prayerful reconviction. Sally's story was no different. Although she did try to "live devoted to Him all the days" of her life, Sally continued to worry about her "crime of breaking the promises so freely made." In times of trial, Sally turned to God for forgiveness, writing, "Oh, I can say nothing in favor of myself but must smite on my breast and say God be merciful to me a Sinner."[7] On April 3, 1813, at Nabby Farrington's funeral, what seemed a culminating moment of epiphany was in reality the threshold to a lifelong struggle between doubt and faith. It was both the ending and the beginning of her search for meaning.

Sally outlined the details of her conversion in a small journal featuring two important figures in her development: Ann Hasseltine Judson, a Baptist missionary to Burma who became a heroic model for Sally's life, and Samuel Wait, a hopeful minister whom she chose as a life partner to facilitate her pious ambitions. Her journal, 6¼ x 4 inches and a half-inch thick, was passed down carefully from generation to generation until it found its way in 1993 to the Special Collections and Archives at Z. Smith

Reynolds Library at Wake Forest University in Winston-Salem, North Carolina, along with a large cache of letters and other documents. Sally's journal and correspondence provide the bulk of the primary sources that inform this work. In addition, I have had access to a handful of letters and a small essay book that are still in the family collection, as well as the handwritten records of the Brandon Baptist Church. The manuscripts provide dates, names, and locations that piece together the events of Sally's early life.

But it is not the simple facts of Sally's writings that help us understand her; it is the nature of the texts themselves that give us nuanced insights into her state of mind. In these surviving sources we witness Sally write herself into being. Her missives and musings reveal the transition from an aspirational missionary to a measured theologian and ministerial helpmeet. Sally's voice transformed as she was influenced by relationships, achievements, and heartbreaking setbacks that shaped her life. Through her intimate and sometimes performative words, we read the articulation of her highest ideals and her most vulnerable doubts.

This narrative begins with Sally's emotional conversion in 1813 and concludes eighteen years later, when Sally follows the call from New England to North Carolina in 1831. At the start of this story, Sally is nineteen, living in her parents' home; in the end, she is thirty-seven and traveling the backwoods of North Carolina in a covered jersey wagon with her husband and young daughter, on the eve of their founding of Wake Forest College (now University). While the establishment of the college would be considered their most significant achievement, I deliberately chose to focus on the early chapters of Sally's life to establish an understanding of the events and people who influenced the early life choices of a young woman coming of age during the Early Republic. What circumstances drew Sally to conversion and Baptist missions? What called her to marry Samuel Wait? What drew the couple to minister to a small Massachusetts church, and what called them away? How were they thrust into the Washington, DC Baptist elite, where they networked with politicians and patricians to advance religious education and missions? Why, to the dismay of Sally's Vermont antislavery family, did they end up permanently in the slaveholding South?

A common theme informs the story of Sally's early life and the broader narrative of the market, ministry, and missions of the Early American Republic: ambition. In the colonial and revolutionary eras of America, ambition was what J. M. Opal described as "rare, exotic, and dangerous," until emerging in the early nineteenth century as our "national creed," when the "prevailing values of a rural and household-based society gave way to those of an urban and individualized one."[8] While secular ambition was focused on upward mobility through the new market opportunities off the farm, the evangelical movement framed ambition through the more pious language of duty. Aspiring ministers or missionaries were given the permission to be ambitious "while combating the worldly visions of that very passion."[9] This held true for women as well: while a materially ambitious woman might be looked down upon, a selfless woman aspiring toward a greater good was heralded. The evangelical mission movement produced high-profile women who served their husbands as religious "helpmeets," providing women like Sally "pious, socially acceptable heroines who were also well-educated, ambitious and adventurous."[10]

It was the power of pious ambition that guided Sally Merriam Wait's journey from convert to helpmeet. Her decisions were shaped by complexities of the evangelical movement, changes in the American economy, the rise and tensions of women's social agency, the fracturing of political tradition, and moral conflicts inherent in a slave economy. Sally's story is the tale of a nineteenth-century woman aspiring to make her mark on the world.

PIOUS AMBITIONS

Part One

SOON FADES THE FLOWER

One

AWAKENING

> I was a poor helpless creature. I felt as though
> I should eternally perish if left to myself.
>
> —Sally Merriam, May 23, 1817

SALLY LISTENED FOR FOOTFALLS ON THE WOODEN FLOORS below. Skirts rustling. Doors closing. Outside, a horse whinnied and thumped its hooves against the ground. A wagon's chassis groaned as the passengers climbed aboard. When the muffled voices of her family became more distant, Sally relaxed, relieved to enjoy a rare moment of solitude from a house full of people, especially her younger brothers. They would be gone for several hours, attending a day of "fasting and humiliation and prayer" that had been called by the brethren in the Brandon Baptist Church. Sally usually enjoyed public worship in the church she had officially joined nearly four years earlier, but today she had invented an excuse to stay back, craving quiet communion with God to retire and "pour out" her soul.[1] It was not long, however, before "Satan came . . . meeting [her] with temptations on every hand." Sally "walked the room," trying to collect her "distracted thoughts and fasten [her] mind on God." But the "poisonous malignant darts of the adversary" flew around her. Plunged into self-doubt, Sally "flung [herself] onto [her] knees before God and cried to him for succor." After confessing her sins and entreating God for mercy, "the tempter flew, [her] soul was set at liberty and [her] tongue was loosed." Sally "melted into contrition before him." At the end of this clash between her pious ideals and all-too-human failings, Sally presumably smoothed her clothes and dried her face, composing herself before her family's return. "I enjoyed a refreshing season," she reported with dry satisfaction.[2]

This was not the first nor the last time Sally found herself on her knees in spiritual turmoil. While her conversion a few years earlier became the fulcrum of her life, it did not provide the "permanent peace and joy" that some nineteenth-century ministers had promised.[3] Rebirth as a permanent state was an ideal continually threatened with the uncertainties of the human experience. To appreciate the tension of Sally's salvific state, it is helpful to view her life in the context of what is now called the Second Great Awakening. Sally's awakening unfolded during a time of tremendous change for professors of faith. During her young life she was influenced by the conversion narrative of the great eighteenth-century evangelical Jonathan Edwards and the modern missionary movement that emerged through the work of William Carey. Examining the issues that influenced her decisions provides the context for Sally's life as a case study in the religious, social, political, and gendered changes during the Early Republic, wrapped in a mantle of ambition in a uniquely aspirational place and time.

Sally Merriam grew up in a comfortable home in Brandon, Vermont. Her father, Jonathan Merriam, was a farmer and tradesman. He held various town offices and was a deacon in the Baptist church. Sally's mother, Sarah Conant Merriam, was the sister of the venerable John Conant, who upon his arrival in Brandon in 1795 acquired a critical parcel of land that would provide all the waterpower in the village.[4] He continued his entrepreneurial efforts by opening a shop, building a stone gristmill, a brick mill, and a furnace for the casting of Conant Cook Stoves in 1819. A major employer in Brandon, Conant was also a powerful town father, holding a number of public offices including postmaster and justice of the peace.[5] In short, Uncle John literally and figuratively held the power in the town where Sally and her family lived. While Conant was a wealthy town dweller, Sally's family eked out a more modest living just outside town on a piece of land later known as the Briggs farm, on what now is Route 7.[6] Beginning in 1787, members of the Merriam and Conant clan migrated west in dribs and drabs, moving from Ashburnham, Massachusetts, and Walpole, New Hampshire.[7] Arriving fifteen years after the incorporation of Brandon as a town, they were not the first white settlers there, but like similar families in the Early Republic, they saw an opportunity to band together, buy inexpensive land, and contribute the various skills necessary to build a town, as if from scratch.[8] By the time they arrived, the native population, consisting of primarily Ibenaki people, had been virtually destroyed, casualties of the brutal French and Indian War that opened up the region for settlement, proving that ambition often came at the price of others.[9]

At the dawn of the nineteenth century, family farms were the engine of rural life in New England, creating a self-sufficient economy where the family grew and manufactured products to satisfy many of their own needs and traded through an elaborate system of accounts with other farmers and tradesmen.[10] The 1810 census indicates that the Merriam household owned two linen wheels, two spinning wheels, a loom, ninety yards of wool cloth, two hundred yards of linen cloth, and thirty sheep.[11] They grew apples and made applesauce, pork butter, and flour.[12] It is also likely they grew wheat and flax, as well as rye, corn, and potatoes, as most farmers in the area did.[13] While Sally's family did not share the enormous wealth of John Conant, they certainly, by association, lacked little and enjoyed influence in the community.[14]

While this description may evoke visions of bucolic nineteenth-century life, the reality was darkly complex, as Sally's conversion narrative reveals. A critical component of Sally's spiritual awakening was the overwhelming and persistent threat of an early death that might come without the blessing of God's grace. For Sally, this fear was influenced by the apocalyptic sermons she heard from the pulpit as well as the personal loss she experienced around her as neighbors and friends fell to illness or harm. In the April 7, 1813 issue of the Vermont *Rutland Herald*, a death notice stands out: "In Brandon, on the 31st ult[imo] Nabby Farrington, amiable daughter of Daniel Farrington Esq., discharged the last debt due to nature after an illness of four days, aged 16 years: cut off in the prime of youth in the midst of her usefulness the pride and boast of her connections and friends. She died a glorious proof of the immortality of the soul; the uncertainty of life, and the satisfaction which flows from religion in a dying hour."[15]

Nabby's death is noteworthy for several reasons. First, thirteen of the fifteen deaths that week warranted only a single line in the *Rutland Herald*. That a sixteen-year-old girl merited so extensive an obituary was a testament to her father's status as a town military hero and statesman as well as her own popularity.[16] Secondly, Nabby's death occurred at the height of a typhoid epidemic in 1812 and 1813. The *Vermont Historical Gazetteer* reported that upwards of sixty people died in the region within a three-month time frame.[17] Given that the population of Brandon in 1820 was just under fifteen hundred, these deaths surely made a grim impression on the living.[18] Three days later, Sally Merriam experienced her conversion. She carefully copied and preserved a poem, titled "A poem written by William A. Finney April 4, 1813, on the occasion of the death of Abigail Farrington," which remains in the Wake Forest University archives. In it, the poet bemoans the loss of "virtue's fallen gem, A half blown rosy plucked from its stem." Young Nabby's funeral, which appears to have taken place on April 3, was attended by a group of her young friends in mourning, most likely including Sally Merriam. Sally's journal indicates that this was the day of her own emotional religious awakening. While it is unlikely Nabby's was the first death Sally experienced, the demise of a popular young friend so close to Sally's age seems to have made a lasting impression on her as well as her friends in Brandon. At a meeting of the Brandon Baptist Church elders a few weeks later, church secretary (and Sally's uncle) John Conant remarked, "There appears . . . an uncommon solemnity . . . on the minds of the youth in this town. . . . Some few are hopefully converted."[19] It is no wonder, with many of their friends dying, that young people would be motivated to repent.

On a more existential level, Sally's fear of dying without salvation was influenced by a pervasive opinion that the end times were near. The possibility of a nearing apocalypse was preached from the pulpit and discussed around the hearth. In the letter that accompanied the 1813 minutes of the Vermont Baptist Association, the writer starts, "The shaking tempest has now begun, God has taken his fan in his hand, and will thoroughly purge his civil and ecclesiastical floor." Sally's uncles John Conant and Isaac Merriam were present at the October 7 meeting when the circular was submitted for approval.[20] Surely the prospect of the apocalypse came up over dinner in the Merriam-Conant household; the specter of death is a recurrent theme throughout Sally's early writings. In fact, it presages and unifies her entire journal, beginning with this poetic fragment on the opening page:

> Soon fades the flower,
> Soon fleets the zephyrs breath
> In midst of life,
> We tread the verge of death.[21]

That Sally organized her journal around this foreboding theme reveals the degree to which it guided this stage of a young New England girl's life. The verse Sally chose to begin her journal came from a poem written by William Leigh Pierce, a young man living in Canandaigua, New York. Published in May 1813, "The Year" is a dramatic recitation of the political and natural events of the previous year. A poem with a Federalist slant, "The Year" comments on a variety of disasters and conflicts, such as devastating earthquakes in the Ohio Valley and Venezuela; a frightful theater fire in Richmond, Virginia; American patriots' battles against Indians and the British; and a Republican/Federalist riot in Baltimore.[22] The account includes gripping descriptions of death and destruction, reinforcing the notion that the end times were nigh. In an ironic footnote that seems to prove the author's point: William Leigh Pierce died of typhoid the following year, at twenty-four years of age.[23]

The events leading up to Sally Merriam's conversion in April 1813 were filled with death. War, illness, and natural disasters were ever-present reminders of the fragility of life and the vulnerability of a young person's soul. The threat of dying prior to achieving salvation was a powerful motivator to convert and lead a life according to God's will. This fear created a sense of urgency that appears again and again throughout Sally's early writings, especially in her journal. Sally's concerns about the state of her salvation vacillated nearly daily. She adopted the language of Jonathan Edwards and then honed it by reading the missives of Sarah Osborn, Harriet Atwood Newell, and other evangelistic women of the late eighteenth and early nineteenth centuries. As an example, on April 3, 1816, her "spiritual birthday," Sally writes, "How sweet was the society of the Saints and how did my heart exult whenever they repeated the name of the adorable Jesus."[24] Happiness and awe filled Sally's memory of her conversion until she recalled how she had fallen short of her promise to God. Then, doubt and despair revealed her shame: "How dreadful appears the crime of breaking so many promises I so freely made. O! I can say nothing in favor of myself but must smite on my breast and say God be merciful to me a Sinner."[25] We can compare Sally's language to a passage by Sarah Osborn, an eighteenth-century Rhode Island revivalist, whose memoir was first published by her Congregationalist minister Samuel Hopkins in Worcester, Massachusetts in 1799.[26] Osborn writes, "And yet, Lord, thou who knowest all things, knowest I love thee. O then, grant my request, and enable me better to keep thy commandments. . . . I love thy precepts, as well as thy benefits: And yet I break them all. Oh wretched one that I am!"[27] It is possible Sally had access to the 1814 edition of Osborn's memoir, as it was published in Catskill, New York, just 140 miles south of her town. Missionary Harriet Newell's memoir, also published in 1814, includes similar language, as she writes, "How great are the changes that take place in my mind in the course of a day! I have felt deeply despaired for the depravity of my heart . . . but the light of divine truth this evening has irradiated my soul."[28] The recursive uncertainty of Sally's salvation and her fear of an early death created a backdrop of both urgency and measured deliberation during her courtship that was to come. Like other evangelicals of her day, Sally careened from hope, to despair, to resolve, to refreshment and then back again to hope.

Following the strictures of the newly converted, Sally often took advantage of significant dates to examine the progress of her life and the state of her salvation. She paused for self-reflection on her spiritual birthday, at Easter, upon each new year, and on her actual birthday in late August 1815, when she wrote, "Another year of my short life has closed. A few more setting suns or a few more years at most and I also shall close my pilgrimage and enter the grave." A few weeks later, she returned to her theme of urgency, lamenting how she had wasted her short life. "I have spent twenty one years of precious time in doing nothing. Surely now it is time to be about my Master's business. O that God would give me grace that I might run and not be weary, walk and not faint."[29]

For inspiration to create a life as an agent for Christ, Sally found female role models featured not only in memoirs, but also in religious publications of her time. On September 19, 1815, she wrote in her journal about two such women, Ann Hasseltine Judson and Harriet Atwood Newell, Baptist missionaries to Burma. "Last evening I had the happiness of perusing a letter from Mrs. Judson to Mrs. Newell. Everything that comes from that quarter is to me highly interesting," Sally wrote. "Sometimes I felt all the zeal of the pious devoted missionary and was ready to sacrifice every enjoyment however endearing to promote the cause of Immanuel."[30] In this entry, Sally seemed to be trying on the role of missionary, flirting with the emotions that such a pious sacrifice might require. To travel to places like India or Burma was high adventure and a life-risking decision. Harriet, in fact, tragically died on an ocean voyage early in her mission, elevating her to martyrdom status in Sally's eyes. "May her piety and virtue serve to succeeding ages as a stimulus to females in particular to be active in the cause of the Redeemer."[31] Sally's "cause of the Redeemer" focused on the marriage of ministry and mission in the modified Calvinist tradition that Sally followed. She was not alone in her admiration of Newell; after Newell's death, dozens of editions of a posthumous memoir were published, and New Englanders named daughters and ships after her.[32] While Harriett Newell's early death inspired avid readers of her memoir, Ann Judson's life in Burma became legendary in the coming decade, with thousands of readers following her exploits through religious tracts.

In the late eighteenth century, evangelizing the faith became fundamental to the expansion of the denomination, when British Baptist leaders Andrew Fuller and William Carey, in a departure from accepted Calvinist doctrine, promoted evangelism as a defining yet controversial characteristic of the Baptist church. As the editors of *Baptists Roots* point out, "The powerful voice of William Carey (1761–1834) could be heard summoning all who believe in Jesus to share the Good News with the 'heathen.'"[33] Religious publications challenged Americans to emulate their British brethren, referring "to 'the amazing power, which American Christians may now exert upon the destinies of men' . . . that New Englanders viewed as gifts from an omnipotent God."[34] Answering this call, Ann Judson and Harriet Newell sailed from Salem, Massachusetts for India with their husbands Adoniram and Samuel in 1814. Most newspaper accounts of the sailing referred only to the ordained missionaries—in other words, the men. However, within a few years, religious tracts and newspapers breathlessly reported the impact of the missionaries' wives, specifically Ann Hasseltine Judson, who became an icon for thousands of evangelical women in England and America. Her mission to convert the "savages" in the remote country of Burma was described as "wild and romantic in the extreme."[35] By traveling to an untamed wilderness like Burma, Ann embodied the romantic ideal of spiritual transcendence through an evangelical lens. In its way, the evangelical cause lashed itself to the Romantic movement, which would inspire a generation of women to move from the background to becoming a force of their own. In a time when women were constrained by patriarchal society, missions and ministry became a viable alternative for a woman wanting to make her mark on the world. As more women like Judson traveled to Asia as missionaries, publications about their travels and travails "capitalized on the potent combination of education, revivalism, and limited career opportunities available to young white women in the Northeast."[36] Thousands of New England women read the stories about Ann Judson and other women missionaries, vowing to follow in their footsteps.

Indeed, it could be argued that foreign missions had more impact in saving souls in America than abroad, with their contribution of evangelical excitement to the domestic scene. As Charles Foster wrote, "Evangelical sermons on foreign missions were stirring: they carried the roll of drums . . . the confident promise of victory under command of a glorious leader. . . . Returning missionaries enthralled congregations with their tales of heathen horrors. . . . Excitement helped to make the wheels go round."[37] The feverish evangelical narrative initially brought more Americans to Christianity than citizens of Burma, for instance, as it was six years before the Judsons had their first convert.[38]

When Sally wrote her journal entry about the Burma mission, she was likely citing the September issue of the *Massachusetts Baptist Missionary*

Magazine, which featured a full report on Harriet's death. Widely circulated throughout New England, this quarterly tract provided essays on theology, news of church leadership, and fascinating reports from missions around the world, all of which Sally anticipated with great interest. As the evolving Judson story riveted both the United States and England, religious papers on both sides of the Atlantic increased their distribution of missionary stories. These tales had a particularly enthusiastic audience in women, and the Baptists increased their promotion to the female market accordingly. Between 1812 and 1817, the number of features on godly women in the *Massachusetts Baptist Missionary Magazine* increased dramatically, with some issues devoted to the theme.[39] The female role models they featured gave Baptist women like Sally a roadmap to their calling. They highlighted women at home supporting their minister husbands, as well as the piously adventurous Ann Judson who braved the wilds of the East to fulfill her redeemer's call. While following Ann's story, Sally imagined herself as a heroine in God's cause to convert infidels. She would continue, throughout her life, to reference Ann's pious sacrifice as an example to follow, giving her the fortitude and resilience she needed to overcome obstacles in her own life.

When Sally converted in 1813, there were limits to the influence that women could exert in the church. While the Baptist power structure enfolded women into church life, they could not be ordained nor serve as deacons. Women had to operate within the sphere dictated to them: as helpmates to their husbands and tending to the other women of their flock. Ann Hasseltine Judson gave women like Sally Merriam permission to explore their calling while still adhering to boundaries of the women's sphere. It would be several years before female missionaries were sent into missionary fields without their husbands, and even then it was rare. Because of this, the recommended and logical course for a pious woman like Sally was to find a husband to complement her desired calling. As we will see, one very suitable prospect showed up in Brandon in 1815.

Two

BECOMING

Brother Isaac joins with me in requesting a copy
of Sister Sally's essay on the divinity of Christ.

—Jonathan Merriam Jr., July 26, 1818

IN THE TRANSFORMATIVE YEARS FOLLOWING SALLY'S
awakening at Brandon Baptist Church, she pondered the tenets of her
faith through reading, reflection, Christian conversation, and writing. As
people often do during times of transition, Sally turned to pen and ink to
aid in her self-discovery. Sally wrote her way through this time of intense
change, emerging from girlhood to become a woman confident in her theology of thought. The extant documents from this part of her life include
a journal, a small essay book, and several letters. Through these sources,
we get a glimpse of Sally's identity in formation, as she, in essence, writes
herself into her ideal of pious womanhood. By the time she married in
1818, Sally's theological voice was developed enough to inspire her older
brothers Isaac and Jonathan, then studying for the ministry, to ask Sally
and Samuel to send them a copy of her essay on the divinity of Christ, a
complex topic for even the most studied theologian. In making the request,
Jonathan asked her to "copy it in the form of a book and send it by mail
in an open letter which may be done without adding her signature."[1] It is
unclear whether they planned to study, share, or plagiarize their younger
sister's work, but the fact that they requested it demonstrates the respect
they had for Sally's theological thinking.

Just months before her conversion, Sally began recording her reflections in an essay on greatness, "one of the first objects of pursuit." She wrote in an exquisitely steady hand in a small booklet with a cover of gray paper that she may have purchased at a store such as Fay and Davidson, where she shopped in nearby Rutland, that advertised "Memorandum Books with Pencils, Writing Books."[2] This writing form, generally known as keeping a commonplace book, was a widely encouraged formula for people to collect original and copied essays, letters, and poetry. Recommended by leaders as diverse as philosopher John Locke and Congregationalist Jonathan Edwards, keeping a commonplace was an opportunity for self-reflection, a place to cull through conflicting ideological debates of the day, and, either by contributing original essays or copying those of others, to create one's private and public identity.

In his 1770 commencement speech to the graduates of Bristol Baptist College, Caleb Evans warned the would-be ministers not to waste time reading useless books or sleeping more than six hours a night. The respected theologian recommended a vigorous course of study and reflection, instructing students to use a "common-place book . . . to insert abstracts of what you read on all subjects . . . for sensibly accumulating a flock of useful knowledge." This recommendation made its way across the Atlantic and was adopted by New World evangelicals, who used the commonplace form to explore theological issues in addition to the moral and educational topics their more secular contemporaries studied.[3] As a newly converted young woman in Brandon, Sally took to this advice diligently, using her commonplace to make original entries as well as to copy notable texts.

Sally's commonplace book is a collection of original essays, copied poetry, and letters of advice she had written to a young friend. She wrote her first entry on "true Greatness" just months before her baptism at Brandon Baptist Church. During the next several years, Sally developed her emerging theology by writing essays and instructional letters to a young friend or relative named Alvira. Her essays are on thoughtfully investigated topics and written in a formal and measured manner. Overlapping the time span of her commonplace is a journal whose entries span from August 24, 1815 to July 10, 1817. Patterned after published memoirs of pious women, Sally's journal reveals the inner turmoil of a humble Christian filled with doubts about her salvation. Where Sally's commonplace is deliberate and academic, her journal is an emotional rollercoaster of intense remorse, grateful reflection, desperate prayers, and recursive hope for salvation. Sally also enjoyed written correspondence with friends and family, but other than the two letters to Alvira copied in her commonplace, there are only a few other pieces of correspondence from this time, including a persuasive 1813 epistle to her brother Jonathan pleading for his conversion to Christ. These early first-person sources—her commonplace book, her journal, and a handful of letters—vary in content, purpose, and voice. Her journal is written from the point of view of a converted sinner in search of salvific affirmation. Her letters also have an evangelical voice, but they are seasoned with the tone of a concerned friend or family member. In contrast, her commonplace book reads like a theologian working through her beliefs. As an "instrument in fashioning self," Sally's commonplace reveals a great deal about her identity during her early Christian life, providing a forum, separate from her journal, to assist in her development of self.[4] Sally's commonplace helped her define her identity in two ways. In the first section recorded in 1813–14, she answered the question of what she believed, helping to shape her private self. The second section, recorded in 1816, investigated her public identity by exploring who she wanted to become.

Sally's early commonplace book entries from January 1813 through February 1814 are her own words, not copied work of others which many times populates the genre. First, she clearly attributes the work of other writers in the 1816 section; all the 1813–14 entries are signed in her name. Second, her essays build upon one another. For instance, she introduces her thoughts about virtue in her essay "Greatness" and expands upon her thinking in the entry titled "Time." She later revisits some of these themes in her journal as well. We can observe the development of Sally's theological voice by examining her original writings: the three essays and two letters to her friend Alvira. Essays titled "Greatness," "Reflections on Death," and "Time" are dated January 1813, December 1813, and January 1814, respectively. In February 1814, Sally copied two instructional letters on the topics of happiness and the depravity of the human heart. After the second letter to Alvira, Sally's commonplace went silent for nearly two years.

As Sally developed her theology, it is possible that a preceptor, teacher, friend, or spiritual mentor was encouraging Sally to write. While no school for girls existed in Brandon during her early years, her sophisticated hand and learned voice indicates she had received instruction. It is unclear who instructed Sally, but like other young evangelicals, she may have looked to her teachers for spiritual direction. A few years before her decision to marry Adoniram Judson and travel to the East as a missionary, the young Ann Hasseltine turned to her preceptor for spiritual guidance.[5] Sometimes friends or relatives suggested topics for commonplace entries, such as this example from the letters of Samuel Frances Smith, a minister from

Waterville, Maine. Corresponding with his sister, Susan, on December 29, 1829, Samuel asked, "You remember the blank book which was not appropriated to any particular use?" Unilaterally assigning it a purpose, he announced, "I am going to give you an extract for it." The quotation from the Bible, he instructed her, is "what you are to write me about in your next."[6] If Sally had a formal spiritual mentor, it is unclear who it might have been. The Brandon Baptist Church had dismissed and publicly rebuked minister Joshua Young the year before for "unlawful connection, with another Man's wife, and of attempts to seduce another woman, also of prevarication, and falsehood."[7] While ministers from around the region stepped in to fill the pulpit, there was not a regular minister serving Brandon until late 1814 when Reverend Abiel Fisher arrived.[8]

While we do not know if there was one person prompting Sally's specific topics, the general narrative in her commonplace reflects a developing Calvinist theology mixed with a strong Enlightenment influence. Her first entry, "Greatness," seems more secular than Christian, as she stresses the concept of "virtue, guided by truth, reason, and revelation. . . . He only is truly great, who is truly good," Sally writes. "He squares his life with reason, and observes order and decorum in all his actions," an observation worthy of followers of John Locke. Sally's idea of greatness eschewed pursuit of external treasures, such as ornaments, beauty, or honor. While this essay does not include overtly Christian references, it does assert a Calvinist rejection of good works over faith when she writes confidently, "It may be asked if those who possess the greatest charities . . . are the most virtuous? I answer no."[9] Sally's subsequent essays fully embrace the Calvinist teachings she was clearly exposed to through her readings. In her "Reflections on Death," Sally writes of a harsh and judgmental God often associated with the Calvinist tradition, explaining that upon the death of "impertinent sinners, their last groans are eternal wretchedness. No guardian angels hover round their dying pillows." She later declares her assured belief in predestination, writing, "Their fates are fixed: fixed by the determinate purpose of Jehovah."[10]

The two remaining original works in Sally's commonplace are letters to a friend identified—in the second correspondence—as Alvira. Sally's letters provide a bridge between the theological voice of her commonplace and her emerging voice as an evangelical. While the letters to Alvira are friendly, they reflect a relationship between the two that served Sally's theological development. Historian Mary Kelley suggests that the act of letter writing and shared reading were "fundamental to articulating an identity with which to act upon the world."[11] Sally used these letters to shape her theology and to take on the role of evangelical missionary. Her February 9 letter begins, "I retire with pleasure from the changing vicissitudes of the active world, to perform the duties of a friend in addressing you by letter." In this statement, Sally indicates that writing to Alvira is a spiritual retreat from the day-to-day world. The act is not purely Sally's sanctuary, however; it is it a duty she takes quite seriously. If her young friend's soul were at risk, Sally's words might deliver her salvation.

In the opening of her February 9 letter, Sally writes, "Your letter dated Jan. 22 I received Fe. 4 in which you requested me to make happiness the subject of my next epistle." Sally is taking on the role of spiritual mentor to the young Alvira, who requests her theological opinions. The entries are both expository essay and personal proselytization. Since these are the only letters recorded in her commonplace, Sally must have felt they complemented the essays that explored her arguments. In this letter, Sally equates happiness to virtue, as she did greatness in her first essay. This time, however, virtue transcends a mere moral high ground; "to be virtuous we must be what is required of us in the gospel of Jesus: we must possess the same benevolent dispositions where were characteristic of his life." Her Christ-inspired ideology continues its mingling with the Enlightenment ideal of reason, as she writes, "We must never . . . be overcome with passion, but must be cool and deliberate in all our determinations." This combination of reason, duty, and pious behavior continues as a theme throughout Sally's 1815–1817 journal.

Sally's next letter to Alvira reveals a clear Calvinist influence as she opens with her reflections on the "depravity of the human heart." The rest of the letter takes on the role of evangelical, exhorting Alvira to turn her back on the "pleasures of youth" and "attend to eternal realities," admonishing Alvira that "procrastination is dangerous in the highest degree." She further warns, "You may perhaps flatter yourself that you shall live a long time. But think not that health, youth or beauty, will exempt you from the cold embraces of relentless death." Sally encourages Alvira to "speedily fly from the tents of sin and wickedness, to the Ark of safety, before the awful deluge shall come when God shall rain a horrible tempest upon the wicked."[12] This is hardly a lighthearted missive from a school chum. In this letter, Sally has assumed the role of evangelical lay preacher with aplomb, a role she had taken on four months earlier when she wrote to her brother Jonathan with a similar mission. After her second letter to Alvira, Sally moved from her essays to a different form of self-reflection. While Sally's commonplace has a large gap of time, from February 1814 to January 1816, she did not set her pen aside. In late August 1815, Sally began keeping a personal journal.

For newly converted Baptists, keeping a journal was itself a spiritual act. In his writings, Jonathan Edwards taught Christians how to lead a pious life.[13] His recommended practices, including study, contemplation, journaling, and secret prayers, had been adopted by the generation before Sally.[14] While she did not study Edwards until the summer of 1821, the influence of his conversion rhetoric was in the "Baptismal water" in early nineteenth-century New England, and Sally followed the example.[15]

The entries in Sally's journal span from August 24, 1815 to July 10, 1817. Because Sally's journal and commonplace overlap in time, the two methods must have served two very different purposes for her. While Sally's journal captures her emotional rhetoric, her commonplace book is a measured document that presents her theology in a more formal and detached manner, written in a careful and exquisite hand. The unevenness of her script varies in her journal, indicating it was written as the events unfolded, with no sign she revised the text after the fact. The construction of her journal indicates that unlike her commonplace book, it was handmade rather than store bought. According to book conservation expert Matt Johnson, the text leaves were folded into folios and then hand cut, possibly with sewing scissors. These folios were sewn together and written on, possibly before the cardboard cover was added. The cover is decorated with hand-blocked paper that may have been a wallpaper remnant. The homemade construction suggests that Sally, or someone close to her, took careful pains in assembling this personal keepsake.[16]

The first page of the journal reads, "Sarah Merriam's Journal Continued."[17] Whether the first journal was lost or is still held by a distant descendant, we do not know. We know a barrel of documents was thrown away after water damage.[18] Although the bulk of Sally's papers were kept intact, certain writings seem to have been bundled and passed down to descendants based on lineal or sentimental ties. It is possible that Sally destroyed the first journal, perhaps because it contained a narrative about a significant suitor other than her future husband, Samuel Wait. What we do know is that her journal did not follow the form of truly private diaries of the time, which were derivative of "workaday forms of record-keeping, the daybook and interleaved almanac," such as that of New England midwife Martha Ballard.[19] While a "truly private diary is predetermined by the topic—the weather, accounts received, visitors, daily occurrences—the public diarist's range of subjects is potentially infinite, generated by the writer's response to the world."[20] In her journal, Sally rarely mentions mundane events like the weather, even when a foot of snow fell on Brandon in early June. Her journal is a curated reflection of her life cast as a religious and moral instruction manual. The format and tone of her journal mimics many of the early diaries published around that time, including those of Sarah Osborn and Harriet Newell, as well as that of Mrs. Abigail Collier, the wife of Rev. William Collier, published in Boston in 1813.[21] The passages in Sally's journal mirror those found in all three of these memoirs, using the prescribed rhetoric of pious women exhorting their faith and worrying about their sins and salvation.

Osborn biographer Catherine Brekus distinguishes between a typical diary "which could be fragmentary and episodic" and memoir, which "was supposed to have a coherent plot."[22] Indeed, interspersed among prescriptive entries on pious prayer and reflection, Sally's journal constructs a story arc beginning with her first meeting with Samuel and continuing through her agreement to marry, culminating with the conclusion of a church crisis. From the first page dated August 24, 1815, which features a meeting with Christian friends, to the final line of an entry dated July 10, 1817 that brings a church scandal to conclusion, Sally rarely misses an opportunity to turn the events of her day into a lesson about courtship, church discipline, redemption, or forgiveness. As Sally went about her days, she was consistently on the lookout for pious lessons for her imagined reader. For instance, in early 1817, Sally, her brother Jonathan, and sister Lydia shared a carriage to nearby Leicester, Vermont to attend a wedding at the home of Henry Olin, Jonathan's future father-in-law. In the entry that followed, Sally wasted no ink on details like the identity of the bride and groom or the names of other guests. She focuses instead on her pleasure at "the simplicity of the celebration," relieved that the couple omitted the "tasteless and endless ceremonies that generally follow the nuptial union which have ever to me been highly disgusting." Sally felt the seriousness of the ceremony and the plainness of the dress were suitably solemn and dignified for piously humble people, as opposed to those of which the "fashionable part of the world are peculiarly fond."[23] One can imagine Sally in the carriage on the bumpy ride home, mulling over the day's events, trying to decide what lessons might be extracted for her imagined reader. Sally turned this particular life event into a lesson on the proper comportment for the marriage of a good Christian couple.

Throughout her journal, Sally casts herself as a heroine in the story of a young woman's evangelical conversion and courtship during the Second Great Awakening. The pace of the action is lively and the timing of the entries is relatively consistent. Sally seemed to be comfortable with her evangelical voice as it developed over the course of the journal. The genre seemed to suit her. Why, then, did she return to her commonplace book after abandoning it for nearly two years? When she picked it up again, she copied three entries into her book, all in the voices of others. It was common for writers to copy prose or poems written by others into a commonplace book, but this was new for Sally. When we examine the format of the entries, it is easy to see why she used her commonplace rather than her journal to record them; inserting them into her dramatic narrative would have disrupted the storyline. Sally's three final commonplace entries were not randomly selected. With a close reading of their content, we see that they reveal Sally's exploration of a new public self, one in which she imagines taking the stage as a Baptist minister's wife.

The first of the three entries, "A Poem written . . . on The death of Mrs Abigail Collier," is a loving and grief-stricken tribute to the woman, highlighting her role as a minister's wife. In the poem, just after Abigail dies, her son asks his father, "'Where is Mama?' . . . 'She's gone to Yonder skies' The afflicted father, whelm'd in tears replies." The little boy then recalls his mother's important role attending to the spiritual welfare of the family:

> When she was here and pa was gone away,
> To attend the meeting, and to preach and pray,
> She us'd to go with sister and with me,
> Into the room where none but God can see;
> And there she told us we would shortly die,
> And then our bodies in the ground would lie![24]

Despite the poem's morbid message, this entry helped Sally contemplate her role in overseeing the family's spiritual instruction while her minister husband was away preaching and praying. Teaching children that "Jesus and his precious blood" would save them from an early death was the responsible role for any pious mother.

The next entry, "Resolutions of E Parsons," was a list of pious resolves of Erasmus Parsons, the twenty-five-year-old son of minister Silas Parsons, who had died in nearby Sudbury, Vermont a few years earlier.[25] By copying this young man's resolutions, Sally seems to be adopting his resolve to resist temptation, behave in a chaste and sober manner, and practice secret prayer. Deists including Benjamin Franklin and devout Christians such as Jonathan Edwards modeled the practice of committing to writing one's intentions to lead a virtuous or pious life. That Sally copied this list written by a young man who also was the son of a minister seems to again

imply that she was considering the possibility of being part of a ministerial family. The final entry in her commonplace is a poem she copied a
few months later, in April 1816. She seems to have transcribed it from the
November 18, 1815 issue of *The Christian Visitant*, a weekly Christian tract
published in Albany, New York. The *Visitant* contributor copied the poem,
in turn, from a popular book at the time, *Guide to Domestic Happiness*. The
essence of the poem's theme is to ask God to help find a marriage partner
who will walk with one in God. "Ah! Should I e'er so lost, so wretched be,
to give my heart to one who loved not thee!"[26] The timing and themes of
these three entries are significant in that they coincide with her future
suitor Samuel Wait's move to Bellingham, Massachusetts, which launched a
long-distance, two-year correspondence. These three commonplace entries
illustrate that Sally was privately auditioning the idea of a new public self
as the possible Mrs. Samuel Wait. Through the narrative of her personal
journal, Sally details for us how her future came to pass.

Three

COURTING

I now find myself under the influence
of a very strong attachment.

—Sally Merriam, February 17, 1817

FROM 1815, WHEN SHE FIRST MET SAMUEL WAIT, UNTIL
their marriage in 1818, Sally agonized about her salvation and viewed her
calling through the lens of a potential marriage. During this time, she
carefully weighed her duty against her affections, ultimately admitting
her fondness for Samuel after nearly two years of correspondence. On
February 17, 1817, she wrote, "I now find myself under the influence of a
very strong attachment."[1] Sally, twenty years old and living in her parents'
home in Brandon, Vermont, had met the handsome and hopeful minister about seventeen months earlier. It would be another sixteen months
before they married and set up housekeeping in Sharon, Massachusetts.
While Sally's age suggests she may have been anxious to find a suitable
mate when she met Samuel, she dragged her feet getting to the altar. The
emotional and spiritual journey that spanned the three years of their courtship reflects many of the dynamics their contemporaries experienced in
early nineteenth-century New England: autonomy from parents to choose
a mate, the concept of romantic love and the companionate ideal, and the
complex gender dynamics of the courtship process. However, as a woman
newly converted to the Baptist faith, Sally had to negotiate an additional
layer of courtship concerns. Sally was anxious to get on with her spiritual
life, and the strictures of the woman's sphere in the Baptist church meant
marrying a man with a compatible evangelical ambition; it was "a passport

to influence, deference, and power."[2] Like many women, Sally "saw marriage to a missionary as simply a means for fulfilling their own calling—a way to achieve a greater level of significance with their lives than they could as single women in New England."[3] Finding a suitable match in the Baptist church was not "a trifling thing," as Sally wrote during her deliberations.[4] She had experienced firsthand the influence a minister's wife had upon the church community, observing her friend and mentor Betsy Fisher in the role of helpmate to her husband and prayerful counselor to the flock. She also read with interest the stories of godly women who courageously agreed to lead a missionary's life with their husbands in far-flung places that were depicted in religious magazines and tracts. The courtship of an evangelical couple during the Second Great Awakening followed the emerging social changes brought on by the Enlightenment and the American Revolution. However, the teachings of a modified Calvinist belief system also required deep spiritual reflection to seek God's consent and to fulfill one's spiritual calling. Sally Merriam and Samuel Wait's courtship, as it is revealed through Sally's writings, offers a case study in how the dynamics of an evangelical courtship played out.

For a newly converted Baptist in the Early Republic, the stakes of courtship were high, affecting not just one's earthly experience, but also one's eternal salvation. In a time where early death or the end times loomed, choosing one's mate was a critical component of the calling to lead a Christian life. The godly women Sally read about modeled the normative strictures of a conversionist relationship—one that was to be God directed and duty bound. God should condone a couple's match, and Sally searched for His blessing throughout her courtship. The relationship should also be God centered: according to the religious conduct literature that Sally read, pure love was assigned to one's relationship with Christ, not to the affection of one's earthly marriage partner. As such, Sally cautioned herself and her imagined reader to put love for God above attachment to her husband. Of paramount importance was choosing a mate on the prospects of one's duty to lead a gospel-driven life. Sally carefully weighed with deliberate reason how her potential marriage would enable and enhance her walk with God. Sally Merriam documented her courtship with Samuel Wait in a way that gives us a glimpse into her inner thoughts and a roadmap into her decision-making process.

Despite the volumes of letters between Sally and Samuel following their marriage, when they spent years separated because of work and study, there are scant letters during their courtship, and none addressed to each other.

The absence of letters during this period is conspicuous, since most of their courtship transpired while they were living in separate towns. Only a few missives between family members, friends, and colleagues remain from this period, although references to continued correspondence between Sally and Samuel exist. When Samuel departed for Massachusetts, Sally wrote that she "shall probably see him no more at present" and consoled herself that "a mutual exchange of thoughts by letters will seem to shorten the hours."[5] We may never know if these letters were lost over time, passed down in a separate bundle to an unknown descendent, or later destroyed by Sally to prevent others from reading the couple's most intimate premarital discussions. Even without letters, Sally's reflections through her journal and commonplace book document a study of the courtship of a nineteenth-century couple in New England during the Second Great Awakening.

Sally's journal begins with a seemingly innocuous entry about a visit with her minister Abiel (sometimes spelled Abial) Fisher and his wife Betsy, who served as spiritual mentors to Sally and became longtime friends. "I have just returned from Elder Fisher's," Sally wrote in her opening entry. "I still find that one hour spent with the humble Christian is better than whole weeks spent in the society of those who know not God."[6] Sally omits whether anyone else was present at the meeting, but it is quite likely Samuel Wait was there. Just a few months before, Samuel had been given a letter of introduction and license to preach by Silvanus Haynes, the minister of the Middlebury Baptist Church near Samuel's hometown of Tinmouth, Vermont, encouraging him to improve his gift "wherever God in his providence shall open the door."[7] This is the first of several "licenses" Samuel received over the course of the next several years, each one presaging a new opportunity for Samuel to pursue Sally's hand in marriage. The license of July 1815 served as an introduction as Samuel moved to Brandon to further his ministerial studies with Abiel Fisher.

When Samuel's parents Joseph and Martha Wait moved their home to rural Tinmouth during Samuel's childhood, Samuel's spiritual anchor remained his grandfather's church at Waite's Corner in Washington County, New York. He had some formal education there, possibly living with his grandfather, Baptist minister William Wait.[8] Judging from the grammar of the infrequent letters from his siblings throughout Samuel's life, most of the Waits were less educated than their Merriam counterparts. Other than an occasional message passed on to Samuel by his siblings, there are no extant letters from either his mother or father, calling into question the extent of their literacy, or at least their comfort with the pen. Given the circumstances of Samuel's upbringing, it's possible that his immediate family didn't place much emphasis on education since most "rural households regarded schools as supplements to the family economy, and often as taxes on it."[9] As such, "most children only went to school intermittently for the one or two months per year that their parents did not need them" to work the farm.[10] Being the eldest son who showed a propensity for studies, Samuel was allowed to pursue an education rather than be tied to the family farm.

After Samuel's formal education at Salem Academy, Reverend Haynes (or Grandfather Wait) presumably used the Baptist network to find a minister under whom Samuel could study, which was found in Elder Fisher. The details of the arrangement are not certain, but it is likely he moved into the Fisher home, becoming an extended member of their family while in Brandon.[11] It would not be far-fetched to assume that the Fishers would be on the lookout for a suitable partner for Abiel's promising young student; matching good Christian souls for Christ's work was part of the Baptist culture. For instance, when a fervent Ann Hasseltine met Adoniram Judson and learned of his plans for mission work, she secured a proposal forthwith. On October 20, 1810, just days after Ann and Adoniram were engaged, Ann visited her young friend Harriet Atwood to tell her of their plans to sail East to preach to the heathens. Harriet nearly swooned with admiration, writing, "How did this news affect my heart! Is she willing to do all this for God, and shall I refuse to lend my little aid?"[12] Ann demonstrates her power of pious persuasion through her ability to recruit companions for her daring adventure. To make the venture possible, Harriet needed a missionary husband. Ann had an answer to that as well. Just three days later, Samuel Newell, colleague of Adoniram Judson, appeared at the Atwell family's door to begin a series of visits. By June the next year, Harriet and Samuel Newell were engaged. In February 1812, when the tumultuous events of "The Year" were beginning to unfold, the Judsons and Newells set sail from Salem, Massachusetts, two model missionary couples with the eyes of the world, and those of Sally Merriam, upon them. Unfortunately, as Sally later read in her missionary tract, by the fall, Harriet and her newborn were dead, having succumbed to disease and the hardships of travel.[13]

While the Fishers may have been encouraging a match between Samuel and Sally during late summer, Sally did not explicitly mention him in her journal until December 1815, when she wrote about "a new and unexpected scene, but I feel not much elated."[14] In the larger context, it appears that Sally is referring to an advance made by Samuel Wait, probably the request for correspondence to which she later referred. Sally elaborated on her lack of uncertainty about Samuel's advances, writing, "I humbly hope that God will direct me in the path of wisdom, for without his assistance I should in all probability not only destroy my own happiness for this life but make those around me wretched and miserable."[15] Clearly, the gravity of the situation weighed heavily on her. And the development was not likely "unexpected" as Sally describes. One assumes Sally and Samuel had been interacting at the Fishers' and perhaps attending church together during the previous months; a proposed correspondence did not come out of no-where. Sally's hesitancy may have reflected the discretion women favored in this period, seeking "above all to avoid public scrutiny in the course of courtship."[16] Sally was writing in her journal for an imagined audience and was therefore careful not to reveal too much. Even then, she did not mention Samuel by name; in fact, it was not until June 1817, months after she had agreed to marry, that she even brought herself to identify him as "Mr. W."

It was an impending move to Bellingham, Massachusetts in early 1816 that prompted Samuel to approach Sally about starting a correspondence. Abiel Fisher had been called to minister at the Baptist church in Belling-ham, and Samuel planned to follow along to continue his training. Again, a letter of recommendation from Silvanus Haynes had provided a prelude to this next step in Samuel Wait's life,[17] as Sally's December entry preceded the Haynes recommendation by just ten days. Samuel was making plans to move, but not before creating a lasting connection with Sally. Her lukewarm response includes an important element in her deliberations: her plea to God for direction. Sally repeated this prayer for God's guidance over and over again during the coming year, as she vacillated between marrying Samuel and breaking off their connection. While she repeatedly pleaded for God's blessing, she mentioned the possible approval of her parents only once. Martha Ballard's diary shows children in the mid-eighteenth century began enjoying the freedom of choosing their own spouses, and this seems to be the case with Sally.[18] In a later entry she wrote, "The feel-ings of my Parents must be consulted before I proceed any farther." But while she hoped for their blessing, she knew they would likely allow her to make the decision, opining, "Should they leave me to act for myself I hope I shall conduct with prudence and propriety so as not to dishonour myself and friends and the bleeding cause of Immanuel."[19] Sally's situation played out similarly to Harriet Atwood's when she was faced with the decision to marry Samuel Newell and sail off to the East. In her journal, Harriet wrote, "Gladly would I leave with [my mother] . . . her kind decision. But no. Although she will not refuse her consent, nor oppose any determination I may come to, yet she will not advise. Who then shall guide and direct me? . . . Oh for the direction of Jehovah!"[20]

In secular courtship of the time, potential brides enjoyed the freedom of their choice in marriage; ostensibly so did newly converted women like Sally and Harriet. They may have wished their mothers would make their decisions for them, but when they did not, a woman of the gospel turned to God for answers. Time and again in the coming months, Sally would plead for a sign from heaven. While she may not have required her mother's permission, Sally hoped that God would provide clear direction.

The ambivalent tone in Sally's entry about the "new and unexpected scene" may indicate Sally had some hesitations about leaving her family for marriage in general, or to marry Samuel in particular. Alternatively, her hesitation may have been an attempt to cast any unseemly affections that she might have in a detached and godly light. Throughout her journal, following much conduct literature of the time, Sally cautioned herself to use reason, not passion, in making her choice for marriage, writing, "The judgments should be founded on reason . . . before the softer passions are suffered to operate in the least on the mind.[21] Here, Sally begins in earnest the agonizing process of weighing duty against affection, a dynamic unique to evangelical courtship. Ann Hasseltine Judson's nineteenth-century memoirist, James Knowles, found it necessary to address this theme, lest the reader come to think she followed her earthly passions rather than her Christ-centered heart to Burma, explaining that "her embarrassment was increased, by the conflict which might arise between affection and duty." The author made a point to assure the reader that Ann was "uninfluenced by any personal considerations."[22] In fact, the deliberations she and other women missionaries made regarding duty seemed to have become a running joke at the time. Knowles notes the "remark of one lady respecting Mrs. J would express the feelings of many others. 'I hear,' said she, 'that Miss H. is going to India. Why does she go?' 'Why, she thinks it her duty; would you not go, if you thought it your duty?' 'But,' replied the good lady with emphasis, '*I would not think it my duty.*'"[23] Sally was not choosing between, at least for now, a life in the savage wilds of India or Burma and the comfortable existence she hoped for in New England, but she still wanted her imagined reader to know she was making her decision with her head and not her heart. She was reticent to reveal the details of girlish romance that she recalled to Samuel later, such as the "pleasure of many seasons in which we, hand-in-hand, accompanied each other to the house of prayer."[24]

Choosing reason over passion became an important recurring theme in her journal entries in the coming year, as well as in her commonplace book when she copied the poem exhorting the reader to dodge cupid's arrow and instead choose a mate who will walk with one in God: "From pangs of hopeless love my bosom spare, Nor let its torturing arrow fasten there."[25] While companionate love was emerging as a dynamic in courtship, pious women considered it with caution.

The day after Sally's January 6, 1816 agreement to correspond with Samuel, she wrote an entry about her heartbreaking farewell to Betsy and Abiel Fisher. One wonders if at least some of her sorrow was aimed at Samuel when she wrote, "My heart was too full for utterance . . . a thousand things rushed into my mind to remind me of what I was losing." She obliquely wished Samuel well in his own mission, writing, "May he be successful in his calling."[26] The intensity of the parting does seem to indicate affection for Samuel, but as their courtship continued during the next year, Sally kept her thoughts close and her options open. One detail in Sally's January 6, 1816 entry was subtle, but its dynamics played out over the following year of long-distance courtship. She wrote, "I have finally consented to comply" with Samuel's request to correspond.[27] Presumably, he asked her to correspond just prior to her December 17, 1815 entry, so it took ten days of deliberation (and perhaps cajoling by the Fishers) before she said yes. While she did not view her agreement to correspond as a formal engagement, it would be a public declaration of a relationship—and for the moment, Sally was in the driver's seat. In the Early Republic, a woman's influence reached its peak during courtship.[28] This aspect of their relationship continued throughout 1816, including the possibility of another suitor who presented himself in April. "Mr. H. and his sister" tarried in Brandon several days while he and Sally got acquainted, causing Sally to declare, "I am much pleased with their society. I think they are the real friends of Immanuel."[29] Sally's interest in him ended, however, when in July Mr. H. conveyed his interest through Sally's brother Isaac who "informs me that Mr. H conversed with him respecting myself on a subject very unexpected and not very pleasant," a comment not unlike her reaction to Samuel's early advances. Isaac gave Mr. H. "but little encouragement. . . . I should still less," she wrote with blunt confidence.[30] Sally was an active player in her courtship, exerting control over the process by exploring other suitors, similar to other young women during that time. Women "sought to continue their explorations in courtship. . . . As long as they entertained numerous admirers, courting girls could prolong their influence."[31] While Sally ultimately rejected at least one other suitor to choose Samuel Wait, her vacillation reveals the complex gender dynamics of courtship in the Early Republic.

Because no letters between Sally and Samuel remain from that time, we do not know the nuances of their relationship, but a letter to Sally from Betsy Fisher does shed some light. In her letters, Betsy indicates that she knew the two were corresponding, which would have been obvious since he was living in their home across the Green Mountains of Vermont. "He has been to Sharon to preach as I expect he informed you," writes Betsy. "I had thoughts about petitioning for a repeal of that embargo law that passed January 7th . . . your courtship must be very cool for the green mountain over which your love has to pass is covered with snow."[32] Betsy seems to be pleading Samuel's case. In her word choice, Betsy was practicing badinage on behalf of Samuel, a technique whereby a lady or a gentleman would hint to the other about their interest by using metaphor so as to remain discrete.[33] In this case, as "petitioner," Betsy chose the allusion of an embargo, referencing the disastrous economic policy of the second Thomas Jefferson administration that would have affected the region in which they lived. The Merriam "embargo" to which Betsy refers must have been a condition that Sally put on their courtship when the Fishers and Wait left Brandon on January 7; presumably, that they could correspond, but that no personal visits would be forthcoming until she said otherwise. In the letter, Betsy became the petitioner to promote Samuel's case that they might see each other. The plea on Samuel's behalf did not move things along, however; Sally's journal lacks entries from early May to early July, and her correspondence seems to have lapsed during that time as well. On July 5, she wrote, "The concerns of Life engross almost my whole attention . . . of late I seldom have an opportunity to employ my pen."[34] Here she may be referring to Vermont's "year without a summer." Caused by fallout from a volcanic eruption in Indonesia, a foot of snow fell in June 1816, ruining all the crops in the area.[35] Perhaps the disruption of her father's harvest required more spinning and needlework than usual to contribute to the family income. By October, Sally had resumed correspondence, writing, "[I] have written a letter to my dear friend Mrs. F and attended our covenant meeting to day." In an entry two days later, after writing about the success of recent revivals, she added, "God grant that the church in S may share largely in the outpouring of the divine spirit."[36] The "S" she refers to is Sharon, Massachusetts, where Samuel had just received a contract to preach for $200 a year.[37] Once again a new career opportunity spurred Samuel to move toward his desire to make Sally his bride, and once again she reacted with apparent ambivalence.

Samuel's official proposal in November 1816 seemed to fall flat. On November 4, Sally wrote that he had tarried with the family the night before and used the next morning to introduce a subject that "on account of my present situation was unpleasant though not unexpected." Like her earlier depictions of romance, Sally described the proposal as "unpleasant," reporting that she "gave a negative answer though with much diffidence."[38] Sally's deflection is in keeping with her earlier reluctance to admit her attraction to Samuel. It seems to be part of a larger strategy not only to exert control by feigning disinterest, but to delay what was, to her, an increasingly difficult decision. And it was a decision that Sally would have to make. Although a nineteenth-century suitor might have the "illusion of control, a woman knew that her role in the early stages of courtship was a reactive one: she might accept, defer, or decline a suitor's offer."[39]

Sally's "present situation" may have referred in part to her distress that she was "still in the gall of bitterness" regarding her salvific state.[40] Of more concern than everlasting damnation, however, was Sally's worry about her unfolding courtship. Her anxiety reflected the concerns many women had about marriage at the time, including fear of childbirth, the loss of one's relative autonomy, and moving from one's familiar and comfortable nuclear family to setting up housekeeping on one's own. And there was an additional consideration that weighed on Sally's mind: the pressure that the status of a minister's wife would bring. Courtship in the Early Republic could be "a transforming and potentially angst-ridden period for many young women."[41] Sally's entry of January 25 illustrates this. After her "diffident" refusal, Samuel, undaunted, returned to Brandon for several days the following January, pressing for an answer. As the time for decision making approached, Sally's mind was filled with despair and confusion, and she was losing sleep from the "perturbation" of her mind. She was "a poor weak frail creature" and could not trust her judgment, afraid she was "destitute of many qualifications which are requisite for me to possess in order to fill with propriety the station to which I am invited."[42] Earlier in her journal, Sally wrote about the elevated position of a minister's wife, writing that the "station of the minister of the gospel is the most dignified the most exalted in which any mere man could be placed."[43] This comment belies her own pious ambition, since through marriage she would achieve such a station herself. In Christian conduct literature at the turn of the century, writers like Thomas Gisborne wrote specific instructions for a minister's wife's comportment, suggesting if she erred in her duty, it would contribute "not a little to lessen the general effect of her husband's instructions from the pulpit."[44] Being the wife of such a dignified character was a great responsibility for a young woman like Sally. For her, "a subject of this magnitude ought to be duly and prayerfully weighed. . . . It is for life."[45]

During the late eighteenth and early nineteenth centuries, the companionate marriage ideal was on the rise. English poet John Milton introduced his theory about companionate marriage in the mid-seventeenth century, ironically, in his tracts on divorce, writing "that marriage is essentially and principally a conjunction of minds, hearts and souls."[46] The norm in Sally's lifetime emerged that a suitable marriage should be not only economically and socially appropriate, but should reflect a complementary match of personalities. As such, "women sought to fulfill their own interests in matrimony."[47] This was true for Sally, but with the added weight that God's interest in her own calling had to be considered as well. For Sally and other evangelicals of the time, when it came to a life decision as important as marriage, the stakes were high. It was not simply a life choice; it could be the decision between eternal life and everlasting damnation.

Another more worldly concern may have caused Sally pause to marry: the subtle yet significant contrast between the Merriam and Wait family economic and educational status. The difference between the Waits' rural Tinmouth, Vermont location and that of the Merriams' in Brandon is still evident today. Tinmouth is and was a series of family farms nestled in the rolling hills, with no real town center. By contrast, Brandon was a moderately populated village "compactly built" like the ideal communities promoted by the "New York booster, William Cooper."[48] Homes in towns like Brandon were clustered closely alongside shops, churches, and usually a Masonic hall. According to Cooper, "They preserved the simple virtue of farm communities while stimulating 'more civility and civilization . . . than was feasible in the remote neighborhoods.'"[49] Sally must have taken into account the differences in their families' education and class while she considered marriage.

Given the weight of her decision, Sally turned once more to God, asking that he reveal her duty and direct her footsteps, writing, "May we both act in thy fear and in such a manner as thou wilt approve and bless that our conduct may bring glory to God and peace and happiness to ourselves."[50] In this passage, Sally shifts for the first time to consider that Samuel might have a role in the decision to marry, hoping that they would "both act in thy fear." The closer she came to accepting the proposal, the more she considered the possibility of being part of a couple. With regard to her prayer for direction, God presumably answered. Two weeks later, she "publicly" declared her affection for Samuel by admitting in her journal "a decision in my own mind has partially relieved it from the perturbation which has of late possessed it."[51] While the decision had been made, obtaining tacit approval from both families was desirable and politic. Sally's family knew Samuel well from his time in Brandon, where they had spent time together at church and in the Merriam home. Not long after Sally and Samuel were engaged, Sally's brother Isaac and his wife Mary named their first son Samuel. This and other fond written references indicate the Merriam family approved of the promising young preacher, who was setting his course to advance the Baptist mission to which they prescribed. It is not clear whether Sally had met any of Samuel's family members before Samuel planned a Valentine's Day visit to nearby Tinmouth in 1817. Sally was highly embarrassed about the awkward feeling of being on display, writing, "While there I not infrequently wished myself alone in Brandon that I might give vent to my feelings by a feast of tears."[52] Until this public evaluation of her suitability to be a minister's wife, Sally had, as many young women of her day, concealed her courtship to all but a few close friends and family.[53] While she tried to hide her embarrassment and appear cheerful, one "old Lady" suggested she was homesick and that "she thought she had discovered that I was restless and unhappy."[54] Perhaps, like many newly betrothed women meeting a houseful of soon-to-be in-laws, Sally wondered what she was getting herself into when confronted with the variance in class and education between the two families. In the end, Sally recovered her composure, writing, "The morning before I returned I felt less embarrassed and more cheerful. I am not now sorry I went."[55] Just a few days later, Sally finally admitted that her heart was inclined toward Samuel. On February 17, 1817, she wrote, "I now find myself under the influence of a very strong attachment. It was long before I dare own this to my own heart. But at length I have been constrained to. When I did I felt my pride greatly wounded. I felt as though I had done violence to my former delicacy."[56] Sally felt her delicacy—her innocence—had been threatened by her feelings for Samuel, and therefore took great caution before succumbing to her heart.

It is significant that in this confession, she never uses the word *love*. The idea of romantic love evolved during Sally's time, "becoming an essential ingredient in the marital equation."[57] That may have been true for Sally's secular contemporaries, but she was careful in her journal to communicate a more puritan idea of affection than a romantic idea of love. Sally did write liberally about love to describe her relationship with Christ, "a character of spotless purity and boundless love." But the teachings of the

Baptist church warned against becoming too attached to worldly things, including one's own spouse or children. To that point, Sally later admonished herself for thinking about Samuel too much and too often, to the exclusion of God, writing, "I am ashamed of myself. Why is not my mind raised above the low pursuit of time things? Why is not my soul absorbed in love to him?"[58] By "him," she meant God, not Samuel Wait. In her same February declaration of attachment, Sally admitted how thoroughly perplexed she was to not have full control over her feelings. "The thought that I was not as formerly complete and sole mistress of my own heart made me blush prodigiously and I felt greatly confused." Her embarrassment continued after she and Samuel were engaged, as she wrote, "Even now I frequently blush to acknowledge it to my own heart." Although she ceded ground to her emotions, she assured herself that God had guided her decision, and that decision was made by reason, not passion: "I have not made up my mind on the subject without mature deliberation. I think I have earnestly and sincerely sought the direction of Heaven and I now feel some very strong assurances that I now pursue the path appointed me by my heavenly Father."[59]

By the time Sally revealed her emotions in her journal, she had known Samuel for approximately seventeen months, throughout which time they had corresponded and visited off and on. For nearly three months, she weighed his marriage proposal through prayer and Christian reflection, yet during all that time, she never dared to make explicit note of her feelings about him. Courtship included careful attention to timing and word choice, so as not to confess one's feelings too soon. For instance, the 1817 letters between Massachusetts brothers Harry and Robert Sedgwick illustrate this delicate balance, when Robert warned Harry that "you cannot be in love until you are engaged."[60] This social norm seemed to have played out in Sally's life, since she waited until she and Samuel were committed before declaring her feelings in her journal.

Just after the acknowledgement of her feelings, the narrative of Sally's journal took an interesting twist. During the five months after her engagement, there were only a few mentions of Samuel. Faithful to the genre of spiritual memoir, Sally returned to her worries about her salvation, making no mention of pre-wedding arrangements or plans to set up housekeeping that might have populated a workaday journal. Instead, she continued her pious narrative with a new, riveting storyline, one that advanced instructions on how to behave in a pious marriage. Engagement, after all, was not the end of a story, but the beginning. Closing her journal with an agreement to marry would ignore the most important element of a prescriptive Christian memoir: how to move forward in a God-centered relationship. Just as the story arc of her courtship wound down, a scandalous and instructive story heated up. Two days after Sally opened her heart about Samuel, she introduced a startling new topic: adultery. Sally wrote in a prayer, "Teach me submissiveness in all things nor let my heart wander from the fountain of life. My constant feet would never rove."[61]

It is not without reason that Sally moved from the subject of innocent delicacy to the possibility of unfaithfulness. In late February 1817 she had an important role in the investigation of a church scandal: the secret affair of Elder Starkwether, the minister of Brandon Baptist Church, with a married parishioner, Mrs. Hall. Although Sally does not reveal the details of how her role in the scandal developed, she was appointed the lead church member on the committee investigating the allegations. Then, along with an elder from a neighboring town, they were to investigate and confront the two wretched sinners and render judgment on the sincerity of their confessions. Sally's appointment to the committee likely reflected the high regard in which she was held, as well as her powerful uncle's influence on church business. In the Baptist tradition, as a condition of church membership, potential members were required to state a public confession of faith. The church judged the quality and veracity of the person's testimony based on perceived sincerity and the use of conversionist rhetoric. In church discipline hearings, such as the one Sally oversaw, the accused were expected to render a convincing and heartfelt change of heart. Mrs. Hall's confession did not disappoint. According to Sally, the accused woman spewed her regret fervently, saying, "I mourn my folly and repent in dust and ashes. . . . I loathe and abhor myself. I am a complete Judas. O my aching, my wretched heart."[62] Mrs. Hall's dramatic confession spans four pages of Sally's journal. Of the exchange, Sally wrote in a remarkable understatement, "I found her apparently very humble." A similar scene unfolded in Elder Starkwether's case. Eight journal pages in length, Starkwether's confession as recorded by Sally used the same language of humiliation and regret as Mrs. Hall's. At the end, Sally declared that he felt "truly humble. If he does not he is a very great deceiver indeed."[63] The church members seemed to agree. A few months later in front of a packed meetinghouse, "Elder Elisha Starkwether . . . gave a relation of the unhappy affair between him and Mrs. Hall."

His confession must have resonated contrition, because records show that he "appears to have a deep sense of the impropriety of this conduct as a Christian and as a Minister of Christ."[64] Sally's journal ends on July 10,

1817 with the dramatic conclusion of the scandal, her last lines squeezed onto the bottom of the final page. In all, the climax of the Starkwether affair takes up the last thirteen pages of Sally's 124-page journal.

The ultimate fates of both Starkwether and Hall could have come straight from a piece of evangelical conduct literature. According to a letter in early 1819 from Sally's cousin Cynthia Conant, the church determined Starkwether should no longer preach there, although it's not clear whether he continued to preach elsewhere.[65] Mrs. Hall's story was more pitiable. After the Starkwether situation was publicly revealed, another scandal came to light, this one between Mrs. Hall and Elder Young, the corpulent, round-shouldered minister that preceded Starkwether. The public humiliation seems to have weighed heavily on Mrs. Hall; by January she had become "evidently delirious" and failing in health.[66] By April, Mrs. Hall had "closed her mortal career." Sally's sister Lydia hoped that her "foibles be buried in the grave of oblivion; and never more be remembered otherwise."[67]

In the context of Christian courtship literature, it is interesting to consider why Sally had included the narrative in her journal. The Starkwether storyline was relevant in that it illustrated sin and redemption in the Baptist tradition, an instructional lesson for the imagined reader. The conclusion provided a dramatic ending to her journal, which was in essence a moral tale of Christian conduct. At the close of Starkwether's confession, Sally wrapped up her memoir with a message of Christ's forgiveness, writing, "I am not without hope that they will yet reign with Christ in Heaven." Then, she concluded with a moral imperative to "watch and pray continually lest we also fall into temptation and are foiled on the field by the subtle adversary of souls. Merciful God will thou keep us."[68] The Starkwether story also gave Sally credibility as a spiritual memoirist for her imagined reader. By relating her leadership role in the crisis, Sally demonstrated the degree to which she had, as a young, unmarried woman, assumed enough tacit leadership in the church to head the investigative committee. Her spiritual leadership at the age of twenty-one presaged the future of her God-directed and duty-driven life as a minister's wife.

Sally and Samuel married nearly eleven months later, in June 1818, two weeks after his ordination at Sharon Baptist Church. Other than a few letters between Samuel Wait and various family documents, no records of the months approaching the wedding exist. We know that they married in one of the front rooms of her parents' house in Brandon in a simple ceremony, presumably foregoing the "tasteless and endless ceremonies" that Sally found so "highly disgusting," as she had written earlier of the wedding in the Olin home.[69] In the five years that had passed during those early writings, things had changed significantly for Sally and the world around her. She had transitioned from a single, newly converted woman to a minister's wife. The War of 1812 had ended, trade had resumed, and the dynamics of the family farm economy were changing. As the nation's new president began ushering in his "Era of Good Feelings," Sally's emotions were mixed. She expressed doubts about her ability to rise to the station to which she was called and seemed worried about leaving the maternal roof to set up housekeeping in a strange town. Yet her journal reveals her steadfast resolve to follow in the footsteps of women like Ann Judson whose faith had guided them into an unknown future. Sally's would begin in Sharon, Massachusetts, where the Waits began their marriage moored to ministry and missions.

Part Two

FACING THE FROWNS OF LIFE

Four

SETTLING

Somebody must live in Sharon, poor
and wicked as the town is.

—Samuel to Sally, August 18, 1820

I feel it is my duty, and of course happiness,
to be content with my lot, and submit to the
dispensations of Divine Providence.

—Sally to Samuel, April 14, 1822

IN MAY 1820, SALLY CAREFULLY FOLDED HER BELONGINGS
into a trunk and fastened its clasps, setting aside a few books and winter
clothes for storage. After bidding goodbye to the Hewins family, with whom
she and Samuel had likely boarded for nearly two years, she endured a
jostling twenty-two-mile journey by stagecoach to Bellingham, Massachusetts, a small town near the Rhode Island border. There she spent a few
days with Betsy and Abiel Fisher, the closest Christian friends she had since
her conversion in Brandon, Vermont seven years earlier. From Bellingham,
she traveled to Boston, where she spent twenty dollars on clothes, taking
time to shop for a crepe shawl for her sister Lydia.[1] She arrived in Brandon
a few weeks later, about to spend months, or perhaps years, without the
husband she had recently married.[2] Sally Merriam Wait's imagined and
ideal evangelical life had just undergone a distressing setback. Her religious conversion and marriage were life-defining transitions that ignited

her pious ambitions. Sally's aspirations were about to be challenged by the limitations of a woman's station in the Early Republic.

In his 1801 *An Enquiry into the Duties of the Female Sex*, Thomas Gisborne described the sphere in which ministers' wives should reside. Of a ministerial wife's qualifications, he wrote, "If religion have its genuine effect on her manners and dispositions; if it render her humble and mild, benevolent and candid, sedate, modest and devout . . . if it lead her to activity in searching out and alleviating the wants of the neighboring poor . . . she is a 'fellow-laborer' with him 'in the Gospel.'"[3] In Gisborne's world at the turn of the nineteenth century, there was no room for a leading lady in the ministry; a woman's place was to be deferential, thrifty, and pious. Yet he described her as a "fellow laborer," a quasi-equal partner in their mission. The calling was shared, but the woman subservient. By the time Sally came of age a decade later, she saw evidence that women were making gains in the evangelical world. Religious tracts Sally read featured women as heroic helpmeets who supported their earthly partners in their shared mission. Contrast Gisborne's words with Jonathan Allen's 1812 sermon in Haverhill, Massachusetts, "On the Occasion of Two Young Ladies Being About to Embark as the wives of Rev. Messieurs Judson and Newell," when he challenged Ann Hasseltine Judson and Harriet Atwood Newell to "teach these women to whom your husband can have but little or no access . . . to realize, that they are not an inferior race of creatures; but stand upon a par with men."[4] While Adoniram Judson spent years translating the bible and preaching to the men of Burma, Ann oversaw a household situated at the edge of a jungle and ministered to the women and children in nearby communities. While she remained relegated to the women's sphere, Ann's courageous actions were celebrated in a way that inspired women to emulate them. Sally hoped to cast herself in that same mold, patterning her early life after female missionaries and ministers' wives whose stories were told in an emotional, sacrificial, and idealized light. Their roles were limited by gender, but the women worked side by side with their husbands in the mission field. These and other women who were featured in publications including the *Latter Day Luminary* and *Massachusetts Baptist Missionary Magazine* provided models for Sally Merriam Wait's own spiritual ambitions. Sally's mother described this dynamic when she wrote just after Sally's wedding, "God of his infinite mercy grant that your companion may prove a faithful Minister of Christ . . . may you both be useful members in Zion and *mutual helpers* to each other through life in supporting the best of all causes."[5] Sally envisioned her role as a mutual laborer working alongside Samuel, as Ann Judson was to Adoniram Judson in Burma.

When she became a minister's wife, Sally put her journaling aside to attend to her new role. The couple's life in Sharon, Massachusetts remains largely undocumented, save a few letters that can be pieced together to frame out their story. Judging by her friendships with church members that lasted many years, we can surmise that Sally played an active role in the community as a minister's wife. We do not know much of her day-to-day activities during their first year in Sharon until new developments began to threaten Sally's ability to work side by side with her husband. When Samuel decided to further his education without her in Philadelphia, economic realities exposed the stubborn limitations that women still encountered. While despondent about this reality, Sally mustered her Calvinist faith to be resigned to her "lot, and to submit to the dispensations of Divine Providence."[6]

In Brandon, Sally seemed to have valued her identity as a scholar and respected church member, even when some conservative members at Brandon Baptist Church, including her uncle John Conant, believed in Paul's admonition in 1 Corinthians that women should remain silent in church. Uncle John wrote to Samuel Wait in 1820 that "nature has assigned" women and Paul was "of the opinion that they in this respect ought to keep silence." It is possible Uncle John was referring to his niece's outspokenness in church, considering his letter was written just after Sally's return to Brandon.[7] Despite Conant's feelings on the topic, Brandon Baptist Church where he served as deacon had, in its original covenant in 1791, agreed that "the Brethren of the Church ought to consult the sisters in all Cases of Discipline," which placed women as members of powerful committees.[8] As she had outlined in her journal months prior, Sally had already been assigned the unenviable, yet esteemed, position of investigating the minister's affair with a parishioner. In addition to serving on discipline committees, the Merriam women attended statewide association meetings, developed female societies, and raised money for domestic missions.[9]

As Sally approached her role of minister's wife, she envisioned herself as a mutual contributor to the Baptist mission. A successful minister's wife was an educated helpmeet who could hold her own in theological, intellectual, and social discourse. In a letter to Sally early in their marriage, Samuel stressed that "there is no place, where human beings can be found ... but what a woman, the wife of a minister in particular, will derive much benefit from a respectable stock of information."[10] Before they were married, Sally and Samuel began to contemplate their future in the ministry, considering a missionary stint overseas in the footsteps of the Judsons.[11] While such a move might have been attractive to the young couple from a standpoint of demonstrating their commitment to the Baptist cause, it would have been fraught with peril. A position in the mission field was treacherous, often requiring the evangelists to risk their lives to meet the task.[12] While they would reconsider more exotic missions later, their first assignment was a more mundane ministry at the recently formed Sharon Baptist Church. How they came to choose Sharon for their first assignment requires examining the early Baptist network set against the practicalities of day-to-day secular life that played out through gender, family, and economic dynamics.

In 1815, when Samuel first moved to Brandon to study and live with Abiel Fisher, few theological seminaries existed. Despite evangelical Lyman Beecher's 1814 call to attract five thousand new recruits to institutions such as Yale University for theological training, in reality ministers were often trained in an apprenticeship of sorts, like Samuel's initial relationship with Abiel Fisher.[13] Sally's brothers Isaac and Jonathan, who also seem to have been conducting studies with Fisher, became friendly with Samuel when he was in Brandon. When Abiel was called to Bellingham, Wait moved with the Fishers to this Baptist-dominated town to continue his studies. Within a few months, Wait was visiting nearby Sharon to preach some Sundays.[14] A cryptic remark in Sally's journal indicates that "friends from S" visited Brandon on Valentine's Day that year; it is possible that the visitors included not only her suitor Samuel but also some town leaders from the Baptist church to ascertain Sally's suitability as a potential minister's wife.[15] If so, she must have passed muster, because within the year, Wait was invited by town elder Dr. Elijah Hewins to lead the church at an annual salary of $200.[16] It would be another eighteen months before Wait was officially ordained at Sharon, followed in quick order by his marriage to Sally in June 1818.[17] When they moved to Sharon, the small membership expressed concern they would not be able to support a full-time minister, which Hewins reminded him later, writing, "You will recollect . . . we expressed having doubt whether we should be able to support preaching all the time."[18] As a middling town with a population of around one thousand people, Sharon did not show much promise for a young couple hoping to make a mark on the Baptist movement.[19] Yet, as Samuel wrote to Sally, "somebody must live in Sharon, poor and wicked as the town is, while others may enjoy a more favoured spot."[20] To the Waits, settling in Sharon was, well, *settling*.

To understand what a future as a minister in a small New England town might have held for the Waits—and why they ultimately chose another path—it is helpful to see the life that Samuel's mentor Abiel Fisher experienced in nearby Bellingham. He lived "on bread and milk half the time,

[had] no tea, and board[ed] for seven shillings a week."[21] In defense of his infrequent letters to Wait, Fisher wrote, "I have traveled more than twelve hundred miles since I received yours. Had from 4 to 20 scholars all this time had a family of from 8 to 12 and attended to all my missionary ministerial duties. In general when I have done all what must be done I have felt no time to write even to a good old friend."[22] Underpaid ministers had brutal schedules and few prospects to move up. Fisher wrote to Wait that he would "continue here a year longer at least although it is by no means a very pleasant place." When he did have an offer from a church in New Hampshire, Fisher turned it down from a sense of duty he felt to meet the needs of his parishioners. "After I gave my answer Mrs. Fisher was almost inconsolable." This could have easily been the future of the Waits, who envisioned making a greater impact on the world.

The backdrop of the Waits' deliberations was the newly formed Triennial Convention, which began meeting every three years starting in 1814. Inspired by the initial success of Burma missionaries Ann and Adoniram Judson, the meeting was ambitious in its design to organize Baptists, described in Judson's biography as a "scattered and feeble folk," on a national scale.[23] The gathering was led by former missionary Luther Rice and a Baptist immigrant from Bristol College, William Staughton, among others. While the initial purpose of the organization was to support evangelical missions overseas and in the American West, its leaders quickly began investigating the feasibility of starting a national Baptist college for the education of ministers.[24] The formal religious education that emerged during the Early Republic "embodied and created a new, more exclusively 'professional' form of ministerial consciousness" to which the Baptists aspired.[25] "Baptist leaders, mostly centered in the urban areas of the northeast, were engaged in a quest for 'respectability,'" writes Ashley Moreshead. As they focused on domestic missions and revivals, they saw the need "to improve the educational levels of their clergy to meet the standards of the older churches."[26]

In 1817, Triennial leaders selected British Baptist William Staughton to open a theological seminary in Philadelphia. Staughton had migrated to America to answer an appeal that Charleston Baptist Richard Furman made to London Reverend John Rippon in 1793 requesting an able and educated minister to fill the demands of the growing Baptist churches in America. Specifically, South Carolina Baptists needed a pastor for the church in Georgetown, a growing community ten miles northeast of Charleston. While Staughton was being groomed for a ministry in Northampton, England, he had declined the invitation to move there because, according to his memoir, he was "strongly impressed with the duty of extending his labors" in America.[27]

But there was more to the story. Church records reveal that Staughton was romantically involved with a married woman, Maria (or Mary) Martin Hanson (or Hansen), a parishioner at Bromsgrove (England) Baptist Church.[28] By the time the request from Richard Furman came in early 1793, Thomas Hanson was dead and Maria was free to marry, but she refused to go to Northampton with Staughton and instead crossed the Atlantic.[29] Although the burial of a Thomas Hansen was recorded in London in 1795, there does not seem to be a record of a death of a Thomas Hanson/Hansen in the Bromsgrove church notes in 1792 or 1793. At this time in England, obtaining a divorce required a literal Act of Parliament and dissatisfied spouses on both sides of the Atlantic sometimes emigrated rather than live an unhappy life.[30] Whether or not Thomas Hanson had actually met his demise, he certainly was dead to Maria. When Furman's letter asking for a minister arrived in England, it solved a lot of problems. As it was read at a minister's meeting, they looked around the table and exclaimed, "Staughton is the man!"[31] Rippon and the other Baptist ministers knew of Staughton's desire to cross the Atlantic and recognized that it may have been less about the Holy Spirit and more about the human heart, but the published record is discreet. Staughton's memoir reads that "his mind had been directed to this country, as his future home, before the letter of Mr. Furman reached England."[32] He appears to have set sail in late summer of 1793, likely from Bristol, a busy port serving the transatlantic trade. It is not clear whether he traveled with Maria or followed after her. Regardless, they had both arrived on American soil before October 26 that year, when the Reverend Richard Furman united William Staughton and Maria Hanson in marriage. An eleven-year-old "niece" named Amelia had made the crossing with one (or both) of them; whose daughter she was, records do not show.

Staughton took the pastorate at the Georgetown church, but the American South did not agree with him, due to the "Horrors of slavery" and "the Sickliness of the place."[33] He used his English and American connections to pave a path to the Northeast, eventually settling in Philadelphia where he made a name for himself with the Baptist elite, becoming a leader in the Philadelphia Baptist Association. When Staughton was offered the pastorate of the venerable First Baptist Church in Philadelphia in 1805, "a new era dawned. The congregation increased, and the building was soon crowded in every part with interested hearers."[34] Staughton oversaw the construction of a new church building in 1808, as well as the two-story

"Baptisterion" in 1810 to provide a changing area for the many immersion candidates who gathered at the edge of the Schuylkill River. In these years, the church was "so prosperous . . . that they were able to pledge to their pastor fifteen hundred dollars and the free use of the parsonage."[35] The influence that Staughton accumulated in the Philadelphia community would lay the groundwork for his leadership in the Baptist educational movement into which Samuel Wait would later be drawn.

In early 1811, as potential war with the British neared, a dispute broke out and a new church was formed out of the schism, not without painful animosity between some members and the minister. In his resignation letter, Staughton wrote that he felt "national discrimination" was a "violation of Christian principles." He defended his home country, writing, "I never regret that I was born in England. Its national policies, in many respects, I disapprove; but it is a land where genius and piety have long been eminent. It is the land of my fathers, as is America the land of my children."[36] After nearly two decades in America, Staughton became a citizen of the United States in October 1811 in response to church members' concerns about his allegiance to the country.[37] The church membership must have been wealthy and influential, because they built a new church that seated an astonishing twenty-five hundred people for an unprecedented $40,000, more than half a million dollars by today's standards.[38] The congregation and their minister hired the up-and-coming architect Robert Mills (who later designed the Washington Monument) to develop the building plans.[39] To pay for it, the income from "pew rents and collections [were] said to be between four and five thousand dollars a year."[40] When the Triennial leaders noticed Staughton's "zeal and spirit" dedicated to "educational and missionary enterprises," he was an obvious choice to create a national Baptist institute."[41]

Several connections caused Samuel Wait and the Merriam brothers to consider attending the theological institute that Staughton began. In early America, the Baptist network was tightly coordinated and close-knit. A number of representatives from New England were in attendance at the 1817 meeting, including Thomas Baldwin of Boston who had preached the dedication sermon at Bellingham's new meetinghouse in 1802.[42] There were additional connections between Baptist leaders and the Merriam-Wait family, including Luther Rice himself. After a short stint overseas with the Judsons, Rice had returned to America, deciding his higher purpose was to raise funds rather than face missionary work in the jungle.[43] A persuasive and captivating preacher, he embarked on a series of "extensive and frequent tours" to spread the news and raise money to fund the missionaries.[44]

In the fall of 1818, not long after the leaders at the 1817 Triennial voted to start the Philadelphia seminary, Rice preached at the Vermont Association meeting in Poultney, Vermont, which Sally's sister Lydia attended. He was there to raise money for missions, which he did handsomely. Lydia noted that Rice raised "in the whole seventy dollars . . . including a number of earrings, finger rings, a silver clasp . . . which they continued to give him, until the moment of his departure."[45] Judging from the enthusiastic response, with the women practically throwing their jewelry at him, Rice's power of persuasion seemed particularly moving to a female audience.

Luther Rice traveled up and down the east coast of the Early Republic, roiling up fervor and funds to supply the Triennial's ambitious plans. At the first Triennial, he reported that seventeen women's societies were in formation. Under Rice's fundraising campaign, the number grew sevenfold by 1817.[46] Rice seemed adept at employing his charisma to raise money from a female audience, although not everyone was as enamored with Rice's abilities to make an impression on women. Traveling bookseller Samuel Whitcomb met Rice when they were both visiting Kentucky in 1818. Whitcomb's landlord hosted Rice to preach at his home but "he did not like him much," commenting, "He brought a young Lady in the gig with him!" Whitcomb's landlady was aghast, pointing out that it was "not reputable here for unmarried men & women to ride or walk out together."[47] Other Kentuckians took a more emphatic offense against Rice. John Taylor, an anti-missionary Baptist minister, wrote a scathing condemnation on Rice in his 1819 essay, "Thoughts on Missions," most pointedly regarding Rice's persuasive fundraising skills. "He spoke handsome things about the kingdom of Christ; but every stroke he gave seemed to mean MONEY," Taylor wrote.[48]

When Rice visited the Vermont Association, he undoubtedly communicated the Triennial's new enthusiasm for educational missions; at the meeting, the Vermont leaders passed a constitution for the Vermont Education Society. In Rice's early years traveling the country, he often promoted and raised money for what was supposed to be the separate educational effort.[49] Indeed, the Baptist leaders would later severely reprimand Rice for his sloppy bookkeeping practices, which resulted in co-mingling of funds raised for missions and those raised for education, among a number of other accounting irregularities.[50] This later made Rice and Samuel Wait arch enemies when the latter was a tutor and trying to save Columbian College from financial hardship, stating that he "shall neither say nor do anything more to be on comfortable terms with [Rice]."[51]

While Lydia watched Rice captivate his audience at the Vermont Baptist

Association meeting in Poultney, it is probable that her parents and older brothers were there too. In fact, it is likely that Rice's charismatic style sparked Isaac's interest in attending the new seminary in Philadelphia, a prospect that would have to be funded by the Merriam family. It was an accepted norm that as the eldest son, Isaac would be entitled to a favorable advantage in his educational aspirations, despite the strain it created on family finances. Jonathan Merriam Sr. and his wife Sarah Conant Merriam relied on family and hired labor to support their enterprise. Fathers depended on sons to help on the farm; mothers employed their daughters to help with spinning, weaving, and needle arts until they left for marriage. With Sally and Samuel in Sharon and Isaac in Philadelphia, father Merriam was doing all he could to make ends meet, including considering sending apples and applesauce from his farm to sell in Sharon.[52]

Their second son, Jonathan Jr., was twenty-eight years old and unmarried in 1819. With Isaac's departure, this left him to help tend the family farm. The three younger boys, Abel, age fifteen; Charles Rollin, age thirteen; and Mylon, age eight, would have worked the farm in addition to their studies, but could not yet be expected to take on the level of responsibility the parents required. There are gaps in the record to tell us where Jonathan was during his early twenties, but by 1813 he was living in nearby Salisbury, Vermont (or Leicester, a nearby town served by the Salisbury post office) and had suffered an extensive illness. He was also apparently living a less than pious life, because Sally sent him a lengthy letter pleading that he "renounce the world the flesh and the devil and come up to the help of the Lord against the mighty." She had signed off as "your affectionate sister who God assisting will ever pray to heaven that your soul may not sink into hell." It had taken Jonathan a full year to reply that he was grateful for her concern, contrite about his wavering faith, and noncommittal about change. At the time, he did not sound much like the aspiring minister he would soon become.

By 1819 Sally and Samuel had set up housekeeping in Sharon, and Samuel had his eye on following in his brother-in-law Isaac's footsteps, although the financial burden to do so was daunting. While Samuel's $200 salary as a minster was meager, Sally could stretch the budget with gifts of food and clothing. The couple likely boarded free of charge in the home of Dr. Hewins, who first recruited Samuel for the job.[53] Attending seminary would mean giving up Samuel's salary as well as undertaking expenses in a city where the couple had no safety net—financial or otherwise. The school was set up to accommodate young men, not couples; Sally's presence in Philadelphia would require additional expenses that the family would have to bear. Complicating the situation was the fact that these deliberations were unfolding in the midst of a devastating economic decline. Several challenging agricultural years in New England, beginning in 1816 with the "year without a summer," brought a sharp downturn in business.

On the heels of these difficult years, a panic over credit beginning in the summer of 1818 led to a depression in 1819 that modest merchant farmers like Sally's father would have felt. Indeed, many families "struggled to hold onto the farms and businesses that they had used as collateral for their loans."[54] John Conant likely experienced the stress of recession in his general store and mill businesses as his customers suffered setbacks.[55] Despite these financial strains, the Merriams had been committed to send their oldest son Isaac to Philadelphia for studies. Anxious to obtain students, the governing board of the institution was generous with regard to tuition, but expenses for travel, board, and books would require cash.[56] Even in good times, cash was scarce in the family farm economy. As Thomas Wermuth points out, barter and trade were less risky than accepting cash, and "almost all products needed by farmers would be acquired without cash" by trading goods and services.[57] In a tightened economy, second son Jonathan helping to make the farm profitable back home would provide relief for the family.

By April 1820, a disturbing development had taken place: Jonathan Jr., apparently newly taken by the Holy Spirit, planned to leave the farm to pursue the ministry as well. This decision marked an apparent change in his life plans, as he wrote, "I have for a long time been persuaded that trials & disappointments awaited me in future life. . . . The usual scenes which were once so delightful are now fled forever."[58] His first attempt at a career, whatever it was, did not seem to end well. News of a son aspiring to the ministry was a point of pride on the one hand and fraught with economic repercussions on the other. The fever of the Second Great Awakening emptied family farms of much-needed field hands as men were called to the ministry, and the Merriam family felt this pressure.

Jonathan's decision to pursue the ministry in his older brother's footsteps upended family expectations. In the traditional farm family economy, sons were expected to be "industrious . . . a reliable contributor to the working household, not a go-getter with discrete aspirations."[59] But this dynamic began to change in the 1820s, when market forces shifted from an insular, family-focused economy to an individualized economy based on ease of trade. By the second decade of the nineteenth century, more than four thousand miles of road in New York alone "pulled fertile farmland from the rural interior into direct market competition with former privileged producing regions." This transformation produced a new self-identity for the Early American Republic man, one of "enterprise, self-importance, and a spirit of independence," which translated to ministerial as well as market aspirations.[60]

Jonathan's ministerial decision was a surprise, perhaps because of his earlier irreligious behavior and, judging from later comments, his somewhat mediocre preaching ability. When young men announced their intention to pursue the ministry, friends and family weren't always supportive. Charles Harding, a Vermonter who decided to follow a call in 1827, experienced derision from his sneering neighbors: "While a few thought him 'called of God.' Still others made the scurrilous charge that he sought to 'get my liveing, without work.' His own pastor 'laughed outright,' Harding claims, and his plan in general 'was treated by many with ridicule.'"[61] While Jonathan's skeptics didn't seem to be nearly so scathing, the women in the Merriam family were distressed, especially at the financial repercussions of Jonathon's decision to pursue the ministry. In a letter to Sally, her sister Lydia wrote, "Our dear parents are again left with the care of the estate. By this time, you say—surely Jonathan has not left them. . . . Yes, Sally, he . . . has left the care of the family for the pulpit."[62]

Sally shared her sister's concern for reasons beyond her parents' welfare. Sally's mother, Sarah Conant Merriam, wrote to Sally, "I am sorry to learn the perturbation of your mind on this affair," noting that they had struggled with Jonathan's decision. In the end, what could they do if a son was called to sound the "gospel trumpet"? Despite the financial trials ahead, mother Merriam wrote, "No, no, we must say go, go my son, go my Brother, proclaim Salvation to a dying world." She explained how this news would affect the family, "on account we are growing old and feeble of course must hire help indoor and out which will take off considerable of the profits of the farm."[63] Sally's mother, who at fifty years old was six years younger than her husband, continued, "Considering our embarrassments we shall not be able to help our children according to our former calculation." She reminded Sally that there were three young promising brothers yet at home, and wondered, "What if God should convert their hearts and call them to forsake Father and Mother and . . . tell them to lift up their voices like trumpets and show unto the people the way of salvation."[64] The implication was clear: because of economic uncertainty, the family could no longer support all their children as they planned—the shortfall would mean depriving the girls of financial assistance. It had been less than two years since the family had supported Sally in her transition to marriage. Since providing household goods was a joint responsibility of the parents and their children, the Merriams likely helped supply the newlyweds with household items when they moved to Sharon.[65] Now facing hard times, Sally's parents had five sons to worry about. Mother reported in her letter that Lydia had given up any expectations of monetary support and implied that Sally should do the same.[66] In September 1819, members of the Merriam family, including Sally's parents Sarah and Jonathan Merriam Sr., and her brother Isaac, visited Sharon before Isaac was to depart for Philadelphia. Jonathan Jr. likely stayed back in Brandon to tend to the farm while his parents were away.[67] Shortly after, Isaac began his journey to Philadelphia, leaving in Brandon his wife of six years, Mary Powers Merriam of Groton, Connecticut, along with their four year old and eighteen month old. Isaac's seemingly indifferent leaving behind of Mary and their young children later brought so much distress that her mental health would be threatened.[68]

Once in Philadelphia, Isaac started his studies and immediately began lobbying for both his brother Jonathan's and Samuel Wait's admittance to the school. Samuel Wait and the Merriam brothers, all in their late twenties, were representative of many "ministers-in-training," according to Moreshead. "The demographic composition of New England's ministry was changing, as older young men from humble backgrounds pursued higher education for the specific purpose of joining the ministry as a vocation."[69] Still unmarried, Jonathan's application was relatively straightforward, especially since the family had now agreed to cover his expenses. He soon joined his brother.[70] Samuel's attendance at the theological institute would be more complicated, because unlike Isaac, he very much wished to bring his wife along, and she very much wanted to go. She worried about her own intellectual growth in comparison to Samuel's, writing to him, "Every step you advance leaves me one farther behind."[71] Once Samuel was accepted, Isaac made efforts to find his sister Sally employment as an instructor "in Geography and drawing maps also in English grammar," but he was hampered by the recession under which the city still suffered. He reported, "As respects to Sally I have some fears that I may not be able to find a suitable place. Thousands here are out of employment." He continued, "The professor would choose to have his scholars free from all cares and . . . fears that having a wife would impede . . . the student."[72] Isaac probably agreed since he left behind his own wife and children; Samuel bringing Sally along would make Isaac look thoughtless in comparison. On February 4, 1820, once Samuel was admitted, Isaac urged a hasty departure and promised to continue his "exertion to obtain some employment for Sally notwithstanding the discouraging prospect."[73]

News of Samuel's enrollment sparked a flurry of activity to prepare for his journey. In two months, Samuel raised money for his expenses by soliciting donations from townspeople and selling off their family stores, including meat, bacon, and hay.[74] Once at the institute, he contributed to his expenses by taking on the tutelage of a young Quaker girl whom he taught for more than a year.[75] Samuel must have been heady with the excitement about his journey south. One can imagine Sally's distress as she emptied out bureau drawers and arranged to store their belongings, readying her husband for a new adventure while she anxiously awaited news about potential employment for herself. Weeks after Samuel arrived in Philadelphia, Sally made excuses to linger in Sharon, just twenty-five miles from the port of Providence, Rhode Island, which would allow her quick passage south if she were sent for. On April 24, she wrote, "I felt a strong inclination to stay here a few days longer in hope soon to hear from you again, though I dare not indulge much hope of following you. Do you think . . . I shall be able to fill the place you mention?"[76] Alas, no notice of employment or call for Sally came, and she was resigned to return to Brandon without Samuel.

In the course of just a few short months, both her older brothers and her husband had moved to Philadelphia to embark on an education Sally could only dream of. The sting of her favorite brother Jonathan's last-minute decision to attend the institute had administered the final blow to her hopes of keeping up with her husband's educational endeavors. On the same day she wrote Samuel a long letter outlining the financial and logistical details of his removal to Philadelphia, Sally penned a hasty letter to Jonathan. Her usual steady and florid hand was shaky and scrawled, belying the emotional state she was hoping to hide. "My dear Brother," she wrote, "I sometimes feel grateful to God that you are permitted to enjoy such advantages, although it should often cause the lone sigh to steal from my bosom." She did her best to seem happy for his "present situation"; still, Sally was resigned to the lot that God's will directed, not just with this particular turn of events, but in the larger providential forces behind them. "Happiness does not consist so much in our actual situation as in resignation to the allotments of Providence," Sally wrote. "When we can feel the supporting hand of God we can face the frowns of life undaunted."[77]

With that, Sally packed up her belongings, bid adieu to her friends, and began her journey back to Brandon alone.

Five

STRIVING

I have been much hurried a fortnight past
with making straw bonnets and have now a
fortnight's work on hand—so you see I have
not much time to read and write as you wisely
recommended.

—Sally to Samuel, June 6, 1820

SALLY KNEW FROM HER MOTHER'S LETTERS THAT ISAAC'S
wife Mary had been "desponding" since her husband's departure for Philadelphia, but until she arrived in Brandon, Sally did not understand the
darkness of Mary's "melancholy nerves" that she was expected to "break."[1]
Soon after her return to Vermont, Sally reported that Mary "appears rather
unwilling to have me absent from her long enough to make a satisfactory
visit at my father's."[2] Sally's plan to move back to her parents' farmhouse
was put on hold while she moved into brother Isaac's home to help her
sister-in-law. With two young children and her husband in Philadelphia at
his studies, Mary had her hands full, but the situation was more delicate
than a need for childcare. Sally and the rest of the family were worried
about her "gloomy state of mind . . . I hardly dare whisper, mental derange-
ment."[3] Whether Mary's emotional instability predated Isaac's departure to
Philadelphia, we cannot be sure, but it was clearly aggravated by it. Later,
after some months of distress, the family would intervene and convince
Isaac that his wife needed to return to her family in Groton.[4] Unlike Mary,
Sally was able to come to terms with her future as one-half of an evangelical

couple. When Samuel left her in Sharon to finish packing, she felt alone. While she exhibited "a depression of spirit" when she and Samuel parted in April 1820, the overland trip to Brandon had given her plenty of time to collect her thoughts, reflect on her situation, and check her faith.[5] As she did, Sally drew upon the same reserve that had helped her make the critical life decision to marry Samuel in the first place: the weight of duty that God put upon her.

This would not be the last time Sally suffered setbacks in her mission journey, and she responded with a spiritual and emotional resilience that would typify her life. She wrote to Samuel a few weeks after her return home, "A constant and abiding conviction that this is the path of duty generally make me feel reconciled to my situation. I am happy to learn that you are pleased and contented with your situation. I am glad you are there."[6] Whether she meant those words or not, Sally was beginning to experience the limitations of a woman's role, regardless of her ambitions. Sally drew from a reservoir of resilience that Ann Judson had modeled during setbacks and trials. It came from a theology locked in faith, which Sally was able to later articulate after studying the works of Jonathan Edwards. The orator's theories explained that the dogged Calvinism belief in total depravity and predestination were compatible with the concept of free will. It took some mental gymnastics to get there, but Edwards asserted that man had the ability to choose his actions, even though he was destined to behave in accordance to his true nature. Sally summed up Edwards neatly, writing that her duty called her to be content with her lot. "I do not mean a mere necessitous submission, which arises from the conviction that we cannot alter our case, but a cheerful acquiescence in the Divine Will."[7]

In the end, there was no mission experience that did not include sacrifice; it was woven into the fabric of the undertaking. If Samuel's current mission was to study in Philadelphia, Sally's was to support him from afar. In her words, "The privileges . . . are distinguished blessings. True, they bring with them privations, but they were voluntarily entered into and are no ground of complaint."[8] In this comment, Sally seems to accept the reality of a male's superiority and his freedom of choice. The letters during this separation demonstrate Sally's struggle to come to terms with the situation. In June, she had conveyed her feelings in first person, writing, "I am glad you are there." A few months later, her missive was more performative in nature, using a formal language that distanced herself from "complaints" about the "privations" of being back in Brandon, without a husband or income to rely on. Sally seemed to be experimenting with her pen to find her way forward in her relationship with Samuel and her place in the world.

It was not unusual for women in the Early Republic to run household affairs while their husbands traveled for work. Midwife Martha Ballard spent long stretches juggling her Hallowell, Maine homestead and her professional responsibilities while her husband Ephraim set out to unsettled lands as a surveyor, often risking attack from unhappy squatters.[9] Mary Palmer Tyler, wife of judge and playwright Royall Tyler, commented in her memoir that her husband was absent most of the year in 1802 after he joined the Vermont Supreme Court.[10] In fact, Mary mistakenly assumed that a minister was more apt to stay home to assist the wife in household matters, commenting, "I had always considered the wife of a clergyman the most enviable of women, as she could always have her husband with her . . . whereas my husband is absent much of the time and all the care devolves upon me."[11] A homebound minister's life may have been Mary Palmer Tyler's observation, but the burgeoning evangelical movement more often required ministers to travel on mission trips, attend association meetings, and accept prolonged assignments away from home, a situation with which Sally was now becoming all too familiar.

At the time of Samuel's departure, the couple anticipated a year of study, leaving their furniture in storage in Sharon for their eventual return. Once Samuel arrived in Philadelphia, however, conversation among Baptist leaders turned to the idea of relocating the school to Washington, DC, where it would perhaps garner the support of government leaders and play to the legacy of George Washington, who had advocated for a university in the new capital.[12] Sally hoped it would move, if for no other reason than Philadelphia's frequent epidemics. She considered the new capital to be healthier. In fact, Samuel was in Philadelphia only a few months before the students fled to the countryside to escape the fever.[13] For more than a year Sally wrote to Samuel pressing for an answer he did not have, as he replied, "I am still entirely in the dark concerning the time when I shall return."[14] The ambiguity about the length of his stay contributed to Sally's ability to surrender to the "allotments that Providence" dealt her and helped her muster the fortitude and ingenuity to face the challenges ahead.

Two major issues were on Sally's mind when Samuel left for Philadelphia: her own continued education and the couple's shared financial challenges. These two matters would become interwoven and overarching themes for the next two years, driven in part by Sally's own ambitions. Both Mary and Sally set out to improve themselves by reading books recommended to them from Philadelphia, hoping not to be left behind to "rust." While Sally labored to supply Samuel with much-needed cash to buy books for his studies and hers, she had no spare time to keep up with the reading he prescribed to her. This situation became an ongoing source of frustration, as Sally noted, "I have not much time to read and write as you wisely recommended."[15] While Sally was "convinced of [the] necessity and importance" of reading, it seems Mary took this possibility more to heart than she did, adding to Mary's already anxious state of mind.[16] Mary's early education in her hometown of Groton is not known, but her spelling and handwriting indicate that while she had a good foundation, she lacked the refinement and complexity that her sister-in-law's writings display, suggesting limited schooling.

What we know about Sally's early education we can piece together from contemporary reports, histories, and inference in family letters. By the time Sally began writing in her commonplace book in 1813, she had clearly received education beyond the basics, and her grammar, spelling, and composition suggest her parents (or Uncle John Conant) had been underwriting private instruction. She may have undertaken more formal studies after March 1813, when the Brandon school committee gathered at "early candle lighting" and chose John Arnold as clerk and Sally's father Jonathan Merriam Sr. as moderator. There being extra money in the coffers after paying "Mr. Jonathan Barlow for keeping School last winter," the committee voted to fund a "woman's school this summer which is to be kept three months."[17] While this is the first known record of a school for women in Brandon, early American leaders like Benjamin Rush had advocated educating women as early as 1787. In his published speech *Thoughts Upon Female Education*, Rush suggested that the "appropriate education of women would contribute to the general uplifting of the morals and manners of the country."[18] Republican leaders believed education would provide foundational advancements in America, and they devised plans for comprehensive school systems. Yet in the early years of the new country, "few of these . . . educational plans came to fruition," especially in rural areas like Brandon, where farmers needed their children in the fields and an aversion to taxes delayed implementation.[19]

Although Sally was nearly nineteen by the time the school committee voted for a women's school in Brandon, it is likely she and her sister Lydia took advantage of the opportunity. In 1818, just after Sally moved to Sharon, Lydia wrote, "I expect to attend the Academy this fall; my studies I am not determined on but think they will be rhetoric, reviewing grammar, arithmetic, and perhaps geography."[20] She would have been twenty-two at the time. Indeed, like many young women of the day, Lydia continued her studies while also running a small school before she married.[21]

The sporadic education provided to Sally by a tutor or infrequent sessions at the Brandon women's academy would not hold a candle to the classic training in languages, rhetoric, and sciences that Samuel was about to receive. Despite the miles between them, Sally wanted to learn with her husband, hoping that "the light you gain, may, while I remain at a distance, reflect on me."[22] Sally and Samuel's collective desire to acquire knowledge was an accepted aspiration for ministerial or missionary couples. Missionaries could be intellectually ambitious as long as they "were not motivated by 'a worldly ambition.'" Ambition to acquire classical knowledge was viewed as virtuous when "incorporated into the pious character of a missionary."[23] According to later correspondence, Samuel studied Greek, Hebrew, geography, philosophy, the *Harmony of the Gospels*, and other disciplines.[24] In addition, Columbian College President Staughton taught the sciences in the fashionable Charles Willson Peale museum in Philadelphia "as most of the animals . . . in his lectures may there be seen—in their skins."[25]

In the last decades of the eighteenth century, Peale, an accomplished and well-connected artist, began adding "curiosities" to his hall of portraits, advertising in papers for donations from collectors who would include Benjamin Franklin and Thomas Jefferson.[26] At the time of its "peak of prosperity" in 1816, the museum in Independence Hall, just blocks from the Baptisterion where converts were baptized by Staughton, was filled with Peale's portraits of Early Republic statesmen and aristocrats, alongside a menagerie of natural artifacts.[27] By the time Wait was in Philadelphia, the financial prospects of the once-profitable museum were "gloomy,"[28] and Peale likely was glad to have the income from the season passes he offered the seminary students.[29] Similarly, Staughton likely was glad to have the attention of such a notable Philadelphian as Peale; in fact, he later donated items brought to America from India by missionaries.[30] A consummate marketer, Peale also knew how to frame his message in a way that would appeal to followers of the Enlightenment as well as religious leaders. Just a few months before Staughton's theological seminary students began visiting the museum, Peale wrote that he was contemplating a "neat address on the subject of Natural history, in order to show the importance of a Museum to diffuse knowledge of the wonderful works of an all wise Creator."[31] Such rhetoric would help allay potential concerns of religious conservatives suspicious of scientific enlightenment.

Sally and Mary were left to learn in a secondhand fashion from their spouses. It was not unusual for male partners to educate their female counterparts; in fact, it could be part of the courting process. In a collection of her writings published by her family in 1925, Mary Palmer Tyler recounted an early conversation during the courtship of her parents. "The first question [Joseph Pearse Palmer] asked was, 'What books have you read?'" When the young woman's answer did not meet his approval, he replied with a sort of intellectual foreplay. "Your reading should be more extensive. I have a large library at college which will be at your service."[32] When Isaac and Samuel arrived in Philadelphia, they took advantage of the plentiful access to books in the busy port city and purchased not only their school texts, but also books to send to Mary and Sally in Brandon. Studying was part of Sally's first report to Samuel when she moved into Isaac and Mary's home. "I am much pleased with the conversations which Br. [Isaac] sent on natural philosophy. I think when I can obtain Leisure, I shall pay some attention to it."[33] By "conversations," Sally was likely referring to *Conversations on Natural Philosophy in Which the Elements of that Science are Familiarly Explained and Adapted to the Comprehension of Young Pupils.* This book by British writer Jane Marcet was hot off the presses in Philadelphia and, following the formula of her earlier works *Conversations on Chemistry* and *Conversations on Political Economy*, explained complex scientific topics through a series of conversations between young female students and their female teacher.[34] Demystifying the sciences to a female audience was becoming a popular trend. In 1817, chemist John Griscom organized a "course of lectures on natural philosophy exclusively for females" in New York City.[35] Letters between Sally and Samuel include a consistent nudging that she study the books he recommended, urging her to "Take time to read and write—nothing will be lost by it."[36] A letter from Isaac portrays a harsher approach, directed to both his sister Sally and his wife Mary. Isaac wrote, "I must give you a gentle reproof for not following my directions with respect to reading the book &.C." He continues, "If you had attended to this as I wished you both would have reapt the double advantage I intended, Information and employment for your minds, so that you would have less time . . . over your gloomy subjects."[37]

This advice is an example of several instances revealing Isaac's impatience with Mary's melancholy, which may have been postpartum depression. In the same letter, he thanked his sister for "alleviating" Mary's "trials," but pointed out that their "disquietude" was a burden that distracted Samuel and him from their studies. "If you can only make yourselves happy," he wrote, dismissing their feelings with a condescending platitude. By this time, Sally had communicated serious concerns about Mary's emotional state, which Isaac's comment brushes off without empathy.

Isaac's admonitions also reinforce the husband's role in schooling his wife, demonstrating that the idea of companionate marriage did not necessarily translate into equal standing between spouses. An exchange between Sally and Samuel early in their separation suggests a tacit agreement about Sally's willingness to be schooled by her husband. In a late July letter, Samuel pauses from sharing news to instruct Sally on her pronunciation, reminding her to "pronounce, been, as though written, bin, are as though spelled ar—quantity as though written quontity—these are not new things to you but sometimes we forget and need to be reminded of common things."[38] Samuel added a suggestion from her brother, who presumably was in the room while Samuel was writing to Sally. "Isaac thinks of another word—have—the a pronounced like a in fat—guard against saying hev—since not sense, when used for an adverb."[39] Sally accepted Samuel and Isaac's patronizing lesson, although perhaps through gritted teeth, writing she was "very grateful for the lesson" and that additional coaching would be "thankfully received."[40] Regardless, in addition to the lessons in diction, Samuel administered paternalistic instructions throughout their separation, suggesting that Sally "devote two hours a day" to studying books including the *Conversations* and *Cummin's Geography*,[41] and later, titles including *Jonathan Edwards on Religious Affections*, Christian conduct book *Thornton Abbey*, and *Stewart's Philosophy*.[42]

Less than a month after she returned to Brandon, another more pressing pursuit began to occupy Sally's attention—an ambition rooted in practical and corporal matters rather than scholarly, pious aspirations. By early June 1820 she wrote, "I have been much hurried a fortnight past with making straw bonnets and have now a fortnight's work on hand."[43] Sally had started a home manufacturing occupation, which would become an overwhelming concern during the ensuing two years. Sally developed her bonnet business as an answer to her family's economic challenges, but it was also a reflection of a national emphasis on domestic manufacture during the Early Republic. In his annual address to the General Assembly in late 1819, Pennsylvania Governor William Findley addressed the extreme economic burdens the citizens of his state were enduring. His speech cited a litany of factors that led to the current depression, including the "excessive importation and consumption of foreign merchandise."[44] While banking irregularities, land speculation, and contraction of credit were central causes of the economic tightening, Findley attributed some of the blame to citizens who preferred "the fabrics of foreign to those of domestic manufacture," which created a weak link in the early American economic cycle. Like other politicians of the time, Findley stressed, "Whatever doubts may exist as to the policy of our becoming a manufacturing people . . . the only safe reliance is upon our own resourses, ingenuity, and enterprise."[45] In other words, American manufacturing could be a deliberate act of patriotism to jumpstart the economy. Sally would have been aware of the grander "homespun" narrative when she began working dried straw into endless braids for bonnets. Extolling the benefits of North American-made home goods had served an economic agenda since at least 1753, when Boston hosted a demonstration of three hundred girls working spinning wheels for Governor William Shirley to launch the Boston Society of Encouraging Industry and Employing the Poor.[46] This narrative peaked at other times, including during the first few decades of the nineteenth century, when local agricultural societies hosted fairs and administered "prizes for flannel, plaids, table linen, colored counterpanes" and the like.[47]

Sally's first and foremost concern was keeping the Merriam-Wait economic engine afloat by earning money in a period when the "locus of responsibility had shifted very so subtly from a familial to individual enterprise."[48] Members of farm families became "part-time manufacturers and entrepreneurs in order to better themselves . . . working with their wives and children spinning cloth or weaving hats."[49] Samuel's occupation with his studies left Sally responsible for the family income at a time when market forces around her were dramatically changing. Her "spinning, weaving, sewing and knitting" would provide for her own livelihood while funding Samuel's education.[50] Given increasing economic pressures, Sally set her sights on a more ambitious endeavor that would give her an entrepreneurial advantage: the construction of fashionable straw bonnets. She seems to have acquired her bonnet-making skills from the time the couple spent in Sharon, Massachusetts. While bonnet making was not an unusual avocation for women of the era, it was laborious, and it included harvesting and drying the appropriate grasses, tedious braiding, and shaping and sewing the hat itself.[51] The area around Sharon was bustling with bonnet-making activity when Sally and Samuel arrived; there was a busy factory in nearby Foxborough, where most of the women and girls were employed.[52] According to oral histories, young girls in Foxborough were "required to braid a length that would reach the ground from the second story window before they could go out and play."[53] It is likely Sally learned the components of bonnet making while there; in fact, she may have brought some projects when she moved home to Brandon, since she already had a backlog just a month after returning.[54]

Sally does not mention bonnet making to Samuel again until the following summer when she announced, "Last summer and this I have been trying experiments continually to see if I could not discover the art of making bonnets in imitation of leghorn. I have at length succeeded. I have employed one girl in the work who has been braiding nearly three weeks and have engaged two or three more who I expect will be with us next week."[55] There are two noteworthy items in her announcement. First of all, Sally was not crafting just any style of bonnet; she was attempting to copy the fashionable bonnets imported from the Italian town of Livorno (called leghorn in America). Sally aimed to capitalize on the market for finely crafted "leghorns" to replace expensive imports. She thought the quality of her manufacture would rival both the Italian-made imports as well as inferior homemade bonnets, suggesting Samuel share samples she sent him in Philadelphia to "ask the opinion of some that are good judges of leghorn likewise the worth of bonnets of the quality of these specimens."[56] Indeed, her workmanship won a "small premium" of five dollars at a fair in nearby Castleton, after which she consigned it for sale by Rutland merchant J. Barret & Company, speculating its price at twenty dollars. Second, Sally was hiring out "girls" to execute the menial and time-consuming task of braiding. She traveled to nearby Rutland, the county seat, for "obtaining girls to work in my 'new bonnet factory.'"

Sally saw a market for leghorn bonnets, and she had ambitions to run a profitable business. There were female role models in New England to follow. While the Sharon-area hat factories were owned by men, a Hartford, Connecticut woman had become an entrepreneurial sensation for her leghorn bonnet business by 1821, making money and winning prizes for her work in her home state as well as in London.[57] Sally was well aware of Sophia Woodhouse's success, writing of her London prize, "The society in England for the promotion of the arts and sciences have awarded the famous Miss Woodhouse . . . for the grass bonnet that she made in 1819, a premium of nearly one hundred dollars, besides the silver medal of the society."[58] She measured her work against that of Woodhouse's, and commented to Samuel, "You will find by comparison that ours is far superior to hers in fineness."[59] Sally's satisfaction with the quality of her work, her perception of market demand, and her need for financial stability propelled her to pursue the leghorn bonnet trade with vigor.

Sally's bonnet business was a part of a larger shift in market dynamics, as women became part of the supply chain to meet the nation's growing demand for products. Households were responding to the "challenges of the sharpened market competition of the early nineteenth century. . . . Families in tenuous economic positions throughout rural New England . . . took part in the out-work production of a variety of products."[60] Rising demand . . . led rural entrepreneurs to look for more ample and cheaper supply of labor," which women could provide.[61] Sally was not simply providing handiwork for someone else; she was creating an ambitious enterprise of her own.

Sally's materially ambitious bonnet business may seem in some ways antithetical to her more religious aspirations, and indeed the two efforts at times seemed to sit in tension with each other. Early American Protestants had a "conflicted relationship with the market economy . . . as they tried to negotiate between religious principles and economic practice."[62] However, when guided by the larger and more purposeful goal to spread the gospel, evangelicals embraced the "tactics of marketing and mechanisms of commerce," as attested by the robust fundraising and publication enterprises constructed to fund missions and ministry.[63] The famous Presbyterian revivalist Charles Finney exhorted his followers to sacrifice for others and practice self-denial. "Wealth and capital were 'tools in which he serves God and his generation.'"[64] In that way, furthering the kingdom by funding missions and education was an honorable public and private affair. Sally viewed her bonnet business as a material means to a virtuous end.

Most of her letters to Samuel during these years included details about the manufacture and marketing of her bonnets to the extent that Samuel began teasing her about the enterprise. In January 1822, he began a letter, "Writing I much fear, my dear Sally, that the bonnet business will suffer for want of attention."[65] Samuel's careless jokes continued through the year, with Sally responding in March, "If I were not satisfied that you designed it merely for a joke I should be a little offended with what you suggested about 'shining in the firmament of grass bonnets.'"[66] Sally was aware of her preoccupation with the business, writing, "I suppose you will perceive that my mind is just now, very much exercised about a bonnet and likely you will pity my weakness."[67] She continued on, however, knowing that her success could mean a boon for the family income. On the completion of a particularly "fine" bonnet, Sally told Samuel that comparable bonnets in New York "went for $110, and the other 95 dollars." However, fetching such an exorbitant price felt unseemly to Sally, writing, "I do not expect success like this. It is making too great profit for Baptist ministers."[68] There was a limit on her ability to square her material success with her nobler ambitions, and that cap seemed to be in the $100 range.

While Sally's focus was on bringing in an income, however modest, rather than answering a patriotic call for American manufactures, she was astute enough to attempt to capitalize on the political benefits when it came to marketing her bonnets. In Brandon, she employed both family members and friends to act as "agents" for her bonnets, asking, for instance, a Mr. Pomeroy to take some hats to New York to sell when he went there on other business.[69] When the institute moved to the nation's new capital in August 1821, Sally hoped to tap into its political influence to use the made-in-America argument to sell her wares. After favorably comparing her work to that of Woodhouse's, Sally wrote to Samuel that friends "have advised to present a bonnet to the lady of president Munroe [*sic*] if he has one."[70] This was not an outrageous suggestion, as the early presidents were expected to "give audience to all comers, from supplicants off the street" to "passing vendors."[71] The following summer, as her expertise on her craft continued to improve, she contemplated, "I wish there could be found a few gentlemen, patriotic enough to pay us a handsome price of it, and make a present of it to the lady of the president of the U.S. I think her Ladyship would not blush to wear it."[72] Sally's instinctive marketing acumen told her that a celebrity endorsement from the First Lady would boost sales. To our knowledge, Samuel never solicited Congress—as Sally also suggested—or the White House to buy Sally's bonnets. He did, however, share her samples with friends in Philadelphia and Washington, DC, some of them members of the social elite, soliciting feedback on her behalf. In early 1823, the fashionable Sarah Miriam Peale, niece to Charles Willson Peale, arguably the first American female professional portrait artist, returned Sally's miniature sample by mail, expressing regret that Sally did not have it in her "power to make the leghorn bonnet for me," because her order had arrived after Sally had given up the enterprise.[73]

Despite her lack of sales to prominent politicians, Sally did manage to sell a number of bonnets before closing her business, one for as much as ninety dollars in Boston, which apparently met Sally's comfort factor in terms of appropriate income for a Baptist. Sally's portion of that income was forty-nine dollars, having shared in its construction with her sister Lydia.[74] Despite the generous price for that particular bonnet—nearly $2,000 in today's dollars—she sold most of her bonnets for between ten and twenty dollars according to her letters. In the end, the cost of manufacturing the leghorns and the difficulty of finding help prevented Sally from making it an ongoing enterprise. As early as a month into her endeavor, Sally wrote, "Grass bonnets cannot be made so cheap as I at first hoped they might be."[75] A few months later, after going to Rutland to obtain "girls" to help her braid the dried grass, she complained it was "difficult to obtain much assistance. There are but few here who would be suitable persons to engage in the business."[76] By the time she stopped making bonnets, she had painstakingly braided and shaped more than seventy-six hats.[77]

Regardless, closing her business had more to do with circumstance than profit. Sally's foremost desires were met when Samuel was hired as a tutor for Columbian College in Washington, DC, thereby allowing Sally to join her husband after two long years of separation. Finally, Sally and Samuel would reunite.

On October 10, 1822, Samuel Wait received an official offer from Enoch Reynolds, secretary of what was by then called Columbian College, to be a tutor. This possibility had been in the works for several months, and Sally had been hopeful that the $200 annual salary would allow her to join her husband in what was then referred to as "Washington City"—now Washington, DC—where the Philadelphia Theological Seminary had moved in early fall 1821. The couple had concealed her potential move from even their closest family members. Sally sidestepped the issue several times with her own father, presumably to keep any objections at bay before the details were settled.[78] A few weeks after the official offer, Samuel wrote Sally that he hoped her health would permit her immediate travel, prompting a flurry of activity, this time to ready Sally for a move southward. While this possibility had been contemplated for months, Sally wrote that the news was "quite unexpected," leading to her being in a "quite perplexed situation." She "did not expect to leave this place until winter; and have now much unfinished work on my hands of my own," including wool that needed to be "worked up" into a pelisse and pantaloons, "two counterpanes to color and weave and also a piece of flannel to weave besides much sewing."[79] The amount of work she faced suggests that she was either doing some of this work for hire or making fresh household goods for her anticipated new living arrangement. As she rushed to finish her tasks, she may not have stopped to consider just how different her marriage would be from the one she had experienced in the little town of Sharon.

Six

LOVING

My heart is constantly inclined to slide off
from the point of my pen.

—Sally to Samuel, March 24, 1822

Do the trustees of the College impose
a vow of celibacy on its professors? If so,
I think it doubtful whether it can ever
rise to much respectability.

—Sally to Samuel, May 19, 1822

AS SALLY BUSIED HERSELF FOR HER RELOCATION TO
Washington City in late 1822, she was moving toward a relationship that had
deepened with separation. The Waits had exchanged more than seventy-
five letters during their time apart, dispatches that two centuries later lift
the veil on their connection. In this chapter, I will pause from the narrative to explore how their thirty-two-month exchange, referred to as the
Columbian correspondence, illuminates Sally and Samuel's relationship
in a new way. Sally's courtship can be viewed through her journal, a semi-
public text that she probably planned to pass down to subsequent generations.[1] As such, what we know about their courtship is what Sally wanted
us to know. Alternatively, during their first two years of marriage, from
1818–1820, other than a few letters between family members, we have no
direct evidence of Sally and Samuel's intimacies. There are no first-person
accounts to examine, no exchange of words to parse, no inner thoughts to

interpret. We are left to reconstruct the Sharon years through the context of the community, church relations, and Merriam-Wait family dynamics, all set against the social, religious, economic, and political undercurrents of the day.

Our insight into their connection changes dramatically with Samuel's April 1820 move to Philadelphia and later DC, which established a four-hundred-mile divide that meant contact only by mail. The distance between the couple created a loss of familiar proximity and the daily subtleties of life—a sidelong glance or brush of hands, an extended silence followed by the clatter of cup on saucer, the familiar fragrance of another after a warm and dusty carriage ride. For more than two and a half years, Sally and Samuel had none of that. They relied on words scratched across a single or double sheet, often written late at night with a faulty pen in a poorly lit room. Reading a stand-alone letter is like listening to one part of a harmony—it does not resonate fully when it is detached from the larger work. A collection of correspondence is more like a full chord progression, its notes blending together to create a larger whole. In this regard, Sally and Samuel's long separation gives us deeper insight into their relationship than had they spent brief periods apart. The Columbian correspondence delivers their story in full harmony, at least in the context of what they wanted to reveal to each other.

Samuel's first course of study when he arrived at the theological institute in Philadelphia was *Harmony of the Gospels*, a text designed to organize and compare the New Testament gospels so that, as Samuel wrote to Sally, "the seeming contradictions, and any other difficulties which present themselves, can be carefully examined."[2] Samuel wrote about the gospel harmony frequently in his first year at the institute to the degree that the word seems to have taken on special meaning between the two. When Sally replied to remarks that Samuel had made in the margins of the *Latter Day Luminary* about the Burma mission, she referred to the passage using his "favorite word," harmony, writing, "I admire its composition, and the sweet and captivating spirit which it breathes."[3]

Sally had expressed enough interest in the gospel harmony that Samuel encouraged her to examine Isaac's copy when he returned home in the spring of 1820.[4] Another association of harmony that had meaning for them, as their daughter Ann Eliza pointed out in a later reminiscence, was their "very kind and conciliatory . . . dispositions." They also "sang very well together, sustaining two parts. This was not as common . . . as it is now." Ann Eliza goes on to relate a story about a presumed fundraising trip where they secured lodging but no promise of meals from a begrudging host. After some time in the house singing, the Waits "heard dishes rattled and finally they were invited to partake of a splendid supper."[5] Apparently, their ability to harmonize became the stuff of family folklore.

The harmony that Sally and Samuel experienced in a literal way—through their dispositions and two-part singing—also manifested metaphorically. In their own words, their relationship depended upon a blending of their complementary roles. Sally's pious ambitions were tempered by her willingness to accept the limits of a woman's role in the secular and evangelical communities. In some ways, she was considered a partner in their shared calling. For instance, as Samuel began imagining their life together after his schooling, he wrote about their future work, referring to "our studies" and joint decisions. "I have often inquired in my own mind what plan we should adopt in relation to our studies when we come to live together again. . . . How happy shall I be when we come to sit down together to make these calculations!"[6] This shared decision making, however, was set within the context of the gender norms that clearly established women subservient to their spouses both outside the home and in the bedroom, to which Sally subscribed. During a report to Samuel on news of friends, Sally wrote of Esquire Douglass's petition for divorce from his wife who, in Sally's words, was "very wrong and in direct violation of the laws of both God and man" by "refusing him admittance into her chamber and has failed in other respects, of yielding that submission to him, which her own happiness, and the religion of Jesus requires."[7]

Secular laws and religious customs required submission and obedience of the wife to her husband, and despite Sally's fiery spirit, she understood her place, though not without internal conflict. In one letter, Sally mentioned Samuel's wish that she be an "obedient wife" and burn his most recent letter after reading it. This request put her into a state of anguish, torn between obeying her husband (and therefore God's will), and parting with a cherished artifact from Samuel. Sally wrote, "I thought of your request, I thought of the very emphatical and significant words, 'Obedient Wife.'" After deliberating, Sally "looked on the 'precious morsel' and the fire alternately." In the end, she refused Samuel's request, writing, "My heart revolted, and my hand refused to lend its aid. What could I do in this dilemma? To burn it, or to be refractory, were either of them distressing."[8] After debating the alternatives, Sally "resolved to be 'obedient,' and burn the letter but not until after [Samuel's] return."[9] This and other letters during the Columbian correspondence demonstrate that Sally struggled with the tension between her own strong will and the "laws of both God and man."

During their thirty-two-month exchange, Sally looked forward to the day when they would no longer be "under the necessity of conversing through the medium of our pen and eyes," but until then the letters were a "welcome guest" and "sweet conversation."[10] Their first letters during their separation reveal a relationship trying to gain a comfortable foothold. In the beginning of this period, the epistles were frustratingly infrequent. A mail system affected by the vagaries of weather contributed to delays, but more to blame was the busyness of both spouses—Samuel with his studies and tutoring, Sally with her contributions to the household economy. Filling a sheet in long hand in pen and ink took time. A full sheet was fifteen by eleven inches, folded over to seven and a half by eleven inches, leaving four pages to fill. Samuel's early letters were rushed, impersonal, and infrequent; Sally's were listless, anxious, and despondent. Samuel's letters, sometimes tucked inside a religious publication, provided Sally with an anxious rush of emotions to her otherwise depressed spirit. When the mail was fetched, it was with "trembling hands and eager eyes" that Sally searched between the pages of a Baptist tract for Samuel's familiar hand. Finding it would bring Sally "an ecstasy of joy" as she declared, "Blessed be God! Blessed be God!"[11]

A close reading of the exchange between the couple reveals gaps in the narrative over the course of their separation, leaving us to speculate as to how or why some letters are missing. Already noted are the manuscripts lost to the rain-damaged barrel that was thrown away by a descendant. To lose a handful of letters from among an otherwise faithful chronology of missives seems unlikely, however. Several circumstances can be theorized to explain the missing letters. First, as noted above, Samuel often tucked letters between the leaves of the *Latter Day Luminary* and later the *Columbian Star*. As Sally reported in October 1820, the comparative cost of a private letter to that of a tract could save the couple money.[12] "Postage on the luminarys 6 cents. A cheap way of conveying letters; do send me a whole sheet in the next," Sally wrote. In the same letter, Sally mentions having "expended $1.34 for letters," not an inconsequential amount for the struggling couple.[13] Therefore, if some of Samuel's letters were tucked into religious tracts, it is possible that an unknowing descendent might have discarded a stack of *Latter Day Luminaries*, not realizing personal notes were hidden inside. A second explanation could be the nature of shared family missives. Since Samuel was living with Sally's brother Isaac, and Sally was living with Isaac's wife Mary, the couples often added personal notes to letters primarily penned by the others. Likewise, a letter from Sally's brothers to their parents would also contain news from Samuel to Sally, since letters were often shared and read aloud to friends, family, and neighbors. Those letters would have been passed down (or not) through the descendants of Isaac and Mary, or Jonathan and his wife Achsah, and are not, for that reason, in the Wait collection. Additionally, as noted, some groups of letters were bundled and handed down to specific descendants. Finally, a last possible explanation for the seeming randomness of missing letters arises from a desire for propriety and privacy about certain topics, as evidenced by Samuel's request that Sally burn the December 1821 letter. In the end, it seems she did burn it, for the letter to which she refers cannot be found in the Wait collection. What topic warranted its destruction, we will never know. In this vein of secrecy, Sally often instructed Samuel to insert separate pages meant just for her into longer letters that she could share with family. This allowed her to "conceal it without exciting any suspicions."[14] It is possible these single sheets filled with private concerns were secreted away, out of the family record.

Despite the dozen or so missing letters, there is an extensive exchange between the couple during the Columbian correspondence. Almost as soon as Samuel arrived in Philadelphia and Sally returned to Brandon, Sally asked Samuel for remembrances to ease the pain of separation. First, she asked for a lock of his hair, admonishing that he not laugh at her romantic request.[15] This practice was a common sentimentality at the time, as the hair of friends and family members often served as keepsakes, put in lockets or braided into intricate designs. Presumably Samuel complied with her request, because it was never mentioned again. A few months later, Sally returned the favor by fashioning a ring of her hair to send to Samuel, which he admitted to treating "foolishly" by wearing it until it frayed.[16]

The exchange of tresses settled, another request proved to be more complicated and became the subject of many letters back and forth for the next fifteen months. "One favor more: do not deny me this. Get your profile taken in painting and send it to me in a letter," Sally wrote. "This I should prize more highly than anything else you can send me. I will send you money to pay for it."[17] There are no fewer than twelve mentions of a painted profile, portrait, or shadow between Sally and Samuel between July 1820 and September 1821, when the institute (and with it, Samuel) relocated to Washington City. The busy city of Philadelphia would have had several options for various types of likenesses during that time, ranging from a full-size oil portrait costing thirty dollars, to a painted miniature for ten dollars, or a miniature profile for two dollars, as Raphaelle Peale solicited in *Poulson's American Daily Advertiser* in 1804.[18] While a large portrait would have been financial folly for Samuel Wait and his brothers-in-law

Isaac and Jonathan Merriam, the three men exerted a good deal of time and effort to satisfy requests for likenesses from the ladies back home. Isaac sat for a portrait, most likely a miniature, in the early summer of 1821 before returning to his family in New England, but the "Sputtering Frenchman," as Samuel nicknamed the artist, never delivered the goods, requiring Samuel and Jonathan to fruitlessly pound on the door of his home.[19] Earlier that spring, Samuel sat for a miniature oil portrait but was unhappy with its result, even though he had brushed up his hair to raise his "foretop" and asked the artist to make him look contented and cheerful, per Sally's instructions.[20] The best quality portrait of the three men was, in Samuel's opinion, the one Jonathan had procured in early April from "the old gentleman." It is possible that the artist in question was James Peale, the brother of the famous artist and museum keeper Charles Willson Peale.

At the time, James, an established artist who painted countless miniatures as well as landscapes and full-scale portraits, was seventy-two and living in financial hardship, as evidenced by his brother's plea to Secretary of War John Calhoun to expedite remittance of his war pension.[21] Despite his advanced age and poor eyesight, James Peale was probably still accepting commissions to support his large family. There are a number of connections between the emerging Baptists and the Peale family, including the friendship between William Staughton and Charles Willson Peale that ultimately led to Staughton's 1829 marriage to James's daughter Anna Claypoole Peale. Another clue to the identity of the artist of the now-lost Jonathan Merriam portrait is Samuel's description of visiting the portraitist's home with Jonathan during his sitting. While there, Samuel saw the unfinished portrait of legendary English Baptist missionary William Ward, who had visited Columbian College in March.[22] As Wait reported, Ward sat for Peale, who had "drawn it for Dr. Staughton and the Dr. is not to know of it till it is presented to him." Wait described the painting of Ward "sitting in a chair with his head reclined on one hand, or rather on the fingers of one hand—this is as large as real life."[23] This work, which seems to be lost, was possibly the last portrait of Ward, who returned to the mission field in Serampore and died two years later.

While most Philadelphians could not count on influential Baptist connections for a treasured miniature by the likes of James Peale, they could take advantage of new technology that was helping to democratize American portraiture. The Charles Willson Peale museum boasted a physiognotrace, a device that allowed the sitter to trace his profile to the page. In an 1803 advertisement, the museum announced that the "ingenious Mr. John I.

Hawkins, has presented to C.W. Peale's Museum . . . a curious machine . . . for the use of the Visitors." Hawkins, an inventor who collaborated on projects with the likes of Thomas Jefferson, Charles Willson Peale, and Columbian College board member Burgess Allison, developed his machine based on the 1787 invention of Gilles-Louis Chretien.[24] It was just before the institute moved in September 1821 that Samuel stopped at the museum for a profile made by the physiognotrace, which was usually operated by Moses Williams, once enslaved by Charles Willson Peale.[25] The outlines of the subject were typically impressed on folded banknote paper, producing four identical silhouettes when they were cut.[26] Having spent less than a dollar, Samuel was able to give one to the institute, one to Sally, and two to his mother; one for her and one for his favorite sister Betsey.[27]

Apart from this exchange of remembrances, the construction of Sally and Samuel's letters demonstrates the evolution of their familiarity over time. Samuel wrote the first letter of the Columbian correspondence to Sally from the road during a stop in Providence, Rhode Island. Just over a page long, the letter was occupied with details about his travels—mode of transport, church meetings he attended, the cost of small items he purchased along the way. Other than hoping that "a kind Providence will take particular care" of Sally, the letter was brisk and utilitarian, with none of the intimacies a lonesome spouse would have craved. While Sally was happy to receive any communication from Samuel, his early efforts rarely met her expectations. His letters were too short, too infrequent, or too devoid of detail. Thus, she set out to coach him on his letter-writing technique, and Samuel proved to be a teachable student. In response to Samuel's letter tutoring Sally on her pronunciation, she in turn schooled him on letter writing. In August 1820 she wrote, "Do not again, my dear, make excuses about having nothing to write, I am sure you never would. Did you fully realize how much pleasure I receive, from every line you send me. If you have not new things to write, something else, will answer as well."[28]

The letter-writing lessons continued as the months unfolded, with Sally instructing, "I am extremely fond of long letters, but short ones will answer. A half sheet once in three or four weeks is better than whole ones separated by six weeks."[29] And, "Do not say so often 'particulars when I see you,' do give me some of them now."[30] Over time, the frequency and length of Samuel's letters increased, and the particulars Sally asked for came in abundance, as he took the time to fill four sides of a double sheet, outlining details about his studies, her brothers, and the college administration. From the beginning, Sally took more risks of intimacy in her writing than did Samuel, penning just after their separation, "While in your embrace the moments fled on the wings of bliss."[31] Later, Sally's romantic reminiscences caused her to self-censure, writing, "My heart is constantly inclined to slide off from the point of my pen."[32] As for Samuel, it took him longer to express intimacy; it was a year into their correspondence before he called her "my dear Sally," "my Love," or "my dearest earthly friend."[33] In the beginning of the Columbian exchange, Samuel tended to communicate through sometimes dismissive teasing as opposed to Sally's sentimentalism, turning the tables when he admonished her for withholding details, writing, "Supposing some person should ask me what you are doing. I could not for my life tell them whether you were making caps, bonnets, gowns or mending stockings."[34] This comment further illustrates the couple's adherence to the gender roles dictated by society.

Given the cultural assumptions of the time, it is not surprising that Sally, for the most part, willingly lived her life within the women's sphere. In fact, she believed this was her destiny, writing to Samuel in 1821, "That which providence has designed for me, is for me the best."[35] On Sally and Samuel's third anniversary, she mused about their relationship within these terms, writing, "Perhaps God has given me to you to make you humble, and you to me to make me sensible of my weakness and vanity." This reinforced the accepted assumption that men were strong and concerned with greatness, while women were weak and preoccupied with the superficial. The gender norms were so entrenched in Sally's time that women not only accepted this construct, but also looked to it as a source of inspiration. Sally considered it her calling to spread the gospel through her role as helpmeet to Samuel's ministry, and while she pushed against the ideological boundaries of the women's sphere, she by and large made her place within it. With regard to her acceptance of her role as background to Samuel's achievements, she wrote, "I would not retard your progress by endeavoring to hold you back, or to draw you aside. It is in my heart to assist you, to do you good, and to make your days glide serenely on."[36] In this sentiment, Sally framed her destiny in the context of sacrifice to a higher purpose, adding, "Not all the allurements this world can possibly present, would tempt me to exchange situations with any female on earth."[37]

This type of sentiment, however, was balanced with an occasional outburst against the inherent power structure. When Sally first contemplated her move to Washington City in the spring of 1822, the college administration was unprepared to accommodate the young couple since the main college building was constructed to school and house single men. Sally protested to Samuel, "Do the trustees of the College impose a vow of celibacy on its professors? If so, I think it doubtful whether it can ever rise to much respectability."[38] Sally was careful to frame her insistence on their living together within the context that it was in the best interests of the college. Sally suggested that most men, "once they happen to be deeply in love, would much soon relinquish a professorship however respectable, than their fair one. This would subject a College to a continual change of professors, which would in my opinion have a tendency to sink its reputation and worth."[39]

While Sally lived within the role dictated by general society and the evangelical community, she expressed her own mind in letters and, presumably, in person. A woman living a life of purpose in the early nineteenth century required a compromise of temperament, one that enabled her to straddle the worlds of submission and ambition. Creating harmony in a relationship depended on each partner playing his or her role, and Sally's letters illustrate her ability to follow the strictures of her providential destiny while defending her positions. The couple's interdependent roles fluctuated with the changes in Samuel's vocational circumstances, which were dictated not by Sally, but by her parents or husband. While in Sharon, Sally took on the role as helpmate to her husband's primary function as minister. When Samuel pursued his studies in Philadelphia, Sally took on the additional responsibility to sustain the family economy by starting a bonnet-making enterprise. Sally's drive and adaptability gave the couple the necessary framework to pursue their perceived mutual calling. Their Columbian correspondence reveals a complex relationship that defies a neat categorization during a time when gender roles were changing. Sally's ability to negotiate the grey areas of minister, provider, and helpmeet would prove valuable as she entered the capital of the Early Republic and the new seat of Baptist influence. In December 1822, after nearly three years apart, Sally was moving to Washington City, a place where the status quo was being questioned and traditional conventions upturned.

Oil painting of Sally's mother, Sarah Conant Merriam, date unknown. This was likely painted by an itinerant artist passing through Brandon, Vermont. In the author's possession; photo by Ken Bennett. (45 x 41 cm)

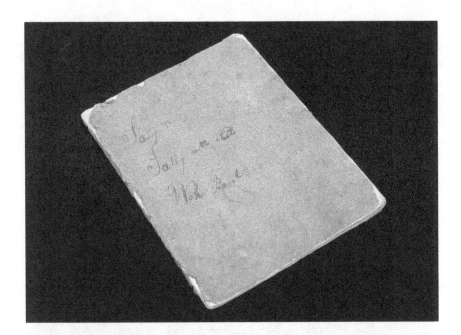

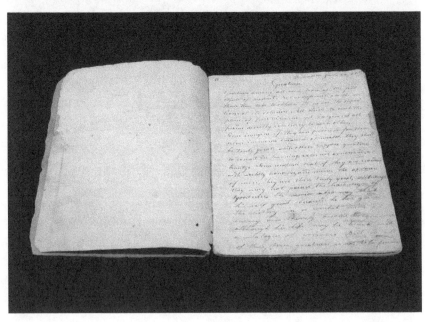

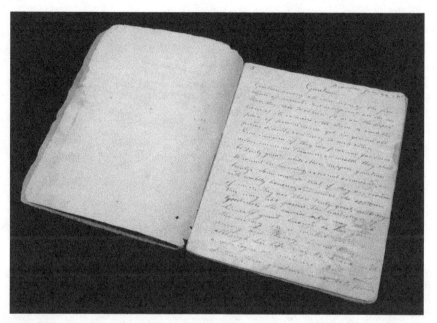

Sally Merriam's commonplace book, 1812–1814. A commonplace book was a popular genre for gathering knowledge by copying the writing of others or working out essays of one's own. Most of the entries in Sally's store-bought booklet are authored by her. In the author's possession; photo by Ken Bennett. (19.05 x 15.24 cm)

Masonic membership certificate showing Samuel Wait as a member of the Rain-bow Lodge in Middleton Vermont. It is dated in the Anno Lucis year 5814, using the ceremonial Masonic dating system which is based on the Gregorian year plus four thousand, in this case signifying 1814. Samuel would have been twenty-five when he joined the Masons, not long before he met Sally. © Special Collections & University Archives/Wake Forest University; photo by Ken Bennett. (20.5 x 28.5 cm)

Small trunk belonging to Samuel Wait. It is lined with newspaper articles describing the Battle of Waterloo in 1815, the year Samuel arrived in Brandon to study with Sally's minister Abiel Fisher. © Special Collections & University Archives/Wake Forest University; photo by Ken Bennett. (18.5 x 45.7 x 25.5 cm)

The exterior of Sally's journal, 1815–1817. Sally likely constructed this journal herself, hand cutting the text leaves and sewing them together before adding the cardboard cover. The patterned hand-blocked paper may have been a wallpaper remnant. © Special Collections & University Archives/Wake Forest University; photo by Ken Bennett. (16 x 10.5 cm)

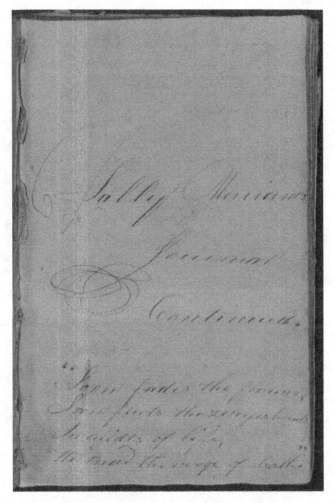

The title page of Sally's journal, 1815–1817, reads "Sally Merriam's Journal Continued," indicating an earlier version existed. Unfortunately, it has been lost or destroyed. © Special Collections & University Archives/Wake Forest University; photo by Ken Bennett. (16 x 10.5 cm)

The first page of Sally's journal, 1815–1817, describing a gathering at Elder F[isher]'s, which likely included Samuel Wait. © Special Collections & University Archives/Wake Forest University; photo by Ken Bennett. (16 x 10.5 cm)

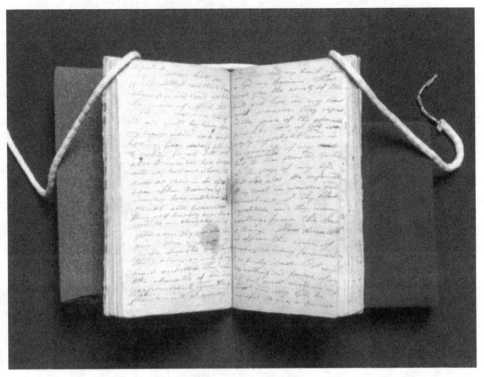

Interior of Sally's journal, 1815–1817. On this page Sally describes her
conversion, writing, "Jesus said to me daughter be of good cheer thy sins
are forgiven thee." © Special Collections & University Archives/Wake Forest
University; photo by Ken Bennett. (16 x 10.5 cm)

Pastel still life painted by Sally Merriam Wait, date unknown. This is an example of a theorem painting, which were popular stenciled still-life arrangements during the 1800s. © Special Collections & University Archives/ Wake Forest University; photo by Ken Bennett. (30.8 x 23.6 cm)

Watercolor by Sally Merriam Wait, 1820. Sally seems to have painted a
number of theorem paintings as well as freehand portraits of her hosts
when she and Samuel traveled raising money. Given the date, Sally may have
painted this after Samuel left for his studies in Philadelphia. In the author's
possession; photo by Ken Bennett. (56 x 46 cm)

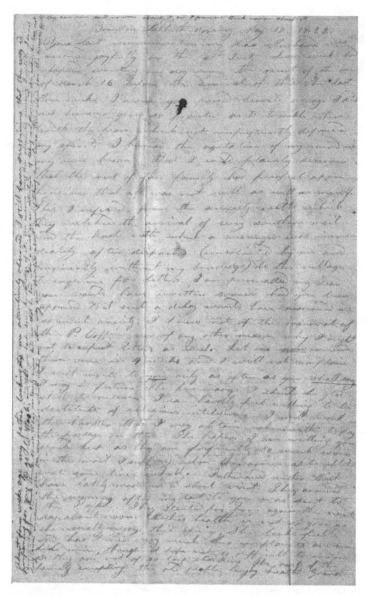

One of the hundreds of letters between the Waits when they were separated during their marriage. This letter from Sally to Samuel was written 1822 when he was at Columbian College and she was in Brandon, hoping to join him. She writes, "Do the trustees of the College impose a vow of celibacy on its professors? If so, I think it doubtful whether it can ever rise to much respectability."
© Special Collections & University Archives/Wake Forest University; photo by Ken Bennett. (20.7 x 33.1 cm)

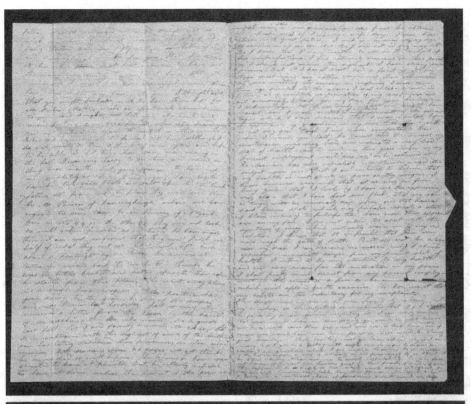
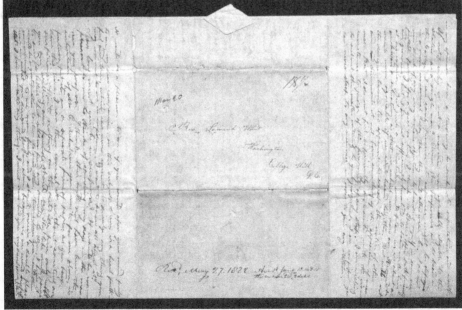

Ann Eliza Wait's christening gown, c. 1826, most likely sewn by Sally Merriam
Wait. Ann Eliza was born in Washington City while the couple lived at Colum-
bian College. © Wake Forest Historical Museum, Wake Forest, NC; photo by
Sean Wilkinson. (66.04 x 45.085 cm)

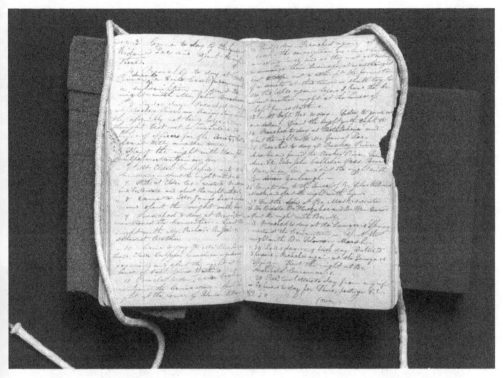

Diary of travels and preaching appointments belonging to Samuel Wait, 1826–1833. Unlike the performative narrative of Sally's journal, Samuel's diary is a workaday accounting of the details of his travels, preaching, and fundraising efforts. © Special Collections & University Archives/Wake Forest University; photo by Ken Bennett. (16 x 10.5 cm)

State of North Carolina Wake County

Know all men by these presents That I Benjamin
G Harrison of the County of Wake and State
aforesaid as administrator to the estate of Nancy
Smith dec'd for and in Consideration of the Sum
of Three hundred and twenty six dollars and fifty
Cents of lawful money of the sd State to me
in hand paid by Samuel Wait of sd County
at or before the Sealing and delivery of these
presents the receipt whereof I the sd Benjamin G
Harrison do hereby acknowledge have granted bargained and Sold and by these presents do grant
bargain and Sell unto the sd Samuel Wait his
executors administrators and assigns two Negroes Viz
Dicy and Mary to have and to hold sd Negroes and
Other the above bargained and Sold or mention or intended
to do to be to the sd Saml Wait his executors administrators and assigns forever and I the sd Benjamin G
Harrison as administrator to the Estate of sd Nancy Smith
all and Singular the sd two Negroes unto the sd
Saml Wait his executors administrators and assigns
against me the sd Benjamin G Harrison as administrator to the Estate of the sd Nancy Smith and against all
and every other person and Persons whomsoever shall
and will warrant and forever defend by these presents,
of all and Singular which sd Negroes I the sd Benjamin
G Harrison have put the sd Saml Wait in full possession by delivering to him the sd S Wait two Negroes
at the Sealing and delivery of these presents in the name
of the sd Dicy & Mary hereby bargained and Sold or
Mentioned or intended to to be, unto him the sd Saml
Wait as aforesaid In Witness whereof I the sd
Benjamin G Harrison have Set my hand & Seal &
this the 2nd Jany 1839   Benjamin G Harrison {Seal}
Witness Wm R Thomas Junr

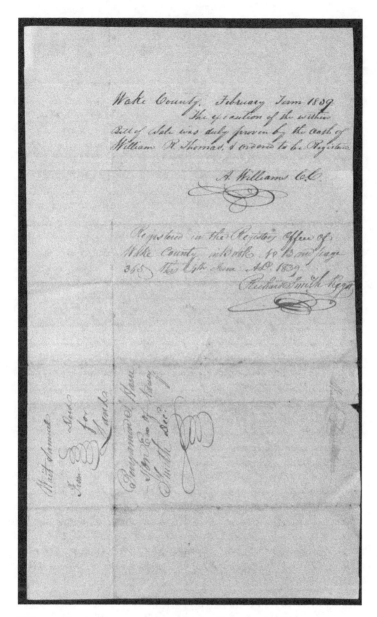

Sales receipt indicating the purchase of two enslaved women named Dicey and Mary by Samuel Wait, signed by S. Harrison, the executor of the estate of Nancy Smith. The Waits seemed to have purchased these enslaved workers to assist them in running a boarding house they were planning to open. © Special Collections & University Archives/Wake Forest University; photo by Ken Bennett. (32 x 18.7 cm)

Samuel Wait carte de visite, by L. W. Andrews Studio
of the Photographic Art, Raleigh, NC, undated.
© Special Collections and University Archives/
Wake Forest University; photo by Ken Bennett.
(10.5 x 6.4 cm)

Photograph of Sally and Samuel Wait, date unknown. Judging from the suit that Samuel wears in this photograph and his carte de visite, it is possible these photographs were taken during the same studio visit. In the author's possession; photo by Ken Bennett. (29 x 35 cm)

Sally Merriam Wait's New Testament, date unknown. Inside, written in
pencil, "Sarah M. Wait, Wake Forest College." In the author's possession;
photo by Ken Bennett. (22.86 x 14.605 x 2.54 cm)

This portrait of Sally Wait hangs in the vestibule of Wait Chapel at Wake Forest University; the artist and date of the original portrait is unknown. This is a copy completed by Arman Thibault de Navarre in the 1970s or 1980s after the original was stolen, possibly as a student prank. © Special Collections & University Archives/Wake Forest University; photo by Ken Bennett. (90.805 x 73.025 cm)

The companion to Sally's portrait is the original of Samuel Wait, artist and date unknown. It is possible these portraits were made upon Samuel Wait's retirement from the college in 1845, but the university records with such details are lost. © Special Collections & University Archives/Wake Forest University; photo by Ken Bennett. (89.535 x 71.755 cm)

This "wedding basket" from China was a gift to Sally from Eliza Moring
Yates, wife of missionary Matthew Tyson Yates, c. 1850. This was likely
a prized possession of Sally's since it represented the Waits' success in
preparing young men for the foreign mission movement. In the author's
possession; photo by Ken Bennett. (22.86 x 17.78 x 10.16 cm)

Daguerreotype of Samuel Wait, c. 1860. © Special Collections & University Archives/Wake Forest University; photo by Ken Bennett. (9.5 x 8 cm)

Golden Anniversary photo of Ann Eliza and John Brewer and family,
1894. John Brewer is the man with the ample beard seated in the
center; Ann Eliza is to his left. While the Waits had only one surviving
child, Ann Eliza and John Brewer had ten children, resulting in a large
extended family. © Special Collections & University Archives/Wake Forest
University; photo by Ken Bennett. (21.7 x 28 cm)

Part Three

UNSTABLE GROUND

Seven

MOVING

> While on my journey to this place I had the
> happiness to be in company with Mrs. Judson,
> wife of the missionary at Rangoon from Phila-
> delphia to Baltimore. This Privilege I place with
> one of the felicities of my life.
>
> —Sally to Aunt Conant, December 1820

SALLY WAS UNEASY ABOUT TRAVELING SO FAR BY HERSELF. The trip from Brandon to Washington City—as Washington, DC was referred to in the Early Republic—would entail wagons, carriages, a schooner, a steamboat, and overnight accommodations in a strange city. In that era women avoided traveling alone whenever possible, and families often engaged suitable companions to accompany solo travelers on their journeys.[1] Sally approached Judge Charles Rich and Rollin C. Mallary, Vermont acquaintances who were serving in the US House of Representatives, about taking on that role, but neither worked out.[2] After citing a number of challenges about finding the proper escort, Sally wrote, "If I was a Mrs. Judson I suppose I should not hesitate about starting the journey alone. But as it is I must confess I lack a little for courage."[3] Sally would have been aware that her Baptist heroine was wending her way to America at that time. In ailing heath, Ann Hasseltine Judson left Adoniram in Burma and traveled west for rest and medical attention. After a stop in England—where she was hosted by philanthropist and Parliamentarian James Butterworth—she visited the United States for the first time since sailing to India ten years earlier.[4]

While in England, Mrs. Judson may have sensed her new celebrity, but it was her arrival in the United States that brought her popularity into focus. American Baptists clamored to spend time with their pious heroine, to the degree that she was forced to turn down invitations in order to rest and heal.[5] Sally could have only dreamed that the two would meet, but meet they did. The details of how the encounter unfolded are unclear, but someone, likely Columbian College President William Staughton, arranged for Sally and Ann to accompany each other on a portion of their individual journeys, on a steamboat from Philadelphia to Baltimore. After their meeting, Sally described her delight in a letter to her aunt: "This privilege I place with one of the felicities of my life. I have often said I would go farther to see Mrs. Judson than any other female on earth of whom I had any knowledge."[6] Sally was "not in the least disappointed" with Ann. Sally described her as a "woman of firm feelings, sensible, discreet, ardent in her piety, possessed of great mental endowments among which fortitude and perseverance shine conspicuously bright."[7] Sally knew her relatives and friends back home would want a full report on what this international celebrity was like in person, down to the color of her eyes and the complexion of her skin. She wrote, "Her person is tall . . . but not very slender, her hair dark, her complexion not very fair. Her features [are] regular and pretty well formed and her eyes of a dark brown, nearly black, and are very expressive."[8] Sally was enamored.

Meeting Mrs. Judson must have reaffirmed the pious ambition that had driven Sally from the time of her conversion, an ambition that had been somewhat derailed over the past five years by her marriage as well as economic and social realities. The couple's first position at Sharon Baptist Church may have met Sally's expectations of spiritual service, but it was a far cry from the dramatic and selfless sacrifice of women of the caliber of Ann Judson or Harriett Newell. Samuel's desire to further his education clearly set the course for a higher calling, but the price was Sally's ability to be on equal intellectual and spiritual footing with her husband. While Sally and Samuel were separated, he was able to increase his knowledge in languages, sciences, philosophy, and religion while Sally remained in the traditional woman's sphere in New England. She had fallen behind in her initial plan to keep up with Samuel's "assignments" when the family's economic situation forced her to spend nearly all her time braiding dried grass to shape into bonnets and finding customers to turn her work into cash. Their separation had become an obstacle to the achievement of the Ann Hasseltine Judson ideal. Her dream of becoming a mutual helpmeet in the mission field, equipped with knowledge to persuade even the most resolute infidel to accept Christ, seemed to be vanishing within constraints that were still all too real. The Baptist tracts and missionary magazines may have been holding up resolute and pious women as models of independence, but most women were still limited by the societal, familial, and economic realities that put men's education and privilege first. Still, Sally was able to frame this setback within the Edwardsian concept of accepting the "dispensations of Providence" willingly. She wrote to Samuel that God's allotments were "appointed by a tender Father, and I feel that I have no cause for complaint, but much for gratitude."[9] Sally's selflessness was expected—of herself and by her husband, her parents, and her church.

Meeting such a celebrated person on her trip south presaged the world she was about to enter. It was a world far away from the little towns of Sharon, Massachusetts and Brandon, Vermont—one where the Waits would attend levees with the president and members of Congress, dine with the Marquis de Lafayette, and become friends with famous artists and descendants of first Virginian settlers. Their time at Columbian College was filled with the promises of a growing denomination that intersected with the celebrity, power, and intrigue of a capital in formation. The ambitions of the Baptists were lofty, and the stakes were high, but their foundations were built on unstable ground.

Sally's nervousness about the move was about more than just travel logistics; she was intimidated by the thought of living in the burgeoning nation's capital. It is unlikely that in her twenty-eight years she had ever been to a town larger than Rutland, where she went to hire braiders for her Brandon bonnet business. Washington City was the seat of government, its political intrigue written about in the Vermont papers. Having spent eighteen months in the city of Philadelphia while the institute was located there, Samuel knew Washington, DC did not compare with cities of larger size and import. "Do not feel any embarrassment about coming to this place," Samuel wrote to Sally a few weeks before she began her journey. "True this is Washington City, but you will be surprised when you come to see it, especially if you should have a view of N.Y. & Phil. first."[10] Indeed, the populations of the three cities in 1820 could not compare, with New York at 123,000, Philadelphia at 63,000, and the nation's capital at under 10,000, a far cry from the original planners' dreams of a city of "160,000 in a few years."[11] The bold and idealistic plans of Washington City took years to emerge, delayed by periods of ambivalence, scarcity, and war. During Jefferson's presidency, the capital city was a "butt for jokes, and poking fun at Washington became something of a national pastime."[12] In 1803, part of the Capitol ceiling fell in and supporting columns split, requiring them to be "wrapped with white muslin to conceal defects," an apt symbol for propping up the government ideals that were not so easily articulated in practice.[13] During a tour through the states just three years before Sally arrived, Nottingham, England, native Emanuel Howitt upon entering the city described his "disappointment in [the city's] appearance, which is rather that of a straggling village, than the capital of this vast empire."[14]

For years, the government struggled to execute the grand plans of Pierre L'Enfant, who was commissioned by George Washington in 1791 to lay out an elegant and sprawling Greek Revival city that would rival any in the world. Even after the executive mansion and Capitol building were constructed, the boggy topography made for unstable trekking. According to historian James Sterling Young, "cows grazed on future plazas ... and hogs rooted in refuse" along the roads.[15] Howitt commented that "the romantic hopes formed of the progress of this city, which was expected to start up into population, wealth, and grandeur, as by magic effect, appears to be vanishing."[16] Samuel Wait agreed that at least part of this commentary rang true, writing to Sally that "having been accustomed for some time to Philadelphia this city exhibits rather a low appearance."[17] Because the ideals of the US Constitution were not yet articulated in a built and cultivated landscape, the city seemed like a shaky artifice struggling for respect while the political leaders in the emerging republic worked to transform their lofty ambitions into a working reality.

The wobbly foundation of Washington City edifices would become a striking metaphor for this phase of Sally's life. It was during this time that the pious ambitions of the Baptist denomination's modern missionary and educational movements would be jeopardized by the all-too-human tendency toward misguided execution. The period from December 1822, when Sally traveled from her hometown to the nation's capital, and April 1826, when she returned to Brandon with a daughter but without her husband, saw the plans for her devout desires veer off course. On one hand, this period provided Sally with a lifetime of stories about attending levees at the White House and meeting Lafayette. On the other hand, it was a time characterized by her constant state of uncertainty, as her circumstances were subject to human frailties that did not necessarily hold up the ideals of American freedom, pious virtue, and selfless service. At times, her reservoir of resilience ran low when faced with the instability of her personal situation, as she negotiated her new role as wife of a college administrator and professor. Thrust into a society that valued the formalities of visiting and entertaining, Sally must have felt rudderless at times with no house to keep and no official role to play that would prove her "usefulness" to

God. She also found herself in a place where a new republic of freedom had been awkwardly imposed onto a Southern landscape "bearing the marks of partial labour and general desertion," as Howitt noted. To him, the uncultivated soil around the capital city seemed to "bear the curse" of slavery, "the morbid evil which will not only operate directly upon the amount of the country's produce, but must blight its moral growth and eat into its very vitals."[18]

The city Sally moved to in 1822 was a study in contrasts, an incomplete testament to the constitutional ideals of liberty. Washington City was designed to be a shining monument to the founders' ideals, but it was built on a muddy foundation by the hands of the enslaved. It magnified the contrasts of the fledgling republic, bringing together the powerful plantation culture, prone to duels and deliberations; the more "austere, moralistic, inner-directed" New Englanders like the Waits; and adventurers from the Western frontier.[19] Indeed, these profiles of people comprised not only the government class, but also members of the Baptist General Convention who lived and visited the new capital to oversee the administration of Columbian College. And while Samuel described the people of Washington City as "generally very plain in their appearance and manners, especially our folks, i.e. Baptists," Sally had imagined something grander and more genteel.[20] Several months before she had revealed to her parents that she was considering a move from their home in Vermont, her suspicious father quizzed her on the possibility that she might join her husband at College Hill. While Sally tried on one of her fashionably crafted bonnets, Jonathan Merriam Sr. teased that she would want a nice one herself when she went to Washington City. He was clearly fishing for information. Sally wrote to Samuel, "I replied laughingly to be sure I shall. I hope then to be able to wear one of the finest cut and to have half dozen servants to wait on me."[21] With her potential move south, Sally seemed to envision herself moving up in society. As it turned out, Sally's expectations of the city's finery and airs were contrasted with the reality of coffles of enslaved bodies. The Baptist General Convention's pious intentions and lavish levees were set against political intrigue and faulty financials. It would take fewer than four years for it all to fall apart.

But in early 1822, the future of the fledgling college looked bright. Former missionary Luther Rice had worked for years to accumulate funds to buy land north of the executive mansion with the assistance of the powerful Reverend O. B. Brown and others, lining up financial support from none other than President Monroe himself, along with many of his cabinet members.[22] The President and members of Congress were all invited to Columbian College President William Staughton's induction on January 9, and while the legislature did not adjourn for the occasion, a number of them did attend.[23] New students included seven sophomores, ten freshmen, three theological students, and seven young men in the preparatory school whom Samuel tutored, hearing them in Greek three times a day.[24]

A classical education was a critical part of the Baptist modern missionary movement. As William Staughton declared during the college's opening ceremony, "When missionaries are passing into almost every region of the earth, it is evident that, to enable them to acquire new languages, and to translate the scriptures from the original text, a sound and extensive education is not only desirable but necessary."[25] The need for an educated ministry was obvious to the convention's governing board; only the location was in question. Looking back now, it is hard to imagine why the Baptist leaders wanted to move from Pennsylvania's largest city. As early as 1790, Philadelphia was a bustling and cosmopolitan city, with many cultural institutions such as a library, bookstores, and theaters. In actuality, the Baptists would not have condoned going to the theater; Staughton's memoir includes a letter in which he admonished his future son-in-law for attending such immoral exhibitions.[26] Bookstores, other than those selling religious texts, probably would not be an advantage for Staughton either. When as a young man Staughton underwent an emotional conversion in his home of Coventry, England, it was fraught with such a prolonged period of mental anguish that doctors were called in. Diagnosing him with "religious frenzy," one physician prescribed the "perusal of novels and romances," which caused Staughton to banish the doctor from his presence for life.[27]

While the secular attractions of Philadelphia may not have been assets to the Baptists, ease of transportation and access to ample housing, trade, and services would have created a more palatable environment compared to the sparsely populated swamp of Washington City. Still, they imagined the new location as a selling point for students, or at least their parents, as Staughton proclaimed in the opening ceremony, "From this hill, as from the eminence on which Aeneas stood, the frequent pupil shall look down and exclaim—'O fortunate! Quorum jam moenia surgunt,'" meaning, *O fortunate ones whose walls now rise.*[28] A "historical sketch" of the city written in 1830 by Washington, DC publisher and promoter Jonathan Elliot touted the college's location just outside the city, painting a bucolic scene that belied the muddy terrain. "Here the student may pursue his studies, apart, and free from, the danger of any dissipation which the Metropolis may contain; and on proper occasions, leave his 'learned lore,' and gain from great and living examples . . . by seeing the theoretical principles . . .

in actual life."[29] In other words, the students would be far enough from town to keep them out of trouble, but close enough to witness the inner workings of a great government in action.

As it turned out, they did have at least one irritating distraction nearby; the Holmead Farm housed a one-mile oval racetrack, where occasional horse racing attracted unsavory visitors and sinful activities. Staughton wrote that managing the consequences of these "wretched races" made their "hands full."[30] Indeed, the perception of innocent country living was eroded away as soon as students made their way into town. Historian Joanne Freeman describes the capital as a city of extremes, influenced in part by the ubiquitous saloons and bars. Between the free-flowing whiskey, the undignified behaviors at horse tracks and cockfights, and the sometimes violent political altercations, Washington City had plenty of vices for the students to explore in their free time.[31]

Philadelphia also had drawbacks in addition to the worldly temptations that might distract young men from their solemn studies. The city had cultivated a reputation as a "yellow fever" town, having endured a number of epidemics since initially losing thirty-five hundred of its citizens to the disease in the last few years of the eighteenth century.[32] Indeed, Samuel Wait and his classmates had fled to the country outside of Philadelphia in the summer of 1820, when the fever once again raged through the city. Even then, the citizens of the Lower Dublin area where Samuel waited out the epidemic grew suspicious of the veracity of board of health reports about the disease.[33] "Localists," those physicians like Benjamin Rush who believed epidemics were a product of the "dirt and filth" of city living, espoused the idea that country living would provide a healthier atmosphere.

The idea of a pastoral setting on a hill overlooking Washington City was seductive beyond the health benefits. It was, by all accounts, a beautiful place. O. B. Brown, Luther Rice, and others found a location on a hill in what is now Columbian Heights, within a mile of the new executive mansion, and just a few miles from the Capitol building. Part of the Holmead estate that dated back to the original eighteenth-century land grants, the Capitol was "in plain sight from the Institute and the President's house would be if not for the tops of a few trees," Samuel commented when he first arrived. "We have a beautiful situation."[34]

However picturesque the setting was, as with most decisions of this kind, power and money played a role. Not unlike the compromise on the location of the nation's capital itself in 1790, there was back room maneuvering to convince the Columbian College governing board to follow the committee's recommendation to settle the college in the South. Just after the vote the Baptist General Convention elected its officers, with Northerners outnumbering Southerners nearly four to one, possibly a compromise related to the decision.[35] This tension between the southern and northern evangelical contingents would intensify over time, especially as the debate over slavery escalated in the 1840s. For now, there was an assumption that New Englanders believed their way of life would be perpetuated through the spread of evangelical denominations. Donald Scott cites evangelist Lyman Beecher, who in 1815 insisted that evangelical Christianity would "extend the 'special influence' that had been New England's blessing and virtue to the South and West and thereby 'produce sameness of views, of feelings, and interests and lay the foundations of the empire on a rock.'"[36] This sentiment could be evidenced by the large number of New Englanders who became faculty and administrators at Columbian as well as at colleges later founded in the South and West.

In the proceedings published in the *Latter Day Luminary*, the committee cited multiple reasons for locating in Washington City, which included the "sacrifice of local partialities," the desire for a central location away from the New England-based missionary activities, and the fact that "the establishment of a college there is already in contemplation."[37] To the latter, there had been a desire for a college in the nation's capital for years, most notably from former President George Washington himself.

In 1897, the *New York Times* published an article with the headline, "Washington's Lost Gift." The article reports that the late president had indicated in his will his desire to fund a national university, which ostensibly he did by designating fifty shares from the Potomac Company, an ambitious endeavor to make the Potomac River navigable. Alas, the effort and the company failed, and the stock was lost, derailing the first US president's good intentions about education. The 1897 story indicates that "great curiosity has recently been aroused in an old subject by the ladies of the Washington University Association, which met here about the middle of the month. Dec 26, 1897."[38] Apparently, the subject had come up repeatedly over the years, with various people and organizations trying to recover the missing donation to shore up different efforts to start a college or university. This persistent rumor was already making its rounds in 1822, prompting Sally to write to Samuel, "I have been told that Gen. Washington left by his will $20000 for the benefit of the first College which should be established in the City. Is this true? If so, has his bequest been obtained?"[39]

Apart from the elusive US president's inheritance, there remained plenty of hopeful pecuniary reasons to locate the college in the new capital; there were donors and influence to be had, and perhaps congressional appropriations down the line. All these factors—health, desirability, and money—contributed to an ambitious plan to expand the Baptist network across the country. It was a heady time for the Baptists, as the denomination transformed from a scrappy and persecuted collection of the faithful to a powerful influence in the Early Republic capital city. This was the culmination of years of toil and inspiration ignited by Ann and Adoniram Judson's mission to Burma a decade before—the same mission that called a young Sally Merriam to her own gospel-led journey. And now, she was right in the middle of it.

The Baptists' lofty ambitions heightened Sally's insecurities about her station as Samuel's helpmeet. Sally felt "illy qualified to be your wife in such a place. . . . You will doubtless frequently have cause to be ashamed of it."[40] Her vulnerability reflected her concern that Samuel had become her intellectual and social superior after several years of advanced study in Philadelphia and Washington City. Her feelings of inadequacy were exacerbated by logistical concerns, especially the lack of housing that would prohibit Sally and Samuel from setting up housekeeping on their own. Not only was the limited number of buildings in the remote setting an issue, the nature of Samuel's position as a tutor in the preparatory department was a further complication. According to the 1822 bulletin, tutors were required to "reside in the College—to attend the tables of the students and ask a blessing."[41] Residing "in the College" referred to living in the main building, which was "117 feet by 26, of five stories, including the basement and the attic, having 48 rooms for students."[42] Samuel roomed on the "third floor, north side of the College, No. 24," just down the hall from Sally's brother Jonathan.[43] Apparently the college had not anticipated having married tutors in their employ, and with the troubles that were to come, the unpredictable living situation created a continual strain on Sally's peace of mind.

An initial solution for Sally's situation came from Dr. Staughton's right hand man, Irah Chase. Like Sally, he was a Vermont native; he was a few years younger than Samuel Wait, but way ahead of him in terms of education, having attended Middlebury College and Andover Theological Seminary. He had been the primary professor in addition to Staughton when the institute was in Philadelphia, and he had been invited to move to the nation's capital to run the theological department at Columbian College. A bachelor when he first joined the institute, in early 1821 he went to "North or South Carolina to change his circumstances."[44] His errand successful, Chase returned married to Harriett Savage, the daughter of a Baptist who was an executive of the West India Company in Wilmington,

North Carolina. Samuel pronounced the diminutive Mrs. Chase "a very modest, amiable, little wife," who appeared "to be well qualified for the place she is now to fill."[45] The Chases generously offered accommodations to Sally in their faculty house, one of two on the property, while Samuel presumably fulfilled the requirements of his position by living in the college building. Harriett was probably happy to have assistance with her new daughter.[46] The Waits and the Chases became close and maintained a deep and abiding friendship, long after Chase left in 1825 to start Newton Theological Seminary, until Harriet died in childbirth in 1834.[47]

Sally's situation with the Chases went well in the first semester of 1823 when she first arrived. But in late summer, Irah Chase went on an extended trip to Europe while Harriett went to Middletown Springs, Vermont to stay with some of Irah's family members. This left Sally in a state of suspension, having to scramble for suitable lodging, which became a common refrain in her time at Columbian College. Other than the time Sally stayed with the Chases, it is not clear what her living arrangements were during the College Hill years. It is possible she (and perhaps Samuel) boarded with Dr. Thomas Sewell's family, judging by their references to him in letters.[48] A physician who served as the professor of anatomy and physiology, Sewell was a fellow New Englander who later became an advocate in the temperance movement.[49] Prior to migrating to Washington City, Sewell was the subject of a scandal in his hometown of Ipswich, Maine when he was arrested for "possession of an 'unsanctioned corpse'" after eight bodies—five white adults, two white children, and one black man named Caesar—were "stolen up from the local graveyard."[50] It was a common practice for physicians and medical schools to resort to grave robbing for research and teaching purposes through the early twentieth century. Even so, the citizens of Ipswich were distraught enough to offer a $500 cash reward for information on "this atrocious villainy."[51] Sewell was befriended by Daniel Webster, who helped set him up at Columbian College after the scandalous event.[52] Despite Sewell's grisly past, he was referred to fondly by his academic colleagues and built a successful career, including a seat on the Washington Board of Health, before his death in 1845.[53]

Samuel's fundraising trip during the August 1824 break put Sally in a quandary with regard to her housing situation. She was left to consider spending the month doing the unthinkable: living in the college building. Upon learning that Sally might board in the college while Samuel was gone, Harriet Chase wrote that it would be "very improper for ladies to visit at such a place." She continued, "it is considered almost a disgrace for a lady to go into Colleges at New Haven. I have heard of one lady that called on her son, and was for some time after an object of ridicule."[54] Despite Harriet's dire warnings, it seems that Sally did indeed spend a month living in the college building. The students would have been out for summer break, but still it must have been both humiliating and unsettling for Sally to be once again without a permanent home on College Hill. Sally's personal living situation was just the beginning of the important cultural shift that her move to Washington City set in motion.

Once she arrived in Washington City, Sally settled into the social fabric of College Hill, as foreign as the setting may have felt to her. Harriet Chase provided a warm, friendly home to Sally, and for her part, Sally probably found some familiar routine in helping care for Harriet's young baby, not unlike her assistance with her sister-in-law Mary Powers Merriam in Brandon. Having grown up in the South, Harriet probably felt more at home in rural Washington City than Sally, having been accustomed to living in a slaveholding state. The 1820 census shows five enslaved people living in her father's household in Wilmington, North Carolina.[55] As a Vermonter where slavery had been abolished in the 1777 state constitution, Sally would be confronted with the pervasiveness of chattel slavery in DC.

With regard to slavery, Washington City "was Southern at its core."[56] Enslaved workers served the families who lived on the college grounds, where a Mr. Anderson served as steward. Anderson, who was mentioned frequently in letters between the Waits, was in charge of "all persons employed as servants in the College," which, in the antebellum South, invariably meant enslaved workers.[57] Off campus, the Waits and other College Hill acquaintances spent a good deal of time with the Misses Holmead at their father John Holmead's home. Likely descendants of the original land grantee, the 1830 census shows John Holmead enslaving eleven workers.[58] This is the same Holmead farm that attracted upwards of five thousand people for the annual horse races, which included gambling and other ill-suited behavior.[59] Irah Chase mentioned the Holmeads in a letter to Samuel, reminding him of "the hours I spent in visiting some of our neighbors and endeavoring like a pastor to converse with them freely on the things that pertain to their spiritual welfare."[60] There are frequent mentions of the Holmeads by the Waits and the Chases in letters, all indicating they found them pleasant neighbors. Even if the Holmeads were not devout Baptists, the College Hill couples must have enjoyed refreshments on their piazza while they tried to save their souls, regardless of how they felt about the enslaved men and women who served the tea.

The administrators and trustees coming to the capital to operate Columbian College in the early 1820s likely brought their prejudices with them.

Race was a complicated construct regardless of one's origins. Northern arrivals may have interacted with black enslaved laborers, but they would not have necessarily been exposed to the Southern plantation system, an institution that differed dramatically from its urban counterpart.[61] Because Sally's home state had banned slavery from its inception, her experience with the practice was minimal. As historian Joanne Freeman explains, plantation-curious Northerners commonly sought out their Southern counterparts to visit their homesteads to see the system in practice. Southern plantation owners were happy to oblige, hoping to shape their opinions on the subject, leaving some Northerners, including New Englander Benjamin French, "pleasantly surprised" to learn that "slaves seemed well-off; the house slaves were 'dressed better than N.[ew] H.[ampshire] Farmers' wives and daughters.'"[62] Experiencing a "sympathetic" enslaver firsthand had the desired effect on French. In his diary, he wrote that the visit "eased his conscience and made him roaring mad at the abolitionists who were threatening the Union."[63] Sally's occasional visits to the Holmead estate and her somewhat bucolic life at College Hill may have had the same effect. In her letters she matter-of-factly referred to people who likely were enslaved. In a letter to Samuel about a thunderstorm and ghost sighting while he was away on a fundraising trip, Sally mentioned "Goodfellow" sitting with "Mr. A" (probably the steward Mr. Anderson) on the north porch during a gathering of College Hill faculty and friends in a family's home, possibly the Sewells'. Given her reference to Goodfellow without an honorific "mister," it is possible he was an enslaved servant.[64] In another note, Harriet Chase wrote that her toddler William, who missed his life on College Hill, asked for "Auntie Wait—please to come here, and bring little Ann Eliza, Uncle Richard, Aunt Betsey, my little hobby horse and whip, I wish to see you very much." Harriet added, "He asked me if God made uncle Richard out of black dust."[65] This indicates Richard and Betsey were probably enslaved workers on College Hill, people that Harriett and her young son were fond enough of to remember them in their letters. It is notable, however, that Sally was "Auntie Wait," while the others were "Uncle Richard" and "Aunt Betsey." Indeed, paternalistic statements and expressions of Christian care were common justifications for slavery in the Early Republic. It was the same mindset that called Samuel Wait to "preach to the Africans" while he was in Philadelphia.[66] In Washington City, free and enslaved blacks attended the First Baptist Church of Reverend O. B. Brown, and "by 1830, these began to join by baptism and by letter, and probably equaled in numbers the white members," according to an early history of Baptists in Washington City. Black members included the "servants of prominent families" such as President James Monroe and At-torney General William Wirt.[67] Biracial worship continued until the black members formed the Nineteenth Street Baptist Church in 1839.[68] Wait's first church in New Bern, North Carolina was also biracial, as were the camp meetings at which he later preached.

Sally's interactions with enslaved individuals were, for the most part, limited to the familiar and "familial" Uncle Richard, Aunt Betsey, and Goodfellow of College Hill, and perhaps the enslaved domestic workers at the Holmead estate. These were situations where Sally might have been able, in her mind, to minimize the dreadful realities of the slavery system. She also had a nurse to attend to her for four weeks after her daughter's birth in 1825, a very intimate although short-term relationship that was likely with an enslaved woman.[69]

Records do not reveal Sally's first impressions of slavery during the Co-lumbian College years. Did she argue with her Southern friends Harriet and the Misses Holmeads about the evils of slavery as her Northern family members would in the decades to come? Or did she politely look away? Sally viewed their assignment in the nation's capital as a temporary one, a stop to accumulate education and contacts that might lead back to New England, as the Chases had done when they moved from Columbian Col-lege to Newton Theological Institute. Perhaps she compartmentalized the slavery issue in her mind, convincing herself that black laborers were not so different from the "girls" she hired in Rutland to braid her straw for fancy bonnets or the daughters of neighbors that her mother and sister employed to keep house and help with the spinning. For Sally, the idea of "girls" working in other families was not uncommon, but "such stints of domestic service presumably ended for free women when they married and began households of their own."[70] In Vermont, household domestic workers would have been lower-class free whites. In Washington City, they were enslaved black people.

Despite familial metaphors, the commoditized underbelly of the slavery system was pervasive and exposed in the nation's capital. Just seven years before Sally's move to Washington City, New York physician Jesse Torrey made his way south to promote educational reform. Along the way he was exposed to both urban and plantation slavery, and while in DC he was shocked to get a "*glimpse* of a light covered waggon, followed by a proces-sion of men, women and children . . . bound together in pairs, with ropes and *chains*."[71] These were enslaved people being transported for trade, a distressingly common sight in Washington, with its location between the slave states of Maryland and Virginia. In response to the scene, Torrey wrote an early abolitionist pamphlet that sparked a national debate. He exposed the cruelties of rural slave life and also called out the "notorious Washington practice of the kidnapping of freed blacks" for sale to the Deep South.[72] This practice was happening in 1822, the year Sally arrived in Washington City, when "Fortune Lewis . . . was knocked unconscious on Baltimore's Pratt Street and conveyed to the District of Columbia for sale."[73] William Lloyd Garrison and other abolitionists used Torrey's exposé in their fight for emancipation. A decade later, visitors continued to express their shock when faced with the evidence of the domestic slave trade in the nation's political center. When English abolitionist Edward Strutt Abdy visited Washington City in 1834, he wrote of the "wretched hovel" where enslaved captives were penned before sale and transport to the Deep South. Only half a mile from the Capitol, the "Yellow House" was said to be "surrounded by a wooden paling fourteen or fifteen feet in height . . . [where] all colors, except white—the guilty one—both sexes, and all ages, are confined."[74]

On trips into the city, Sally must have been exposed to the scenes of the domestic slave trade. Did she know what was taking place behind the high walls of the slave prison? If she saw a coffle of enslaved people, did she divert her eyes or express disgust? Did she wait for a private moment with her husband to murmur distress? How did Sally square the Baptist American ideals of freedom with the slavery she witnessed in Washington City? Other than the few mentions of the enslaved workers who served College Hill, Sally's record is silent on her reaction to slavery while living in the nation's capital. Later, with their more permanent move to North Carolina, Sally and her family would write openly about their distress connected to the consequences of living in a slaveholding state. But during the Columbian College years, Sally's letters were relatively silent on the topic. She seemed to be occupied with the whirling new political and social scene in which she found herself.

Eight

FUSSING

> Invitations have been given to the President
> (Monroe) both houses of congress and all
> the heads of departments & I believe to
> all ministers in the district. . . . Great fuss
> to Mr. Rice's word.
>
> —Samuel to Sally, January 8, 1822

FROM THE TIME THE INSTITUTE CONSIDERED ITS MOVE to Washington City, its leaders—Luther Rice and William Staughton—seized on every opportunity to lobby support from wealthy and influential men. The charismatic Rice, whose "zeal and courage never faltered," was described as "tall, nervous, anxious, often over sanguine."[1] Rice was at heart a promoter, a fundraiser, and a networker, functions that benefit tremendously from a surplus of optimism and hope. Staughton and Rice seemed an inspired match, their polarized dispositions and shared ambitions complementing each other perfectly. Staughton was a "great force of character, of commanding presence and manner, and pleasing address. . . . He was athletic, and fitted to command attention. His voice was strong and musical. In eloquence he had no superior."[2] As corresponding secretary to the Baptist General Convention, an office he held until 1826, Staughton provided a steady vision and considerable control over affairs.[3] Both he and Rice were persuasive orators, but while Staughton's fiery preaching converted people to cleave to Christ, Rice's charisma convinced them to part with their cash.

Luther was born in Massachusetts in 1783 to the quick-tempered Amos Rice, who acquired "habits which proved unfavorable to his future useful-ness" while fighting in the Revolutionary War.[4] He and his wife belonged to the Congregational church, but their membership seems to have been more about social tradition than spiritual fulfillment, leaving Luther vul-nerable to spiritual wandering as the evangelistic spirit swept New En-gland.[5] Luther inherited some of his father's fiery essence, but after the requisite time of youthful folly and tortured self-reflection, he became convinced of Christ's salvation and decided to channel his talents to sup-port the gospel. By the time he was twenty, he was employing his consid-erable art of persuasion to sell subscriptions to the *Massachusetts Baptist Missionary Magazine*, which later became a theological lifeline to a young Sally Merriam Wait.[6] Luther entered Williams College in 1806, about a year after what later became known as the Haystack Prayer Meeting when Samuel Mills and a handful of Congregationalist students sought shelter under a haystack in a field during a rainstorm, and later adopted the cause of foreign missions.[7] Luther went on to attend Andover Theological Seminary, where he joined these and other young men to fervently take up the evangelical call, including Adoniram Judson. The Judsons and the Newells had set sail in 1812 from the busy port of Salem, Massachusetts. Rice left port in Philadelphia, not far from the recently built Baptisterion. It was with much fanfare that these first American missionaries sailed to Calcutta on the eve of war with England. The religious and secular press covered their every move in the ensuing years, igniting the American and English public with the piously adventurous tales of their mission for God. The first news from India included a major plot twist; on the long crossing, Adoniram Judson, after carefully studying the New Testament, concluded that the scripture did not support pedobaptism, the sprinkling of infants that the Congregationalists (and most Catholic and Protestant faiths) prac-ticed. After much study and prayer, Judson came to the conclusion that Baptism required a declaration of faith followed by full immersion. Ann and Adoniram left America as Congregationalists, but they arrived in India as Baptists. Once there, they and Luther Rice, who they convinced of their theological arguments, were baptized and received in Calcutta by none other than the great William Carey, and they began mapping out plans for their missions in their newfound faith.

The details of how the next several months unfolded are complex, but after some time, Ann and Adoniram Judson landed in Burma. Fellow missionary Harriett Newell and her baby tragically died on a voyage, and Luther Rice returned home to the United States, his health and perhaps enthusiasm shaken when faced with the harsh realities of the climate and living conditions.[8] He left suggesting he would come back, but despite Adoniram Judson's pleas for Rice to return, he never did.[9] It was just as well, because Rice was better suited to help solve the missionaries' new challenge to graciously sever ties with their Congregational church funders and garner support among American Baptists for the unexpected, newly baptized missionaries. Luther Rice was the man for the task.

Rice knew the value of connections, and he put them to work to influence the move of Dr. Staughton's fledgling seminary to the nation's new capital. Along with the powerful Reverend O. B. Brown, Enoch Reynolds, and others, Rice began soliciting support for the college from every possible sector, especially in the political world, as evidenced by the number of early donations from President Monroe and members of his cabinet. Rice also knew the value of ceremony and celebrations attended by celebrities, and he liked to "make a fuss" when entertaining the influential. For the college's first ceremony in the capital, Rice sent invitations to President Monroe, both houses of Congress, and just about every other politician in Washington City. Like a true showman, "Mr. R. says he does not care whether they can all get into the College or not, if they will only come."[10] This party took place before Sally moved there, leaving her to imagine the pageantry of the inaugural celebration while she was still home in Brandon worrying about the most recent visitation of smallpox on the town.[11]

With Sally's relocation to Washington City in late 1822, her lifestyle would undergo a tremendous change. In her young life in Brandon, much of her activity revolved around family life, practicing needle arts, weaving, spinning, and making money amid a crumbling farm economy. Most of her social time was limited to sleighing season, when the farms did not need attention and families and friends could travel easily across the snow-covered ground. Church, of course, provided a primary focus of life off the farm too. In Washington City, Sally would not have a house to keep. There was no wool to be carded, no flax to be spun. While she surely helped with the housekeeping in the homes where she boarded, her daily farmhouse routine was gone. This was not her first time off the farm, of course. While Samuel led the church in Sharon, Sally was learning the duties of a minister's wife, honing the art of bonnet making, and performing other household tasks. After Samuel's first departure to Philadelphia, she had lived in town in Brandon with Mary Powers Merriam. During that time, Sally was continually busy helping care for Mary's two small children, keeping up her studies, and most significantly, running her leghorn bonnet business. Washington City would provide a different experience.

Sally's first several months on College Hill were occupied with deliberations about an urgent call to duty. After the "felicity of her lifetime,"
meeting Burma missionary Ann Judson, Sally felt her call to mission re-
vived. During their steamboat conversation on the overnight sojourn to
Baltimore, Ann would not have missed the opportunity to stress the need
for additional missionaries in the field to advance their work. Indeed,
while she had traveled to England and the United States primarily for
her health, she spent countless hours lobbying influential friends in both
countries to increase their support. While Ann convalesced at the home
of her brother-in-law Elnathan Judson in Baltimore, Dr. Staughton invited
her to join the meeting of the 1823 Triennial Convention, which would be
held in Washington City.[12] There she formally petitioned for additional
missionaries in Burma: "I would take the liberty to request . . . that two
missionaries . . . may be sent to the Rangoon station, and two others, as
early as possible, to Chittagong."[13] Sally likely visited with her role model
while she was in town for the convention, and Ann Judson surely put her
charismatic and persuasive powers to work, hoping to recruit Sally to the
mission field.

Sally corresponded with her family about the possibility, but few were
supportive of the venture. In the months leading up to and following Ann
Judson's appearance at the Triennial Convention, Sally received no fewer
than seven letters from various family members trying to talk her out of undertaking a mission to Burma with varying degrees of concern. Her future
sister-in-law Achsah wrote optimistically (and incorrectly), "Your mother
smiles whilst tears trinkle down her cheeks, but I believe she would be very
merry if you should finally go."[14] Her cousin Cynthia reiterated the common
family argument that the "unhealthy climate of India" would send Sally to
an "early grave."[15] That argument was not misguided, as missionaries to the
east had high mortality rates. Other family members, like Samuel's sister
Betsey Burrington, decided no aspect of the idea had merit. She wrote, "It
must be something like 10 or 12 thousands Miles from your native land,
almost half round the Globe. The inhabitants of Burma I suspect is a most
uncivilized unpleasant people who have different grades of worshipping."[16]
It was Sally's mother Sarah Merriam who was most resolute in her arguments against the idea. In several firm missives she outlined the reasons
why a trip to Burma would be an imprudent undertaking. Given all the
perils of travel, her mother argued, Sally's recent poor health made the
idea foolhardy. "If your calling was from the great head of the [church]
to go to Burmah, would he not give both of you soundness and health of
body in some measure equal to the task?"[17] She also thought it would be a

waste of the convention's money, wondering how they could "squander of publick property, are they not bound to send the young robust and strong who have not been impaired by sickness and diseases."[18] But it was Sally's older brother Isaac who summed up the most revealing of arguments in his usual ham-handed fashion, suggesting the Waits were just not cut from the mission cloth. After attending the examination at Hamilton College of the Wades—a couple who followed Ann Judson's call and sailed back with her to Burma—Isaac was "satisfied that God designed them for the Mission. I was convinced God called them rather than you."[19] His undertone reinforces the judgmental nature of the family's eldest son.

Experiencing Ann's "fortitude and perseverance" had clearly rekindled Sally's own pious ambitions. For now, however, she and Samuel remained on College Hill, where Samuel spent his time running the preparatory school and Sally adjusted to her new life by getting to know other wives, neighbors, and the Washington City elite. She still held concerns about being "illy suited" compared to others. Regarding Harriet Chase, she asked Samuel, "has Mrs. Chase enjoyed superior advantages in point of education?"[20] After the initial whirlwind of Burma deliberations, however, she settled in. We do not have much information about Sally's day-to-day life in Washington City until the arrival of a disturbing letter later that year. Jonathan, who had been performing mission work in Norfolk, Virginia during the summer break, became ill with fever and severe dysentery. Despite his grave affliction, he somehow was able to make his way to College Hill by October, where Sally spent several weeks nursing him to health. It is possible that anatomy professor and physician Dr. Sewell took Jonathan into his care during that time, as Sally may have been boarding with his family after the first of the year. [21] Jonathan's illness was so severe that it was doubtful he would recover, and Sally spent day and night by his side, following her mother's request to "fill a mother and sister's place" in nursing him.[22] A flurry of letters between family members, including one from double cousin and physician Isaac Foster Merriam, offered medical advice. Sally's mother handed the same out abundantly, asking Sally, "Do you feed him with boiled rice high spiced with cinnamon, nutmeg, cloves, &c do you fill a foot glass half full of loaf shugar and then fill it up with good peach brandy and give him once an hour too do you give a strong reduction of rose tea with allum and has he had bark of hemlock. . . . Do you lay cloaths wet with hot spirit on his bowels?"[23] Mother's detailed prescriptive advice reveals her assumption that Sally would act as nursemaid to her older brother around the clock. She kept up the exhausting routine until early November, when Jonathan decided to make the three-week journey to his parental home in Brandon. After some months, Jonathan improved, but he never completely regained his health.

After Jonathan's departure from College Hill, Sally and Samuel were able to fully participate in the activities of the college and the nearby city. The Baptists were part of the political social scene, as evidenced by Sally's sister Lydia's breathless curiosity about the parties that they had been attending. By May 1824, Sally had already commented to her sister about a levee hosted by South Carolinian and Secretary of War John Calhoun, and she was expecting to attend one at the President's mansion soon.[24] Lydia asked Sally, "How was the President's lady dressed? Do the gentlemen attend these levees? What is their dress? Do the ladies in Washington possess minds as much superior to ladies in the country as what their dress is?"[25] The early Sally Merriam—the one who penned her pious journal in 1816—would have been shocked by her sister's fascination with parties and fashion some ten years later. Once, she had preferred solemn gatherings with humble Christians over the "society of those who know not God," a sentiment dictated by the religious conduct literature of the time.[26] For instance, in September 1815, after spending the afternoon with a "large and brilliant party of young people," the newly converted Sally had written that despite the "sumptuous entertainment . . . I find that time spent in the fashionable circles of the great profits me but little or nothing."[27] As for fashion, in 1816 Sally had embraced the Baptist New England tradition that people should be "neatly dressed but plainly," even at weddings.[28] Yet by the time she left Washington City in 1826, Sally owned a silk satin spencer (a long-sleeved jacket in the Empire style), a leghorn bonnet with artificial roses, and a dressy velvet bonnet with matching black feathers (picture Scarlett O'Hara's green velvet headpiece with osprey feathers in the movie *Gone with the Wind*). Sally's adoption of mainstream fashion and activities indicates just how far the Baptists had evolved since setting up their power base in the nation's capital.

Others in Columbian College circles approached the Washington fetes with caution. Baron Stow, a New Hampshire student who later rose to prominence through his clashes with Luther Rice, was suspicious about the frequent gatherings, although he preferred the college parties over the levees in the city. After attending two successive College Hill events in March 1824, one at Dr. Sewell's house and the other at president Staughton's home, he was "pleased with seeing the great propriety of conduct manifested by all present—cheerful, but not vain or trifling."[29] He fretted about the irreligious people at President Monroe's levees, writing, "How readily do men do homage to an earthy ruler! But when the Prince of Peace claims their attention and respect, they obstinately refuse him altogether." In all, however, he felt the "company, moreover, was very respectable."[30] Not everyone agreed on the respectability of Monroe's "drawing rooms." Although clearly written with an implicit bias, an oft-quoted article in early histories attributed to the *Intelligencer* caustically described Monroe's gatherings in no uncertain terms. It read, "The secretaries, senators, foreign ministers, consuls, auditors, accountants, officers of the army and navy of every grade, farmers, merchants, parsons, priests, lawyers, judges, auctioneers, and nothingarians—all with their wives and some with the gawky offspring, crowd to the President's house every Wednesday evening; some in shoes most in boots and many in spurs."[31] This description is a far cry from the picture that Sally's sister Lydia seemed to have in her mind when she asked about the ladies' and gentlemen's dress.

The Baptist leaders' penchant for mingling with powerful politicians climbed to new heights in late 1824 when none other than the distinguished and eminent Marquis de Lafayette passed through town during his historic tour. Lafayette's triumphant return to the country whose independence he had helped to win fifty years earlier was made manifest in a widely anticipated year-long series of receptions, speeches, festivals, and parades. When Lafayette's ship docked in New York in August, an estimated eighty thousand fans were on hand, equivalent to more than two-thirds of the city's population.[32] The next month, when Lafayette arrived in Philadelphia, "four cream-colored horses . . . conveyed General La Fayette into the city . . . before a fire of artillery, for the purpose of testing their ability to stand a heavy fire as a salute to the general."[33] Not to be outdone, a huge spectacle was planned for Lafayette's arrival in the nation's capital—and the Baptists were right in the middle of it. Luther Rice, never one to miss an opportunity to make a fuss, joined in a citywide illumination on December 12, 1824, where a "crowd of thousands," according to Baron Stow, welcomed "our distinguished guest and national benefactor." According to an early college history, the edifice was central to the celebration. The description read, "The College building . . . had the lights in the eastern, southern, and western fronts of the building, 'amounting to several hundred,' ignited almost simultaneously."[34] The planners, likely under the direction of Rice, erected a "transparent" eight-foot star on top of the building, and "at ten o'clock all the candles were extinguished simultaneously, as suddenly as they had been lighted."[35]

The *Columbian Star*, the Baptist newspaper then edited by Luther Rice, gushed that the writer "could not recollect having ever seen a more splendid illumination of a single building." Stow was not as impressed, writing in his journal that he thought the "attempt to make a great show . . . was almost a failure." Standing amid a "confused mass of black and white huddled in Capitol Square," the mayor of Washington City "*read* an address" to Lafayette, an embarrassment to the young Baptist, who would have valued extemporaneous orations. Stow went on, "After a salute of twenty-four guns, awkwardly fired, the procession of ill-appearing military marched through clouds of dust from the Capitol to the president's house. . . . There was nothing grand or magnificent in the display, though an attempt at both."[36] Stow's disdain for the ceremony seemed to be motivated by a number of prejudices, including his religious preference for solemnity, his republican distaste for extravagance, and his already growing dislike of Luther Rice, of whom he later became a public nemesis when he took over the *Columbian Star.*

We do not know Sally's impressions of the grand—or lackluster, according to Stow—illumination to celebrate Lafayette's arrival; in fact, we do not know whether she ventured into the throngs in Capitol Square or stayed back to help with the illumination of the building (someone had to blow out all those candles). But she was very likely in attendance two months later when Lafayette returned to Washington City, and this time, to College Hill. On that occasion, the Baptists leveraged their contacts and their loftiest ambitions to host Lafayette at their December commencement of the first graduating class in Washington City. December 15, 1824 must have been bittersweet for William Staughton, as his beloved wife had not lived to see the day when, surrounded by members of Congress, President James Monroe, Secretary of State John Quincy Adams, American foreign ministers, and the faculty and students of Columbian College, Staughton received Lafayette at the Baptist college that he helped found. Maria had died on January 10, 1823 of typhus fever, with William and her two daughters beside her; their son James was studying abroad at the time. According to a letter after her death, the students of the college had agreed to wear "crepe on the left arm for thirty days."[37] The commencement festivities included a procession to the Presbyterian Church on F Street, loaned to the college for the day to accommodate the large number of guests.[38] After the opening exercises, the procession returned to the college for a reception with a "full band of music" and receiving line, followed by a dinner at President Staughton's home on College Hill. While there is no direct evidence that Sally was on hand, it is probable that such a reception with faculty and students would have included wives; in fact, it is hard to imagine the wives not insisting on it.[39] The graduation exercises were quite an event for the college. On the one hand, Lafayette's attendance at the Columbian College commencement was just one in a series of hundreds he attended that year. On the other, that he was present is a noteworthy testament to the political and social capital the Baptists had accumulated in Washington City.

The pomp and ceremony belied troubles that few people beyond the inner circle knew. Months before the College Hill building was illuminated to celebrate Lafayette's return, the unstable foundation of Columbian College began to erode, and Sally's future was once again on shaky ground.

Nine

CRUMBLING

Mr. Rice will apparently commit a kind
of moral suicide, poor deluded fallen man.

—William Ruggles to Elon Galusha, October 1826

SECRETS ARE HARD TO KEEP. BUT IF THE FUTURE OF AN
entire religious movement hangs in the balance, one does one's best. In
June 1824, word was getting out about troubles at Columbian College,
information that did not become public until at least a year later. According to the first college history, the "Superintending committee declared
that 'the confidence of complete ultimate success in relation to the great
objects of the College is unimpaired.'"[1] But in a letter from Harriet Chase
to Sally Wait, it was clear insiders had been tipped off that something was
amiss. Even though Irah Chase was in Europe, Harriet wrote Sally from
Vermont, "I was pained to hear of the embarrassments of the College. I was
not however a stranger to it, before the intelligence I received from your
letter."[2] It is not clear exactly what transpired. It may have had something to
do with Congress's refusal to act on a petition to grant Columbian College
money, although that was common knowledge that was reported in the
Star.[3] This quiet scandal must have been tied to the financial irregularities
of Luther Rice's bookkeeping that later emerged. The situation caused the
Waits' old friends Irah and Harriet Chase a great deal of distress. In a late
June letter to Wait, Irah said he was "astonished—at least I am mortified
at the course pursued by Mr. B[rown] and Mr. R[ice]," notably referring
to them as "mister" rather than the more reverential "brother" used at the

time. Chase goes further to describe his relief that the "superintending committee," a small group that included Brown and Rice, disbanded, taking the time to write five lines from Psalm 37 in Hebrew. Translated, the message reads, "I have seen a wicked and ruthless man flourishing like a green tree in its native soil, but he soon passed away and was no more; though I looked for him he could not be found."[4] The animosity against Rice would soon be in the open. A few months later, Columbian College professor William Ruggles wrote to Vermont Baptist leader Elon Galusha with surprising candor, commenting, "Mr. Rice will apparently commit a kind of moral suicide, poor deluded fallen man."[5] By the end of that year, Mr. Anderson, the steward, apparently banned Rice from his dining table, forcing Rice to go "into the closet [to eat] there."[6]

Whatever the exact nature of the troubles that arose in June, they prompted Samuel and Sally to consider an immediate departure from College Hill, which Harriet Chase begged them to reconsider. "I am so well acquainted with my husband's views of Mr. Wait's leaving the institution . . . he had said to me repeatedly, that Mr. Wait must not, ought not to leave."[7] While Sally's exchange with Harriet was relatively direct regarding the financial "embarrassments" and the rumors about the culprit, Samuel's letters to friends and family were more oblique. In an early August letter, Sally's brother Isaac asked, "We cannot guess at the reason why your 'place must be filled.' Are you going away? . . . Is there any difficulty so that you feel induced to leave to avoid trouble?"[8] Just as that letter was mailed, Samuel left on a month-long trip to Virginia to raise money and solicit subscriptions to the *Columbian Star* during the August recess, his first foray into fundraising for the college. Throughout the early years, "printed appeals for funds were constantly being issued," and it seems that the board was looking to anyone at the college who might be adept at delivering a fundraising pitch.[9] From this point in his career going forward, Wait juggled his preaching, teaching, and fundraising skills to lay the groundwork for a career in administration.

While Samuel went west, Sally remained in Washington City, lodging, much to her and Harriet Chase's chagrin, in the college building, although she spent as much time as possible in more familiar surroundings, likely the home of Dr. Sewell.[10] During his month in Virginia, Samuel wrote to Sally at least ten times, sometimes more than once a day: "You must not get angry with me for writing so often Sally. It is now about 12 and my other was written about 2 or 3 hours ago."[11] The frequency of Samuel's letters was not because he missed her, but because she was serving as his ad hoc secretary. When he secured a pledge or sold a subscription, Samuel wrote Sally and she passed the information along to college administrators. On August 28, he wrote, "After I wrote you yesterday, from Sharpsburg, I obtained another Subscriber for the Star—Jacob Miller Sharpsburg Washington Co. Md. This gentleman paid in advance, be sure to mention this."[12] For the summer, Sally's role as helpmate had shifted from minister's wife to administrative assistant.

Once the school term began, Wait returned to campus, and the drama with the college's financial woes and discontent continued. The promising Alva Woods, another Vermonter with degrees from Harvard and Andover, abruptly left for a professorship at Brown. He had been inducted into Columbian on its opening day in 1822, then in 1823 was sent on an extensive and expensive year-long buying trip to Europe with William Staughton's son James, sending back books and equipment worth nearly a thousand pounds.[13] Not long after the pair returned in 1824, Woods resigned, his departure sending a foreboding sign to insiders. When Sally's brother Jonathan learned the news, he told Isaac, "There has been a blow up at Washington, you may depend on it."[14] His comment turned out to be predictive, for things were indeed about to explode. Meanwhile, however, there were levees to be hosted, buildings to be illuminated, and a French marquis to be entertained.

The next few years the college reeled between its pretense of success and anxiety from financial duress, the board seemingly executing their strategic plans based on Godly hope. As the college's history points out, "The founding fathers . . . were men of great faith. . . . Some way or the other, God would provide."[15] Samuel Wait was not so sure; by early 1825, he was at least surreptitiously investigating other career options. In March, Harriett Reynolds, a leader in his old church in Sharon, asked Samuel "whether you would choose to come to S[haron]."[16] Several months later, Samuel made a trip north during the August break, stopping to see Sally's family in Brandon on his way to investigate possible opportunities. The family was saddened when Sally did not come along, "the more so as it was occasioned by your ill health," her sister Lydia wrote.[17] Judging by the family's letters in August and September, everyone had expected Sally on the visit and was disappointed when Samuel showed up without her. It is quite possible Sally opted to stay back in Washington City because she was, at that point, two and a half months pregnant. This was Sally's first known pregnancy, at nearly thirty-one years of age and after just under seven years of marriage. Of those seven years, the couple had spent a little over four of them living together—plenty of time to have started a family. However, Sally often suffered from ill health, so it is possible that contributed to not conceiving, or perhaps she had experienced early miscarriages. Spring 1821 through summer 1822 had been a particularly trying time for Sally, who wrote that she had "lost some flesh, that my skin is tinged with an unusually deep yellow and that several dark brown spots which may perhaps indicate a state of blood inclining to putrefaction, have made their appearance on my face."[18] Sally's illness seemed to be related to her liver, given her jaundiced state and complaint of pains in her side. In the fall of 1822, just before Sally moved south, she visited Saratoga Springs, New York, a popular destination about seventy miles southwest of Brandon, for improvement of her health. She was gone three weeks and spent ten dollars plus the cost of a chaise to travel there, and she reported to Samuel that "the waters together with my journey has improved my health. . . . For a week previous to my return and a week afterwards I was entirely free from pain in my stomach and side." Unfortunately, the relief was brief. "Since that period I have occasionally felt something of my former complaints."[19]

Sally's childless state may have precipitated their consideration of adopting an eight-year-old orphan in 1822. Shortly after the first mention that Samuel might be offered a place at the college, Sally twice wrote about the possibility that Samuel might return to New England and "fetch little Eliza Elin, an orphan, home with you when you come."[20] This prospect remained a real one until Samuel pushed Sally on a decision in August, just a month or so before she traveled to Saratoga Springs for her health. Samuel wrote that Sister Redman, possibly a member of the O. B. Brown First Baptist Church that Samuel attended, "mentioned the case of little Eliza to me again," warning Samuel that she was "rather bold & she think[s] it would not be best to keep her at the college." He asked Sally to "tell me in plain language what is the best case."[21] This she did, when she admitted to Samuel that she had some concerns about adopting a child that she had "no personal acquaintance with." First of all, since it was "all together uncertain when we shall keep house again, to take proper care of her would perhaps be rather difficult," Sally argued. But just as importantly, Sally had concerns about little Eliza's temperament. "I do not much like the word 'bold,'" Sally wrote. "It sounds very disagreeable when attached to a female," affirming an accepted assumption that girls should be compliant. Sally went on to muse about whether the child's shortcomings could be overcome, wondering if she would "discover a becoming modesty as she advanced in knowledge."[22] With that, Sally encouraged her husband to "do as you think best, and I shall be satisfied."[23] It seems remarkable that Sally would leave such an important decision in the hands of Samuel, but she had made her opinions clear. While Samuel probably felt some pressure from church members to take in this orphaned child, in the end, he followed Sally's oblique refusal. There is no mention of Eliza Elin after the late August letter.

Regardless of the couple's 1822 adoption deliberations, Sally was expecting a child in the summer of 1825 when they had planned a trip north, and she probably was not willing to risk travel so early in the pregnancy. Childbearing was a risky business and was referred to as an "illness" that often threatened the life of a mother. In addition to physical peril, Sally must have also felt emotionally vulnerable being pregnant in a place so far from family—especially given the insecure state of the college—and therefore the family's livelihood. By the fall of that year, the couple ratcheted up their intentions to leave College Hill, telling family that they planned to leave "at the expiration of another term," which would be shortly after the birth of the new baby.[24] Considering the situation at the college—the financial troubles, Alva Woods's recent exit, rumors about Staughton's resignation, and now the departure of the Waits' close friends Irah and Harriet Chase to establish a new theological institute in Newton, Massachusetts—the writing was on the wall. Perhaps Sally could have her baby and then return to the fold of her kinfolk in Vermont. Samuel stepped up his inquiries about new positions within his network of family and friends. Sally's family certainly hoped that "providence may open a door . . . in the region," as her sister-in-law Achsah wrote.[25]

In the meantime, the Columbian College troubles roiled. The Triennial Convention would be held in April 1826, its leaders meeting under the cloud of the now well-known financial woes of the college. There was a contentious debate between two factions: one group, led by the powerful Reverend O. B. Brown, defended Rice's management of fiscal affairs; the other group was suspicious of Rice's culpability. Among the anti-Ricers were those who felt he was merely sloppy in his bookkeeping, as well as those including Wait, Chase, and Baron Stow who suspected outright wrongdoing. Isaac Merriam wrote to Samuel about his "distressing anxiety of deciding between conflicting claims."[26] There was tremendous tension between the groups, who heretofore were united in their crusade for Christ. Rumors whirled among the Baptists throughout the Early Republic. The details still were not clear to all, but they were considered seismic in nature. Isaac wrote, "What is the matter!! Has the breathless vesper of Sicily's evening been suddenly disturbed by an earthquake. . . . Has Etna's crater torn of its cap and parted her liquid stream of fire?"[27]

Before now, Wait had done his best to keep his suspicions about Luther Rice quiet. No one wanted a scandal that could jeopardize the foundation that had been built by the Baptists. Isaac complimented his brother-in-law's discretion, praising Wait's "prudence to conceal what you judged injurious sooner to reveal," reminding him he had "never let a lisp of this escape."[28] In early 1826, however, Samuel wrote letters to contacts throughout New England trying to secure a position as a delegate to the convention to influence the governing board to strip Rice of his duties. No one was helpful to his cause. Even Isaac ran out of ideas, writing, "I thought of writing to Br. Knowles or Prof Chase—to get you an appointment—but am inclined to believe the delegation from Boston will be full."[29] Undaunted, Wait continued to work his connections, sending his suggestions for the college's management to Irah Chase, who would be attending in an official capacity.[30]

In the midst of this maelstrom, a blue-eyed baby was born. On February 1, 1826, after less than five hours of labor, Sally Wait gave birth to a daughter they named Ann Eliza. On the morning of her birth, Samuel folded the eight-pound, four-ounce baby into his arms and kissed her cheek, exclaiming, "God bless her little heart! God bless her little heart!"[31] We know a bit more detail of the circumstances of her birth thanks to some "particulars" Samuel shared "only with you and yours" in a letter to Sally's brother Jonathan.[32] Samuel wrote, "Sally's health was generally very good till within 5 weeks of her confinement. . . . On the last day of January, her health was as usual. She took tea with us and in the evening until 9 was only a little indisposed."[33] The labor was a short one. "At 10 she was more unwell, and, the course being called up, we soon found that the moment to which we had looked with so much anxiety had indeed come. Think, my Br[other] and Sister too, how great must have been our joy at the birth of the child in a short time."[34] Ann Eliza's delivery was a relatively easy one, much to their relief. "Perhaps her first [illegible] will in the end, do us no harm," [35] Samuel wrote. While Samuel's letter is generous with details, it omits some information. In a time when a family member—a sister, mother, aunt, or cousin—usually attended to the mother at the time of birth, Sally was without any nearby relatives. Her best friend Harriet Chase had moved away, and Dr. Staughton's wife, Maria, had passed away the year before. Presumably the college's Dr. Sewell would have been the attending physician, but it is unclear which College Hill female friends had been by Sally's side. While Sally was happy and relieved to deliver her child without incident, being so far away from family must have felt like being on unsteady ground.

Only six weeks after the high of Ann Eliza's birth, upsetting news arrived from Uncle John Conant in Brandon. Sally's father, Jonathan Merriam Sr., had fallen gravely ill. Seventeen days later, he was dead. As was customary in the community of Christians, her father's salvific state during his departure was noted as unusually blessed. "I have been much with him and can say I never witnessed so much glory becoming in the mind of a dying person," Uncle John wrote in the typical evangelical rhetoric of a Christian death experience. "He had very unusual manifestations of the divine presents all the time of his sickness."[36] Like most evangelical depictions of passing, the deathbed scene may have been a somewhat fictionalized account. The intent was not to mislead, but to reassure loved ones of the dying person's salvation, as well as to minimize their distress. The act of writing the death-bed narrative was likely soothing to the writer as well, who was usually a parent, sibling, or spouse. Most religious memoirs included a long, detailed description of the subject's death that provided not just family members but admirers with a balm for their grief. When Ann Judson died in Burma just a few months later, her devoted husband Adoniram was not by her side. Instead, locals with little command of English attended to her death, which meant that Adoniram lacked the narrative so important to a grieving relative. In Ann's memoir, Adoniram's sentiment to his mother-in-law illustrates this: "'You perceive, that I have no account whatever of the state of her mind, in view of death or eternity." Other than a few accounts from the Burmese attendants about Ann's confused mental state, Judson had few consoling words to give Ann's mother about her death, which caused them both distress.[37]

As was also the custom, Jonathan Merriam Sr. dictated a "farewell address" to his wife, Sarah Conant Merriam. The thousand-word missive included the requisite declaration that he was "very happy and assured" that he was "bound to the city of our God," bidding "farewell to that sacred volume which has been the unerring guide of my pilgrimage on earth." He continued, "Farewell my dear companion, you have been the faithful associate of my pilgrimage and have bourn with me the toils and the afflictions of life, our cup of domestic blessings has been full and overflowing. . . . Farewell a short farewell. Farewell my children. . . . My work is done. I am going home."[38]

And so was Sally Wait.

Part Four

TO BRING US ALL TOGETHER

Ten

SEEKING

> I pray Him in whose hand is the life of
> us all, to preserve your life and health
> amidst all your wanderings and to bring
> us all together again, around our own
> fireside, and our own family altar.
>
> —Sally to Samuel, September 9, 1830

SALLY SETTLED INTO THE LADIES' CABIN ON THE *OLIVE BRANCH*,
a steamboat that served travelers between Albany and New York City.[1] The
newly launched ship provided a comfortable situation, probably similar in
scope to the Fulton Company's *Chancellor Livingston* that accommodated
"thirty-eight in the main cabin, twenty-four in the ladies' cabin and fifty-six
berths in a forward cabin."[2] For more than a decade the Fulton Company
had held a monopoly on steamboat travel in the state of New York, con-
trolling access to the Hudson River, a critical link between the city and
the recently completed Erie Canal. A new rival company had launched
the *Olive Branch* after a Supreme Court decision broke up the Fulton monopoly in early 1824.[3] Samuel Wait bade goodbye to his wife and child
and left them in the care of Sally's brother Jonathan. Ann Eliza amused
herself by examining the layout of the cabin and inspecting the "different
ladies who came on board." When the "bark began to rock," Sally let out
an "involuntary sigh . . . and cast a despairing look," pressed her tiny baby
"to her bosom," and resigned herself to yet another separation from her
husband of nearly eight years.[4] The details of this letter are shared with

the reader in a new voice, that of Ann Eliza Wait. With the birth of their new daughter, the tone of the couple's missives had shifted again. During their first few months of separation after Ann Eliza was born, Sally wrote to Samuel through the eyes and voice of their infant daughter, and Samuel's replies were often to Ann Eliza, revealing the family's tender affection.

While Samuel had not succeeded in securing an official position at the Triennial Convention, he followed his brother-in-law Isaac's advice to "come to N.Y. to attend" the meeting whether or not he could win a seat.[5] Samuel, Sally, and Ann Eliza traveled together to New York City for the convention. Sally probably visited with other wives while their husbands attended to business, or perhaps she assisted with hospitality and logistics. Neither Samuel Wait nor Isaac Merriam were listed as delegates at the official meeting that opened on April 26, but Jonathan Merriam Jr. and many Wait compatriots in the fight to save Columbian College were. Like-minded delegates included current and past colleagues William Staughton, William Ruggles, and Irah Chase, as well as Sally's Uncle John Conant, Samuel's first mentor Abiel Fisher, and Vermonters Elon Galusha and Joseph Sawyer.[6] In the end, the convention officials upbraided Rice, calling him a "very loose accountant" with "imperfect talents for the disbursement of money." After listening to witnesses against him, it was decided "no charge against Luther Rice as to immoral conduct has been substantiated."[7] They stripped him of his treasurer duties, but his appointment as agent, or fundraiser, for the college would continue.

While that may not have satisfied the anti-Rice hardliners, it was enough of a comeuppance to encourage concerned Columbian College supporters that a new day was dawning. Just as important to the institution's future was the post-convention deliberation held on May 9 at the Oliver Street Baptist Church in Lower Manhattan, which Samuel joined. The attendees, who felt a "deep and lively interest in the welfare of Columbian College," adopted "immediate and efficient measures to relieve said college from embarrassment," which included a new approach to fundraising that apparently Samuel helped create.[8] He wrote Sally that on the ride back to College Hill, Dr. Semple, president of the convention, told Samuel "he feels much encouraged—speaking of our (Mr. Ruggles' and my own) trip to New York he said, you have saved the College."[9] Whether or not that would prove true, this meeting would become a turning point in Wait's career, advancing him confidently into a career of fundraising, a critical skill for a hopeful Baptist leader.

After the meeting, Samuel and Sally parted—Samuel returned to College Hill, and Sally and Ann Eliza boarded the *Olive Branch*, headed toward her family in Brandon. Once the journey was underway, Sally went on deck with Jonathan to take in the sights of the "romantic and beautiful views of the highlands along the Hudson River" while Ann Eliza "listened to the harsh and grating monotonous noise" of the steamboat's machinery. They passed by Fort Putnam, a Revolutionary War garrison, and waved to West Point cadets standing on shore. After enjoying these sights, Sally took Ann Eliza to the cabin to sleep through the rest of the thirty-hour trip, arriving in Albany the next morning.[10] From there, Sally, Ann Eliza, Jonathan, and Rev. Joseph Sawyer, an old friend from Rutland, boarded another boat for the port of Troy, where they had breakfast. By stagecoach they traveled to Bennington, Vermont. There, Uncle John Conant, who had left New York City earlier than the others, collected the travelers in his wagon and delivered them to the Checkered House in Eagle Bridge, New York, a frequent resting place for the Wait family as they traveled to Samuel's hometown of White Creek, New York. The inn, a white-and-red-checkered house, was later made famous in paintings by Eagle Bridge native and early twentieth-century folk artist Anna Mary Robertson, also known as Grandma Moses. From there, Sally and Ann Eliza visited Wait family members in Washington County, New York. It was a grueling ride on a hot New England day. Sally wrote that she was "much fatigued and our little daughter cried harder and longer that evening than I had ever known her to do before." The next day, after jostling along in an open-air wagon with a tiny "babe in [her] arms," Sally wrote that she felt as if "every bone in my body has been broken and my flesh bruised in every part of it."[11]

After visiting Samuel's family, Sally and Ann Eliza traveled to Brandon, Vermont, where she had a tearful reunion with her mother and sister. This was their first time laying eyes on little Ann Eliza and their first reunion since Jonathan Sr.'s death. The house felt very "desolate indeed" in her father's absence. It was "a most affecting meeting. Our hearts were too full for utterance." Leaving their babies at home, Sally and her sister Lydia visited their father's grave, which was just yards away from Nabby Farrington's headstone. Sally must have wept thinking about the challenges she encountered since her spiritual birthday some thirteen years earlier. She knelt in the grass and "plucked a few green leaves from the green sod which cover his ashes" and later enclosed them in a letter to Samuel.[12]

Sally had barely unpacked when troubles again surfaced on College Hill, causing Samuel to indicate that he would leave the institution. In June Sally wrote, "I do not understand why you think of leaving as things in regard to the college have taken so nearly the turn you desired."[13] But Samuel, exhausted by the still-unfolding Luther Rice financial scandal, was making immediate plans to return to New England. In this and her next letter, Sally detailed how and what Samuel should pack or sell prior to his departure. She listed every belonging they owned, from furniture ("I would sell the cot bed and bedstead $2.50"), to mundane clothing ("my woolen stockings I wish brought also likewise my flannel nightgowns, my knit petticoats"), to fancy outfits, such as her silk spencer and bonnets with feathers and artificial roses. She listed crockery, glassware, tin boxes and pans, pillows, pillow cases, blankets, comfortables, coal boxes, iron ware, pails, and books—dozens of personal belongings and kitchenware that reveal—after the fact—that by this time, they had been keeping house somewhere on College Hill, if not in a portion of the Sewell's home, then elsewhere. Sally filled several pages instructing Samuel how to dispose of their plants and a variety of decorative and medicinal fauna that they kept on their "piazza." The dusty miller (used for headaches and to prompt menstruation), pennyroyal geranium (an abortifacient also used for gout), and balm geranium (to treat skin wounds and repel insects) were to be distributed to her female friends, including Matilda Holmead, Ann Smith, Jane Paine, and Mrs. Anderson, the steward's wife.[14] These detailed instructions indicate how settled Sally had become at College Hill, cultivating close relationships as well as a home.

While Sally was sorry to leave her friends, she was happy to restart her life in more familiar surroundings. Despite the freshness of the news that Samuel was returning home, she was already making long-term plans to retrench the family in New England. Shortly after her return north, she gave Samuel's younger brother Hiram four dollars to buy Ann Eliza a sheep, and also planned to appropriate "a small sum for the trifle which is still coming to me from my paternal estate for the purpose of assisting in educating her."[15] She may have felt some financial agency with a potential inheritance from her father's death, a small parcel of cedar land, which she sold to her mother for fifty dollars the following year.[16] As their marriage seasoned and Samuel's travels continued, Sally became more outspoken about their future. Compared to her compliance regarding adoption of an orphan six years earlier, Sally expressed her desires openly, but not without the deference expected of a nineteenth-century wife. After writing how she longed "for the time when we may be permitted to dwell in quiet by our own fire side," she added an oblique apology. "I did not think of saying so much of my own feelings and I scarcely know how it has escaped me, unless it is that when I am writing to you I only think aloud."[17] Despite her strong opinions, Sally continued to straddle the space between obedient duty and defiance, choosing to influence through a measured and gentle resistance rather than through outright demands.

But for now, Samuel was coming north. Before he left Washington City, he took care to get a formal dismissal and recommendation from Columbian College, something he would need to secure a new position. Signed by president William Staughton, professor Ruggles, professor Alexander Caswell (who later became president of Brown University), and Thomas Jefferson Conant (John Conant's son who had recently been hired as a tutor), the letter stated that Samuel Wait had "distinguished himself as a faithful, able, and assiduous officer" of the institution.[18] By early September, Samuel had begun an extended New England job search, primarily in upstate New York, traveling west in a one-horse wagon.[19] His letters to Ann Eliza read like a travelogue as he left his grandfather's hometown of White Creek to visit Brutus, Waterloo, Victory, Montezuma, and Geneva, a region where many of his Wait relatives, including his favorite sister Betsey, had migrated. He was clearly taken by this region, writing to Sally, "There is no comparison, my dear, between this country . . . and any part of the world you have ever visited. Let any man of common sense once see this region, and I have no doubt about the result."[20]

By early October, he had visited Canandaigua, Victor, Pittsford, Rochester, Caledonia Springs, LeRoy, Covington, Bethany, Alexander, and Pembroke.[21] Wait used family and Baptist contacts, and possibly his Masonic brethren, to network along the way. A Mason since 1814, Wait found himself smack in the time and place of the mysterious kidnapping and probable murder of William Morgan. Morgan, an ostracized Mason who had threatened to reveal the fraternal order's secret rituals, had been arrested on trumped-up charges in Batavia, New York, then transported to nearby Canandaigua by brothers loyal to the oath. Samuel was seventeen miles away in Geneva when Morgan disappeared. While the exact unfolding of his disappearance may never be known, most anti-Masons agreed that Morgan was murdered.[22] Some rumors about his death included reports that Morgan suffered the consequences of the Masonic oath to which he once swore, promising that secrets would not be revealed lest he have "my Throat cut, my Tongue taken from the roof of my mouth, my heart pluck'd from under my Left Breast, then to be buried in the Sands of the Sea."[23] While Wait made no mention of the scandal in his letters, he had likely heard talk of the controversy, which became a national sensation leading to the anti-Mason political movement. In fact, during the time that Wait traveled in the region, "*ad hoc* citizens' committees . . . traced [Morgan's abduction route] over 100 miles from Canandaigua west by Rochester to Lewiston and finally to Morgan's last known incarceration at Fort Niagara," a route quite similar to Wait's, putting him in the middle of the continuing controversy.[24] Later, in North Carolina, Samuel also ended up in the middle of anti-Mason sentiment when a conservative Baptist association decreed that church members who joined the Masons or visited lodges and Masonic parades would be barred from church fellowship.[25]

Masonic scandals aside, Samuel took the time in New York to see relatives, network with Baptist ministers, and visit Niagara Falls, which with improved travel was becoming a major tourist attraction. His letter to Ann Eliza describes his powerful experience: "I would, my dear child, were it in my power to do so, give you an adequate description of the great falls on this noble river. . . . I thought, my precious little one; that possible at a future day I should see this wonderful cataract again, in company with yourself and your dear Ma'am."[26] In this letter, Samuel reminded Ann Eliza that she was now nine months old. "My face is now turned towards home, and I almost promise myself the pleasure of pressing you to my bosom one week from next Tuesday." By December 12 he was back in White Creek, New York with Ann Eliza "sleeping by [his] side" as he scratched out responses to a flurry of letters that had awaited him, pleading for him to return to Columbian College, again to save the institution.[27] Two months later, Sally was again left without her husband as Samuel was back on the road to raise money for the Baptist cause.

Had he been a swearing man, Samuel Wait would have cursed Luther Rice on a cold February 14, 1827. Samuel had been called back into service for Columbian College, and he and Dr. Staughton had been traveling since two days after Christmas, crisscrossing the back roads of the Carolinas in a twenty-five-dollar wagon that some female friends of the Baptists had helped outfit into a suitable carriage for the journey. He missed Ann Eliza and Sally, who were now back in Brandon tending to family while he and Staughton raised money for Columbian College, which was once again on the brink of financial ruin. This day was a far cry from the Valentine's Day a decade before, when Sally had traveled with Samuel to meet his family to seal their engagement. It was also a long way from the grand reception they hosted for Lafayette just two years earlier, when the future of the fledgling college seemed unstoppable. Now Wait and Staughton were stranded at a stranger's house in New Bern, North Carolina after a carriage accident caused the fifty-six-year-old college president "serious injury" and threatened to delay them from their critical task.[28]

If Samuel blamed Rice for this disaster, he was not alone. While Samuel was on his walkabout in western New York mapping out a potential future for his family, a barrage of letters had poured in from friends associated with the college, most notably president William Staughton. All of them encouraged Samuel to accept Staughton's invitation to join him on a fundraising tour to salvage the "disastrous circumstances" of the institution. The board, Staughton wrote, having "virtually prohibited" Rice "from the prosecution of any Agency" until he could straighten out his sloppy accounts, had "come to the conclusion that I can render important services by leaving the Hill and proceeding to beg for it." He went on in his letter to Samuel, "On looking around for a brother to assist me, my thoughts have been turned to yourself. I know the kindness of your disposition and you are sufficiently acquainted with me to form a judgment how far our feelings and purposes and exertions can amalgamate & contribute to each other in producing beneficial results."[29] In other words, Staughton thought Samuel Wait would make a good traveling companion. Staughton was vague about Wait's compensation but assured him it would "be such as will communicate to Mrs. Wait and yourself entire satisfaction." Considering Wait was still unemployed after his trip around New York State, it probably did not leave him much choice but to go, much to Sally's disappointment. But a persuasive call to duty may have been a stronger pull than pay. Both Waits, at this point, had invested a great deal of time and emotion in the Baptist mission. The letters to Samuel from college administrators and volunteers provided a flattering appeal to his continued sense of responsibility to the cause.

All things considered, Wait's friend and Columbian College faculty member William Ruggles probably best summed up reasons to tour the South. If Wait were to take this trip, Ruggles argued, "you will have such a grand opportunity to become acquainted with all the important parts of our country & all the distinguished men . . . especially from your denomination." What better way to satisfy Wait's "wish to see the world" and look for a new position at the same time? If Samuel was still trying to figure out his long-term calling, a fundraising trip at the side of the esteemed William Staughton could provide an ideal opportunity to investigate his options. "You could never indulge your society to visit different regions & scenes to better advantage," Ruggles reasoned. "And only think of the vast good you may be accomplishing at the same time."[30] With that, Ruggles had laid out a masterful argument for Samuel to again take up the cause for Columbian College.

Wait had left Sally in Brandon before Christmas to rendezvous with Staughton in Washington City on December 27, 1826. During his two months away, he had already missed Ann Eliza's first steps and the cutting of her first tooth.[31] Sally was lonely and distraught that Samuel was again drawn to the South. In February, she wrote to Samuel about the death of his old mentor Silvanus Haynes, whom he had just seen on his trip in western New York. "Some of our friends have thought of the vacancy as an eligible situation for you," Sally suggested. She took the opportunity to express her distress, writing, "I long for the time when we may be permitted to dwell in quiet by our own fireside . . . and can together bow before the family altar." Sally pined for Samuel in the early part of 1827, writing, "Your absence leaves a void which can be supplied from no other source. I feel that the best half of my existence is torn away."[32] While family members were planning to attend a sleigh riding party with thirty couples, Sally decided to pass, with "no desire to join in such parties of pleasure."[33] She worried about how the separation affected Ann Eliza. Although she could repeat the word "poppa," Sally was not sure she "recollects what the word means." Still, she was determined to put on a show of compliance to the lot of providence and "submit cheerfully to every dispensation."[34]

Apart from her emotional worries, Sally was also concerned about more practical matters such as Samuel's health, fearful that if he traveled too far south in the coming months, he would be "in a climate as warm weather advances, which so often proves fatal to northern constitutions." This was not a baseless assumption to Sally, who had relatives who had suffered on trips south during the summer, including her brother Jonathan's near-fatal experience two years before as well as a cousin who had died. "I cannot express to you, my dear, half of the solicitude I feel on this subject. I think of the fate of poor Alvan Merriam, and of many others."[35] Sally's perception of the South was influenced by these experiences. The hot climate was the stuff of legends. "I suppose the trees are now in bloom in Georgia," she mused in early February.[36]

During Samuel's absence, Sally was living in her parental home, but it was no longer her mother's house. The year prior, the family had made a deal with Jacob Powers, Lydia's husband, to sell his land in Groton, New Hampshire and move to Brandon to take care of her aging parents, who could no longer keep up the farm. Typically, the paternal homeplace would be transferred to the eldest son or willed to the youngest if he stayed home to take care of aging parents. In the Merriams' case, oldest son Isaac was pursuing the ministry and the youngest boys weren't old enough to take over operations, leaving the family to strike a deal with Lydia's new husband. Sally's younger brothers Abel and Charles Rollin helped Powers drive his cattle to move his farmstead to the Merriam home. Powers apparently agreed to invest $700 in the transaction, which meant he would ultimately inherit the farm.[37] Sally's mother's options were constrained by the laws of coverture that often left a widow as a tenant in her former house, and they were complicated by the limitations of her children's living situations. The other boys in the family had set their sights on preaching, teaching, or industry and were constantly moving about and scraping to make ends meet. These young men were members of what Donald Scott called a "dislocated generation, forced to strike out on its own, making its way as it went with few family resources to begin with or fall back on."[38] With Sally determined to follow her calling with Samuel, the agreement with Lydia's husband seemed like a good option at the time. Unfortunately, the long-term repercussions of this family decision would prove dire for Sally's mother. After Lydia's early death in 1830, Powers married twice again and had several more children, expecting his former mother-in-law and tenant to act as housekeeper and nanny to the young children. Sally's brother Charles Rollin later wrote that he was "unwilling that her last days should be spent in drudgery" at the hands of Powers's newest wife.[39] Their mother's last years became a tragic footnote to the changing family dynamics of the Early Republic.

But that would come later. In the meantime, with Samuel traveling the back roads of the South to raise money for the college, there were mouths to feed. Whatever salary Wait was to be paid on his fundraising trip, it probably had not yet made its way to him, much less to Sally, so she and Lydia started up a business in the meantime to help them along. It is not clear exactly what their venture entailed; Sally could have brushed off her old bonnet-making skills, but she had already experienced frustration with her inability to turn a profit. Also, the description of the business in her letter of February 1826 does not indicate she was braiding and shaping bonnets considering the pace of their work. "Not long since we made about 4 dollars on what was made and sold in five days. . . . But this was our best, some weeks we have not made one dollar."[40] Bonnets took much longer to produce. It could be they were spinning, weaving, or producing some form of handiwork for others. Despite their inconsistent sales, Sally remained optimistic that "we shall have as much employment in the spring as we wish."[41]

Meanwhile, however, Sally was in snow-covered Brandon while Samuel Wait was marooned in a near-stranger's house in New Bern, North Carolina. The wagon crash that sidelined him there would later be described as a providential event that called the Waits to North Carolina for their remaining lives. The incident is a critical part of the story of the origins of Wake Forest College, a legend that is repeated today. An early twentieth-century accounting by Wait grandson John Bruce Brewer at the inauguration of ninth Wake Forest President Francis Pendleton Gaines opened with the story: "A horse became frightened, ran, threw a man out of a wagon, injured him and broke the wagon. Result: Samuel Wait became a citizen of N.C. and in 1834 became the first President of W[ake] F[orest] C[ollege]."[42]

The narrative implies that the hand of providence was at work in charting the fate of Sally and Samuel Wait, a sentiment with which Sally herself would have agreed. The accident did indeed have a fateful effect on Sally and Samuel's future, and it could be argued that the college's founding would not have unfolded had the horse not bucked. As it was, the "disaster" detained Wait and Staughton "in Newbern about a week longer," which gave Wait time to inspect the village and its Baptist inhabitants.[43] He liked what he saw, and there was an attractive opening, something he had not found in his travels around western New York. Despite several offers from New England, none of them promised a suitable or sustainable salary. His brother-in-law Jonathan, writing on behalf of the Vermont Association, admitted their opening for an agency "I presume would not please you," as they were looking for an agent "who has no family," meaning someone who needed little salary.[44] The Middlebury, Vermont church could only offer $200, with an additional $100 from the state convention.[45]

The members from Sharon, who had remained loyal to Wait since his departure from that church in 1820—so much so that one member of the congregation named his son Samuel Wait—continued to appeal for Wait's return.[46] Letters had been sent on several occasions beginning in early 1825 inviting Samuel back into the fold, the most recent appeal coming from Leavitt Hewins in February 1827.[47] Invitations from Sharon continued a few years forward, to the extent that Sally's mother opined that their choice to go to North Carolina over Massachusetts was a "Jonah's trip."[48] While the Sharon members were consistently earnest in their appeals, Wait may have doubted their capacity to meet the financial needs of his growing family. He remembered their inability to follow through some four years earlier, and he also knew the shortcomings of leading a struggling Baptist church in a small New England town. He had just seen his old friend and mentor Abiel Fisher, who was still ministering the church in Bellingham, Massachusetts, the small community a few miles from Sharon. His situation was likely not much different than it was in 1820, when he lived "on bread and milk half the time."[49]

The situation looked different in New Bern, a vibrant port village that once served as the colonial capital of North Carolina. Historian Catherine Bishir describes its status as an urban port. Its architecture was sophisticated, its economy urban, and its social life complex.[50] Wait had met Edenton minister Thomas Meredith, a rising North Carolina Baptist leader, who approached Wait about an opening at his former church in New Bern. A Pennsylvania native with some theological training, Meredith was committed to Baptist missions and education in a state that did not always agree. Earlier that year, the conservative Kehukee Baptist Association issued a tract that rejected "Missionary Societies, Tract Societies, Bible Societies, and Theological Seminaries" in no uncertain terms. The association stated they "discountenance them and the practices heretofore resorted to for their support, in begging money from the public to back them."[51] This statement was a shot across the bow to Wait's and Staughton's efforts, and excerpts from the tract were printed with disdainful commentary in the college's *Columbian Star*.[52] There would be many more clashes with the Kehukee Association to come, but for now, Meredith assured Samuel that the New Bern Baptist Church had more liberal views and "mourns over this but could not prevent it."[53] It was in this same circular that the group denounced Masons, forbidding its church members to join the fraternity and denying ministers who were Masons to preach in their pulpits.[54] Considering the strength of the Masonic brotherhood in New Bern at the time, this was likely another reason they took exception to the circular. Although by the time the Kehukee Association administered their directive, the New Bern Masons had gone quiet, most likely due to the William Morgan affair. The March 8, 1826 meeting minutes of Lodge No. 3 are followed by blank pages until March 25, 1835.[55]

When Samuel's horse bucked and his wagon broke down, the Baptists in New Bern began a spirited recruitment to convince him to relocate as their minister. Before the accident, Staughton and Wait had been staying at the home of Brother Handcock, an early member of the church.[56] With the wagon broken down and Staughton injured, Wait was sidelined for a week. It is probable that Wait asked Elijah Clark, the founder of the Baptist church and a carriage maker, to repair the wagon. Clark's store (and later dwelling) were located on East Front Street, between Union and King Streets, a few doors down from William Handcock's business and home.[57] The area was a small Baptist enclave adjacent to the cedar-lined "Baptismal Shores," where members were baptized. Handcock was known to offer up his home as a place for the immersed to change out of their wet clothes.[58] While he was there, Wait got to know Clark and Handcock, who were not only neighbors but also related by marriage, as their wives were sisters.[59] This must have made the subsequent division between the two men that much more awkward. Between the time they began recruiting Wait and his eventual move South, Brother Riggs wrote Wait that "it pains me to the heart that is a difficulty between our Bro[ther] Clark & Handcock a unhappy scene has taken place."[60] Whatever the conflict was, it caused Handcock's name on the original church records membership list to be summarily crossed out. He seems to have been restored in February 1836, only to be excommunicated again in 1843.[61] Listed with Clark's and Handcock's names on the original list of church members was James Riggs, who, together with a handful of others, met in Elijah Clark's home at the corner of Middle and Craven Streets in the early years of the church.[62] Clark and Riggs especially would become important figures in Samuel's recruitment to lead the New Bern Baptist Church.

Once the wagon was repaired and the skittish horse replaced, Wait traveled on to Charleston to continue the Columbian fundraising assignment. Still spooked from the accident, Staughton opted to travel by stage, meeting Wait in Charleston, South Carolina. In March 1827, however, once in Charleston, Dr. Staughton received "some further intelligence . . . in relation to the college—all in a most disastrous condition." The Charleston Baptists were abuzz with the news that, back in Washington City, Luther Rice, O. B. Brown, and others had recaptured control of the board. On March 24, 1827, Dr. Staughton "wrote his resignation and put it into the P.O." in Charleston, ironically in the city where he had begun his American journey.[63] It was a bitter loss for Staughton. As his son-in-law later wrote: "He relinquished his post only when he felt that to remain any longer would embitter his own existence, and bring no relief to the college."[64] At the height of his career, Staughton had been secretary to the influential American Baptist Foreign Mission Society, president of Columbian College, and chaplain to the US Senate. He had been asked to deliver a sermon at the Capitol upon the deaths of former US Presidents Jefferson and Adams. Staughton mingled with Congress, feted Lafayette, and donated artifacts from Indian missions to the fashionable Charles Willson Peale museum.[65] It must have felt like a sudden and precipitous fall when the college he helped found had fallen into the hands of his adversaries. After his resignation Staughton remained in the South for a few weeks before returning to Philadelphia and provided sporadic preaching to area churches until he agreed to assume the presidency at Georgetown Theological Institute in Kentucky in 1829. He quickly married Anna Claypoole Peale, the niece of Charles Willson Peale who was twenty-one years his junior, and loaded up their belongings. They made it only as far as Washington City before Staughton succumbed to illness and passed away, according to his new wife, repeating the words, "Hallelujah! Hallelujah! Hallelujah!"[66]

In Charleston, Samuel resigned his position a few days after Staughton, an inevitability that had been several years in the making.[67] The Columbian College turn of events combined an economic urgency for Samuel and a spiritual opportunity for the New Bern Church. Wait was still on the upward trajectory of his career, and there was an immediate professional option on the table. After bidding goodbye to Staughton and the Charleston Baptists, Samuel returned to New Bern to spend the spring at the church on a trial basis. He spent his time preaching, attending services, meeting with leaders from other churches, and visiting the poorhouse and prison.[68]

On June 1, the church voted to pay Samuel an annual salary of $500, substantially more than churches in New England had offered him. Before and after the vote, the members showered him with gifts. Brother Riggs gave him a pair of shoes, Sister Riggs donated two pairs of "short summer stockings" and a "piece of very elegant shirting," and Sister Handcock gave him a black silk handkerchief. Wait wrote in his diary that Sister Outten donated a "frock for my little daughter."[69] Wait's wardrobe probably needed an upgrade after months of constant travel, especially to citizens who felt that New Bern was a "'vortex of fashion,' where the 'gayest of the gay' lived a life 'full of extravagance and fine dressing.'"[70] Samuel was not only called to duty to North Carolina; he also seemed smitten with the relative sophistication and generosity of the town's Baptist leaders.

The backward attitudes Samuel encountered elsewhere in North Carolina did not dissuade him. While he considered the "state of the ministry all about that region . . . deplorable" due to the narrow thinking of the Kehukee followers, he seemed buoyed by the challenge: "I do not know of a more important opening."[71] Samuel's old friend Irah Chase agreed. "It may be that Newbern is the very best place for commencing our efforts to set our affairs right in N.C." Chase wrote that a North Carolina stronghold would create a "wide and important field of usefulness."[72] From Chase's letter, it is clear that Samuel had asked for Chase's opinion not only on becoming minister at New Bern Baptist Church, but about potential for bigger plans. Chase asked, "Would yours be a private establishment? . . . Could you probably bring under your institution young Baptist brethren from other places?"[73] Chase wrote that New Bern "would be a highly important field for pastoral labour" and that it was "a great distance from Edgefield," meaning far enough from the newly established Baptist

Furman Academy and Theological Institution to avoid competing for donors and students if Wait were to establish an educational institution "where
some of our young brethren might be fitted for college."[74] Here was a place
Samuel Wait could make a mark on the world. But first, he had to sell Sally
on their "duty to come to N.C."[75] He had many arguments to make.

His first order of business was to dispel the persistent perception that
northerners could not survive in the oppressive heat. He was assured that
"there are many northern people in town and that they commonly had
good health," writing to Sally, "We have been mistaken about this region."
People generally did well in the fall and summer, at least "till hard in
July."[76] From there, Samuel used every persuasive argument imaginable,
his letters reading like an early nineteenth-century chamber of commerce
brochure. "It is a most beautiful place. I never saw a town in which there
were so many trees," Samuel wrote. "From the steeple of the Pres[byterian]
meetinghouse, I had a most delightful view of the whole town—these trees
made a fine appearance though not in bloom."[77] Referring to a species
introduced to America in the mid-eighteenth century, Wait goes on, "The
trees are called 'china,' and sometimes 'the Pride of China,' and resemble
a pretty large apple tree."[78] In these and other descriptions, Wait used im-
ages that compared New Bern's topography, people, commerce, location,
and even town layout to those that Sally would recognize, hoping to dispel
the guarded impressions she might have in her mind about the Carolinas.
The church seemed "most like our old friends in Sharon," he wrote. There
were "two banks, one weekly paper, a Court-House and jail. The streets,
generally, cross each other at right angles as those in Phil[adelphia]." In
terms of location and commerce, Samuel wrote, "The shipping is much
more considerable than I was aware of," with packages moving "constantly
to New York and other ports," which would give them speed of mail delivery
and ease of travel to keep in touch with family in the North.

New Bern was a bustling port of five thousand inhabitants, which Samuel
compared to Troy, New York, a city near Albany that they had visited when
traveling to and from Washington City. While not as many grand houses
lined paved streets as in Troy, he had "no doubt but more shipping is
owned here. . . . Many of the vessels are employed in some trade with the
West Indian Islands."[79] His descriptions were quite accurate. The trade in
New Bern provided a fashionable social life with noted North Carolina
families and politicians.[80] In some ways, relocating to New Bern would be
a logical transition from their experience in Washington City. But Sally
had questions about her potential new congregation, asking, "How do
the members of the Baptist church rank with the members of the other

churches, in regard to intelligence, and influence in Society?"[81] This was not an idle question. Baptists were often a middling and scrappy bunch, not always at the height of society. Concerned about status, Sally knew that Clark, while an established and relatively successful carriage maker, was considered part of the "mechanic" class, a term that would have included many types of artisans who worked with their hands.[82] Riggs, a hatter, was known affectionately as "Uncle Jimmy Riggs," not an honorific that conferred status of an elevated class.[83] In New Bern, white artisans ranked higher than the enslaved and those of the white labor class, but lower than the gentry class who owned extensive property or wealth.[84] With the emerging emphasis on formal training of preachers and missionaries, the ministerial field was creating a professional class during the market revolution in the Early Republic. Both Sally and Samuel were aware of this distinction and aspired to ascend accordingly.

The racial composition, class, and social dynamics of New Bern in the mid-1820s were complex. Unlike the District of Columbia, which was a sparsely constructed government center surrounded by swampy planta- tions, New Bern was a thriving port city of five thousand residents when the Baptists were recruiting Samuel. While he overestimated the population by three thousand in a letter to Sally when he wrote, "New Bern is the largest town in N.C.—has about 8000 inhabitants, say half white," his estimate on the ratio of white to black residents was not too far off. Approximately 60 percent of the population was black, with enslaved blacks and freed men and women working as domestics, draymen, port workers, mariners, artisans, businessmen, and farmers. Coastal North Carolina was teeming with diverse mercantile workers. When traveler Moses Curtis arrived on the coast from Boston in 1830, he found the "wharf and stores crowded with blacks, noisy and careless."[85] New Bern's economic system was less like rural Washington City and more akin to Baltimore, encompassing a spectrum of labor categories including enslaved workers, indentured servants, and apprentices.[86] New Bern had varied and complex lines be- tween race, class, and station. For instance, John Carruthers Stanly, a freed black man, was a successful barber serving some of the city's elite whites.[87] Stanly, said to be the son of white New Bern merchant John Wright Stanley and an enslaved Ibo woman, was manumitted by his enslavers, a common practice in Craven County after the Revolutionary War.[88] Over time, as a free man, Stanly became wealthy and at one point was himself one of the largest enslavers in the county before eventually helping free at least forty enslaved people.[89] Stanly's wife was a free black woman, Kitty Green Stanly, who cofounded New Bern First Presbyterian Church alongside twelve other town leaders.[90] One of her cofounders was Eunice Edwards Hunt, a daughter of Jonathan Edwards.[91] While free blacks did not have the rights of the white population, some had enough economic and social agency in enclaves such as New Bern to accumulate wealth and worship alongside whites. While enslaved church members were segregated to the church balcony, the Stanlys purchased two pews on the main level of the sanctuary.[92]

While Sally had experienced slavery during her time at Columbian College, it had been a relatively bucolic setting compared with the dynamics of New Bern. On College Hill, Sally's daily interaction with enslaved people was with the bondsmen and women who served the college, like "Uncle Richard and Aunt Betsey." While Sally had traveled into Washington City occasionally, her day-to-day setting was rural. New Bern would be a different experience, and Samuel needed to paint a picture for Sally that would lessen her concerns about raising their child in a slaveholding state. Samuel made such an effort when he described his visit to New Bern's prison. The Craven County Jail, a few blocks away from the Baptismal Shores, was just a few years old, its four hundred thousand bricks having been supplied by a free black brick mason, Donum Montford. An enslaver and owner of real estate, Montford, as a male tax payer, would have been qualified to vote at the time.[93] In a letter to Sally and Ann Eliza, Wait made a point to tell them that at the prison, he had conversed and prayed with the prisoners, including two who were "confined for murder. One of these unhappy men killed a Negro only 3 or 4 days ago. They both have their trials in October."[94] This was not meaningless commentary. Samuel was sending Sally a message that in New Bern, justice existed for the black population, since a white man was being held in prison for the consequence of killing a black man.

Sally met Samuel's initial letters recruiting her to join him in North Carolina with ambiguity. Samuel was keenly aware that Sally and her family did not want them to move for a number of reasons, and slavery offered a uniquely moral imperative to stay in the North. Sally naturally preferred to stay in New England to be closer to her dear sister and mother. In an early response to Samuel, she wrote that she had "the impression that the prospect of a permanent home in that place is by no means very encouraging." Sally was tired of "tossing to and fro" and longed "for a steady home."[95] She could not imagine the New Bern commission a permanent one, which may have provided some consolation in making the decision to move. Sally was concerned about raising Ann Eliza in North Carolina, a place she described as being filled with "much ignorance and bigotry in this denomination."[96] In this comment Sally was likely referring to the anti-education and anti-missions movement in general, not slavery specifically, but her concerns about a permanent move to the South were clear. "It would be no easy thing to train her up in the way in which we think she should go, when every thing around us was against it," she wrote.[97] While Sally did not convey her concerns about slavery specifically in her early replies to Samuel, her family did. From their first consideration of New Bern, Sally's family reflected the rising abolitionist sentiment in New England by continually communicating their horror at the idea of their settling in a slave economy. Even after they had moved to New Bern, older brother Isaac was sure they would return, unable to "believe you can always endure slavery before your eyes."[98] Brother Jonathan and sister-in-law Achsah were adamant as well, writing, "Our strong and prevailing objection to the south is, slavery slavery."[99] Yet, at least for the time being, Samuel's persuasive arguments prevailed. Sally agreed to move to New Bern, a place far removed from family and a society that was familiar to her.

Eleven

RECKONING

> But, when we think of our accountability to
> God, and when we think of the judgment seat
> of Christ, and of meeting these poor North
> Carolinians there, we dare not [dissent to]
> them without the most convincing proof that
> God has here no more for us to do.
>
> —Sally to Leavitt Hewins, March 1830

> Can you not . . . weigh the consequences of
> endangering the Souls of your children and
> your own life also which is due to them as their
> earthly guardian before you settle again in a
> land of slavery?
>
> —Mother to Sally, April 1830

IN MID-JUNE 1827, BROTHER RIGGS GAVE SAMUEL WAIT
ten dollars cash to add to the fifty-five dollars he had already given him.
Samuel used it toward his fifteen-dollar passage on a schooner heading to
New York.[1] After being stalled offshore several days, the wind picked up and
they took sail, passing by the Cape Hatteras, North Carolina lighthouse as
they headed out to sea. On the morning of June 29, the ship arrived at the
New York harbor, having passed in Wait's estimate nearly a hundred vessels
sailing from the busy port. By July 1, he arrived at the Checkered House
and preached at the church his grandfather led in White Creek, New York,

about seventy miles south of Brandon, Vermont. Sally likely met him there with Ann Eliza, finally reunited with his "dear family once more—having been absent about 6 months and half, and traveled 11 hundred miles out and back again."[2] Wait's plan was to spend the summer and fall in New England to avoid traveling in the blistering heat and to pack for a December move to North Carolina. The little family had agreed to move into a New Bern dwelling that carried significance for the early church members.[3] A modest framed house that still stands at the intersection of Middle and Craven Streets, this was the former home of church founder Elijah Clark, who had since moved to his new home. While some early accounts report that the house was used for the first meetings of the church, the facts are in question.[4] Regardless, there probably had been plenty of gatherings of the faithful under the gambrel roof. The Waits' rent was seventy-two dollars in the first year, seventy-five the next.[5] The Wait family would be living in the heart of New Bern, a few blocks from the Baptismal Shores, the Baptist meeting house, the Presbyterian church, the temporarily shuttered Masonic temple, and the now-feuding Clarks and Handcocks.[6] While Samuel's plans for an academy for young men of the Baptist denomination did not come to fruition, he did decide to open a "female academy" to augment his income.[7] He advertised in the *Newbern Sentinel* and the *Newbern Spectator* for his fall term, stating that "his school will be small, and no effort will be wanting to give satisfaction to all concerned." The tuition was set at six dollars per quarter.[8] While the advertisements clearly promoted the school as his, it is likely that Sally played a hand in the support and perhaps some of the instruction, especially if any domestic arts were included in the students' studies.

As Sally and Samuel prepared to move, Samuel wrote Brother Riggs with a list of questions that Sally most likely had peppered him with when they met in White Creek. Riggs responded on August 10 to confirm plans for the move. Riggs would arrive in New York in October, presumably on unrelated business. He would bring with him "$150 or $200" and then accompany the family on a "pleasant passage to N.C."[9] In between comments about mattresses, ironware, and the dispute between Elder Clark and Brother Handcock, Riggs instructed Samuel, "As to the girl we think that you will do well to bring her with you."[10] He went on to write, "She will be worth in this place from $3 to $4 per month if there is the quality you think. . . . Our servants in this place is worth from $2 to $3 per month & she is better than ours & I think will remain so."[11]

Who did the Waits plan to bring to New Bern? Could she have been an enslaved woman who had made her way with Sally to New England from their time in Washington City? Given Sally's family's opinion about slavery, it is hard to imagine her showing up in Vermont with a black enslaved domestic worker when she returned there in early 1826. Also, the value differential that Brother Riggs outlined between his "servants" (who were indeed enslaved) and his estimate for the Waits' "girl" seems to indicate she may have been a white Vermonter.

Domestic assistance would not have been a foreign idea to Sally, nor would it have been to most of her peers. Historian Joyce Appleby remarks that "in nineteenth century America . . . almost every household—down to the poorest farm—had one or more. To be really poor was to live without a servant."[12] When Sally was in Brandon braiding straw for her leghorn bonnet business, she traveled to nearby Rutland to hire "girls" to complete piecework. Sally's mother often mentioned hired women living with them to help with farm and household activities. After her younger daughter Lydia's removal to Groton to commence housekeeping in 1823, Sally's mother had reported that "one hired girl cleared out the same morning and the other the next."[13] In another letter Mother Merriam wrote that Lydia "hired a girl about the middle of July [to] assist her through haying and harvest and then set to her spinning."[14] In the summer of 1828, Sally's younger brother Abel wrote that "Lydia has a girl with her most of the time."[15] Live-in domestic help was an unremarkable state of affairs for the Merriam women. But, of course, these "girls" were not chattel property. They were likely young, white Vermont girls whose families made ends meet by hiring out their children, a common practice at the time. The selection of a domestic worker to live in one's house was an intimate decision, as it meant inviting a stranger into the most personal aspects of family life.[16] As Sally was planning the move to New Bern, she knew she would need help setting up house and taking care of eighteen-month-old Ann Eliza, while also assuming the responsibilities of being a minister's wife. It is unlikely that she felt comfortable with the idea of enslaving a domestic worker once she moved to New Bern. Is it possible that, to avoid or delay that prospect, Sally decided bringing a Vermont "girl" with them would be a more tolerable alternative?

Another indication that the Waits' domestic help may have been a Vermonter is that Sally's mother seemed to know her. A few months after the Waits set up housekeeping in New Bern, Mother began a string of letters inquiring about a young woman named "Doratha," asking about her in a familiar tone. In February 1828, Mother asked Sally to tell her "all about Doratha and what your prospects are in New Bern."[17] That May, she asked "all about Doratha and whether she can write. . . . Give my respects to D and accept the same for yourselves."[18] Asking after Doratha's schooling seems to indicate familiar concern for the girl. It is possible Mother was following up on a promise Sally had made about educating Doratha, something the young girl may not have been provided in her crowded, disadvantaged family back home. A full year passed before Mother again asked, "What has become of Doratha?"[19] Just as Samuel was tendering his resignation to the New Bern Baptist Church, Mother's questions about Doratha became more pointed, as though the earlier inquiries had gone unanswered. In November 1829, she simply wrote, "Where is Doratha?"[20] This is the last we hear about her. Unfortunately, the letters Sally wrote in response to her mother's questions are not in the archives.

Doratha's unexplained disappearance corresponds with another significant development: the appearance of two enslaved women in the Waits' New Bern household on the 1830 census.[21] The two females at the time of enumeration included a woman between the age of twenty-four and thirty-five, and a girl under the age of ten, most likely mother and daughter. Given the Waits' strained finances, it is likely that these two females were either leased from their enslaver or possibly provided by Elijah Clark or James Riggs, Samuel's Baptist sponsors—and both enslavers.[22] In coastal towns during this time, there were various ways to procure labor, including enslaving, renting from enslavers, or in some cases paying wages directly to "self-hiring" enslaved workers.[23] This was practiced in most every Southern town.[24] There is no known evidence to explain the financial situation regarding this enslaved worker and her daughter, but the census reveals that the Waits clearly had adapted to the slave culture by 1830, despite Sally's unease. Samuel had already acclimated to the system when he had stayed with Brother Clark before Sally moved to town. In his diary, he noted tips to enslaved workers who assisted him in Clark's home, giving them $1.20 and $0.75 on two different occasions, which would have been a customary practice.[25] How did Sally feel about her new living situation? As mentioned before, the idea of domestic live-in help was an established practice for members of the Merriam family. Sally would have been accustomed to differences in class dynamics, but she would not have been as familiar with the complexities that race presented. While we have records of Sally's objections to raising her children in North Carolina in general terms, we have no written record about how she reacted to slavery specifically, and we cannot know what she may have vocalized about it to her friends and family in person.

The 1830 census was taken one month before Samuel's professional plans once again disrupted Sally's world. In late 1829, Wait resigned from

New Bern Baptist Church, giving the members three months' notice as his contract required, although the couple lingered in town for another nine months before Sally returned to Brandon.[26] The decision to leave the church seemed to be driven by finances. After all the promises from Riggs and Clark during Wait's recruitment, it seems the church had not come up with the $500–$600 salary the family expected. After one year of residency, they had renewed Wait's contract for only $400, about a 25 percent pay cut.[27] Wait might have seen this change coming when he first moved to New Bern, since he had started the female academy to supplement the family's income. As it turned out, while New Bern was a thriving port that visitors called the "Athens of North Carolina," its economy was sinking under the weight of a local banking crisis with the fall of Caribbean trade.[28] As tradesmen, Clark, Riggs, and other members of the Baptist church probably experienced financial setbacks, making it difficult to follow through on their generous intentions.

In the interim, Samuel picked up a short-term missionary gig with the Massachusetts Missionary Society and went on the road, leaving Sally behind in New Bern.[29] During that brief appointment, by Samuel's accounting, he "preached 71 sermons, administered the Lord's supper once, and distributed between 4 and 500 tracts."[30] Wait recruited John Armstrong, a Philadelphia native who had attended Columbian College with him, to take his place. "Having no family he can live on what he receives for preaching without a school," Wait wrote.[31] While Armstrong seemed well liked and went on to become one of the first faculty members at Wake Forest College, not everyone was pleased with the choice. Reverend R. B. Howell, who also knew Armstrong from Columbian College, wrote Wait, "I hope he is not what he formally was at the college." Howell added, "Beseech him for the love of God . . . to obtain, if he has not already, a high standard of piety."[32] Apparently Armstrong had sown some wild oats while at College Hill. When Wait resigned from the church, he cited the time commitment necessary to keep the school as a significant reason. "Till a person has tried it, he can not know how unpleasant it is to be in such a situation," Wait complained. The school made him "constantly confined to the town," which kept him from "preaching, at least occasionally, in the country." This was an "important object of coming to this town" in the first place, as the region "20 miles around [him was] lamentably destitute of religious instruction."[33]

Despite Sally's doubts about living in the South, the couple continued to be drawn to North Carolina during a particularly difficult time, specifically as it related to social unrest. In addition to a withering economy, the political and social agency of blacks was moving backward, not forward. In the early nineteenth century in North Carolina, some landowning free blacks had political rights, including the right to vote. These and other civil liberties would be eroded with Draconian laws that were passed as 1830 approached. In the years just following the Revolutionary War, many evangelical churches, particularly the Methodists, had condemned slavery. Bishop Frances Asbury denounced slavery in 1798, but the abolitionist voice of the United Methodist Church was softening by 1818, reflecting the splintering national opinion. [34] A look at Samuel's ministry in New Bern and a few years following instructively illustrates the dynamic of evangelicals' relationship to slavery in North Carolina in the late 1820s and early 1830s.

New Bern black and white citizens "worked alongside one another in shops, on construction sites, and along the wharves and waterways,"[35] and this interaction extended to worship. When Samuel was named minister to the New Bern Baptist Church in 1827, the membership consisted of "22 whites and 8 blacks . . . who reside in town—some are too far off to be able to attend meeting here."[36] Of the eight original "coloured" members listed in church records, only two of them were recorded with first and last names, Philip Wiggins and Peggy Sawyers. The others—Abraham, Phoebe, Judith, Mary, Winnifred and Priscilla—were referenced by their first names only.[37] This document could indicate that the first two were free blacks and the others were the enslaved workers of white members. The Presbyterian church was also biracial, as was the United Methodist church. In fact, the United Methodist church was primarily black, with 390 black members and only thirty white members in 1807,[38] although apparently many attended services without professing faith. Wait looked down on those who were "only seekers" as less than desirable worshippers, referring to them as "rubbish."[39] Like the Northerners who brought their prejudices intact to Washington, DC, Wait carried with him racial biases of the time, like many of the white members who were a part of "the larger Anglo-American world."[40] In his diary, he described a Methodist service as having "much noise . . . chiefly among the blacks." He goes on to write, "I sincerely think that such as possess the least knowledge, make the most noise."[41] His comments reveal the disturbing premise of early evangelical churches.

When British Baptist William Carey inspired the modern missionary movement by traveling to India, members of many denominations enthusiastically followed suit. Tracts were printed, funds were raised, and plans were made to travel to remote and dangerous lands to convert heathens from their sinful and ignorant ways. The altruistic missions often followed opportunistic colonialists motivated by economic gain. The philosophy inherent in both endeavors—exploiting resources and saving souls— presumed the superiority of a paternalistic, white, Christian way of life. Whether a missionary was traveling to Burma to convert "Hindoos," the American West to save Native Americans, or the Carolinas to preach to backwoods whites and their enslaved counterparts, the goal was to elevate men and women from their ignorant state to gospel-educated hearts and minds. This is what Samuel had on his mind when he wrote to his longtime Columbian College friend William Ruggles that the region was destitute in religious instruction.

Wait's abolitionist-leaning cousin Zera Washington Wait, writing from Granville, New York, emphasized the interconnected approach to missions and education in a letter to Wait in 1844. Referring to the last few decades that "realize[d] the mighty moral change that has been affected . . . in opposition to and in spite of the ignorance and idolatry—the superstitions and traditions of a hundred generations, we are constrained to exclaim, 'What God Hath Wrought.'"[42] Cousin "Zery" used his argument to expose the "one dark spot in this bright field of moral vision . . . the institution of slavery."[43] By 1844, when he wrote this letter, the abolitionist movement was in full swing in the North, where they had "almost daily demonstrations of its reality" with fugitives from slavery escaping to Canada to exercise "their inalienable rights . . . endowed by their creator."[44] If Samuel Wait's response to Cousin Zery's letter still existed, we might have a more direct knowledge of the nuances of his opinions about the confluence of religion, race, and slavery. Instead, we are left to interpret his silence on the topic within the context of what other religious leaders around him were articulating, both in defense and condemnation of slavery. In 1820, a Quaker minister—from a denomination active in the abolitionist movement—visiting North Carolina "found that New Bern's slaveholders could 'bear to be reasoned with on the great evils of slavery'" when he preached about it one Sunday.[45] Of course, he was just passing through.

Most ministers who wanted to put down deeper roots in their communities learned to moderate their stance as the political climate changed. Not long after the Waits arrived in eastern North Carolina, an Episcopalian minister sympathetic to the abolitionist cause advised a dying widow in Edenton to leave her enslaved workers to the American Colonization Society, giving them passage and resettlement in Africa. The colonization society, started by a Presbyterian minister in 1817, was an alternative to immediate manumission in the states. Many abolitionists considered colonization impractical and morally deficient, but some offered it as a compromise to integrating additional freed blacks into United States society, an idea that most enslavers disdained. In 1822, many of the powerful ministers in Washington City were officers in the American Colonization Society, including Columbian College trustee Reverend O. B. Brown.[46] As historian Charles I. Foster points out, the "American Colonization Society had been the Evangelical answer to slavery," offering a "bifocal view of satisfying politicians such as Henry Clay and to many others averse to any firm commitment."[47] For a Southerner, colonization offered to "remove troublesome free Negroes by deportation," while in the North it encouraged manumission.[48] Thus, colonization was the prevailing sentiment in the college and the pulpit when Samuel moved to Washington City. After the Edenton widow died, her cousins challenged her will, and the enslaved people in question were hired out instead of being sent to Africa. The minister who had made the suggestion lasted only a year in town, offering up his resignation to the family who had sponsored him.[49] Clearly, being an outspoken abolitionist did not create job security for ministers or missionaries in the slaveholding South.

Richard Furman, a Baptist minister in Charleston, South Carolina, issued an extreme and resolute pro-slavery argument in 1823. He wrote a full-throated defense of slavery citing biblical proof texts after the Denmark Vesey conspiracy, an alleged plot by a free black man in Charleston to incite an insurrection. Furman's letter to South Carolina Governor John Lyde Wilson was designed to "assure the . . . population that the state's Baptists stood foursquare behind slavery . . . and their masters" to calm the fears of the frightened Southern enslavers.[50] Furman was minister of the wealthy and powerful Charleston Baptist Church, whose members had financial and social interests in maintaining the slave economy; the Vesey affair motivated Furman to protect their power. Like most political, social, and moral issues, the situation was fractured and constantly evolving.

As 1830 dawned, rumors of impending insurrections mounted, causing officials to increase slave patrols.[51] It was this fear, along with the entrenchment of a Southern economy dependent on slavery, that led to stricter laws in North Carolina and other Southern states in 1830. New North Carolina legislation was targeted to suppress free and enslaved blacks, forbidding trade with enslaved people and prohibiting teaching them to read and write. Strict laws about harboring fugitives from slavery and the ability of free blacks to live in the state, along with steep fees for whites attempting to emancipate their enslaved workers, were designed to discourage free blacks from mingling with their enslaved counterparts. These laws dramatically altered the state's social climate just as the Waits were contemplating North Carolina as a permanent home.[52] Not incidental to the timing of these laws was the appearance of *David Walker's Appeal—to the Colored Citizens of the World,* an abolitionist tract that justified the use of violent force for freedom. It set off a firestorm of panic when it spread throughout the South in the late 1820s. Walker, born free from slavery in nearby Wilmington, North Carolina, moved to Boston and became an abolitionist leader in the 1820s. Historian David Cecelski points out that Walker used his maritime contacts in Southern ports to share his abolitionist call.[53] On November 27, 1830, the *Newbern Spectator* published a letter from North Carolina Governor John Owen about an "incendiary publication" to "sow sedition among our slaves." He was likely referring to *Walker's Appeal,* in which the author used both political and religious arguments against slavery. Owen noted that there was a "systemic attempt . . . under the cover of pious exertion to enlighten the ignorant, and lead them from sensualizing darkness."[54] The governor's not-so-veiled message warned about the perils of preaching to the enslaved, which the Baptists, Methodists, and others clearly were doing.

The roil about impending rebellion in the South magnified the deep concerns that Sally's family had about the miseries of slavery. By this time, little Ann Eliza had a fourteen-month-old baby brother, whom the Waits had named William Carey, after the famous Baptist missionary. It is unclear how Sally reacted to the growing fears and rumors that swirled in New Bern. She lived a stone's throw from the Neuse River, within view of free and enslaved black watermen traveling with relative ease, perhaps sharing rebellious ideas conveyed from their Northern counterparts. Dryboro, a settlement inhabited by free black families, was a few blocks away.[55] If Sally was already nervous about staying in North Carolina, her mother's letters did not help. Sarah Conant Merriam's hopes soared when she learned her son-in-law had resigned from the church, but they were dashed when she found out they were considering another long-term assignment. Sally had apparently suffered illness attributed to the sultry climate, and her mother warned that after she "barely escaped" with her life from "the malignant disorder of the South," she would be "guilty of suicide" if she stayed another summer.[56] Just as importantly, her mother turned to dire warnings about the moral and physical dangers of slavery, reiterating her early admonition that Sally had "two lovely children whose morals you have got to cultivate." Sally's mother pleaded: "Can you not . . . weigh the consequences of endangering the Souls of your children . . . before you settle again in a land of slavery?"[57]

The concerns expressed by Sally's mother would escalate in the coming year, after the Waits had recommitted to North Carolina as their home. Just two months after their final return to the state, the possibility of violence became very real with Nat Turner's capture after executing a bloody rebellion in Southampton County, Virginia. Just days after Nat Turner was hanged for his role in leading the insurrection, Mother wrote to Sally in frightened language about her "perilous situation. . . . We have such shocking accounts of Negro insurrections and murders." She wrote that they had reports from Norfolk, Virginia and Tarboro, North Carolina, "and other noted places that the whites are very much incensed against the Baptist and Quakers [and] think their liberal principles are one great cause of the tumult and insurrection."[58] In the North, a great deal of the abolitionist thought was coming from these two denominations; in fact, by the mid-1830s, Sally's home church in Brandon, Vermont became a hotbed for supporters of immediate emancipation, which many viewed as a radical approach. While the abolitionist leader Orson Murray had not yet arrived in Brandon, the movement was percolating there among Sally's friends and relatives. Her mother's next comment reflected her own sympathies, at least from a distant vantage point, for the insurrectionists, when she continued that the news "makes my blood almost chill while reading the awful torture and cruelty the blacks are put to when taken."[59] Nat Turner had been not only hanged, but also drawn and quartered as a warning to other potential enslaved insurrectionists.

While many Southern whites were threatening the enslaved population with horrific vengeance, Sally's mother feared retaliation on Sally and Samuel for their religious views. She wrote, "If that is the case you are in danger of imprisonment or assassination. You will therefore be cautious of your words and action."[60] As tensions escalated, Baptist publications cautioned ministers about publicly speaking out against slavery or taking political stands of any kind, writing that it was "'not their business to manage the world.'" An address given by Boston minister Daniel Sharp titled "Counsels and Cautions" that was reviewed in the 1835 edition of the *American Baptist Magazine* made it clear that ministers should stay out of the fray. With "respect to our social and political condition . . . which tend to agitate the whole community, and threaten to dissolve the union of the states . . . ministerial prudence requires that he should not become a party to them." Sharp advised that a minister's job should be to "hush, not to increase the storm of human passions."[61] While white ministers exhorting abolitionist ideas were warned off professionally, black ministers encountered more dire threats, since they were suspected of stirring passions, and therefore danger.[62]

Historian Charles Irons writes about the shifting attitudes of white evangelicals to their black counterparts in the church after the Nat Turner rebellion. While relationships had eroded, many whites worked to reestablish lost trust and continued their zealous commitment to converting the enslaved.[63] This approach seemed to be the case for the Waits. As their time progressed in North Carolina, Samuel continued to preach to blacks, presumably free and enslaved, at the many camp meetings that swept the South in the early 1830s and beyond. He provides a detailed description of such a meeting in a letter to Sally, inviting her to "imagine yourself in a pulpit large enough to hold ten men with a thousand negroes behind you, and twice the number before you of white persons—perhaps a third of the blacks and one quarter of the whites making all the noise they could."[64] Wait went on to describe the revival's tumult, which made the conservative New Englander uncomfortable. But after a few days at the meeting, Wait swallowed his inhibitions and "went in among them, some on their knees, some down flat on the ground, in a word, in all the different postures among them, and talked to them, prayed with them . . . nearly all, within the altar crying aloud for mercy."[65] At these and later meetings, it is probable that black ministers preached alongside Wait and the other white preachers. A few years later, fellow minister Brother Kendall wrote to Wait to let him know that "Ralf Freeman the old negro preacher died last Friday about 10 o'clock P.M."[66] Kendall was referring to the former enslaved worker of fellow Baptist minister John Culpepper, who had been a popular preacher before his death in 1833.[67]

Between 1827 and 1831 the Waits vacillated between duty and family, considering appointments in the South and the North. During this uncertain time in North Carolina, relations between blacks and whites worsened rather than improved, presaging a period of continued conflict that a few decades later would take the country to the brink of destruction. When Samuel was offered a one-year fundraising position with the newly formed North Carolina Baptist Convention, he considered the job with reluctance. The assignment meant he would once again be horse-and-wagon bound, traveling from town to town in search for funds.[68] After all, agency was a lonely life, one that required "a constant sojourn, moving from town to town, meeting with indifference and sometimes with open hostility."[69] An agency in the South would also be "attended with considerable hazard" since he would "be exposed considerably in a warm climate." And, "should

I refuse . . . I do not know who can be obtained to fill my place."[70] In a letter from Sally to Brother Hewins in Sharon, answering yet another invitation from his old church in Massachusetts, she explained the circumstances of their deliberations. The new North Carolina Baptist Convention was formed "to awaken the lethargy and to promote the interest of our denomination," and its leaders seemed to think that Samuel was the only man for the task.[71] She writes to Hewins about the state's "darkness, ignorance, and bigotry" and her concern that "many are bitterly opposed to all religious operations of the day."[72] Still, she had hope that "there also exists a redeeming spirit: light is dawning and in many instances ignorance and bigotry flee before its effulgent rays. We trust in God; that the period is not very far distant when N. C. shall rank with her sister States in deeds of Christian benevolence."[73]

While Sally may have privately regretted Samuel's continued travels in the South, publicly she showed her strength of conviction when communicating with others. As it was, Samuel's own ambitions had once again created uncertainty in Sally's life. With two young children it was not practical for her to go along on Samuel's travels, and there was also not enough money for her to stay in New Bern while he toured the state. While at this point Sally felt that "in a pecuniary view [their] prospects would be better" in the North, duty called. She wrote, "When we think of our accountability to God, and . . . the judgment seat of Christ, and of meeting these poor North Carolinians there, we dare not [dissent to] them without the most convincing proof that God has here no more for us to do."[74] Despite Sally's "objections to bringing up our children" in the South, which remained "with all their force," the call to duty tugged at her skirts.[75]

The couple would part once again: Samuel to the interior of North Carolina and Sally back home to Brandon, Vermont. In early August 1830, Sally, in companionship with a Mrs. Saunders, boarded a ship bound for New York, feeling "empty and desolate" to begin yet another journey home without her husband.[76] The passage took twelve days, with "head winds and calms almost all the way interspersed with occasional squalls."[77] Sally was sick the whole time at sea, as was Mrs. Saunders. Neither Ann Eliza, then four and a half, nor William Carey, eighteen months, showed signs of seasickness but were "highly delighted to get on shore." Their son W. C. was a handful, acting "like a pig just let loose from the stye, delighted with everybody and everything."[78] While Sally was excited to see her family, she was not prepared for the dramatic changes that awaited her in Brandon.

Twelve

CHOOSING HOME

O how I want to be within visiting distance
of my dear parents and all our family
friends. But North Carolina for distance,
is nothing to Burmah.

—Samuel to Sally, January 1831

WHEN SALLY ARRIVED HOME IN 1830, IT FELT LIKE EVERY-
thing had changed. She had left her husband in a tenuous situation, her
"heart agitated with fear" for his health and safety as insurrection threatened.[1] While Sally's faith stood strong, the idyllic dreams of her newly
converted nineteen-year-old self to follow in the footsteps of the legendary missionary Ann Hasseltine Judson probably seemed hazy and illusive,
complicated by finances, logistics, and unpredictable health. Her role
model had been dead for nearly four years, overtaken by fever in Burma.
Sally's optimistic and entrepreneurial ideas of selling homemade bonnets
with her sister Lydia and sisters-in-law Mary and Achsah as part of the
homespun manufacturing movement may have seemed naïve to her now.
Achsah was now often ill, her complaint diagnosed as being "caused by the
sulphuric scent taken into the lungs when bleaching bonnets."[2] The political landscape of Vermont had shifted from regional concerns to national
conflicts, foreshadowing the bitter divide the country would soon face. The
rising influence of the populist Jacksonian Democrats coupled with the
fallout from the William Morgan affair had led to an ardent anti-Masonic
movement that ripped at the fabric of the region. Isaac had mentioned

this development when he warned Samuel that in order to move back to New England, he would be required to "denounce Masonry. . . . The Anti Masonic mania" had reached such a fever pitch.[3] Ministers became targets, whether because they were brothers themselves or "because they simply . . . refused to condemn Masonry fully."[4] When Samuel wrote to Jonathan about the anti-Mason movement, his brother-in-law wrote back what appears to be a startling response: "Although you have never been hood-winked & had a cable thrown around your neck . . . tell the people you free . . . yourself from any obligations to obey any call, sign, signal or summons from that institution and all will be well."[5]

While the bitter conflict created a mob-like mentality on both sides of the movement, Jonathan was not suggesting that Masons were being kidnapped and threatened with hanging, despite the alleged violence perpetrated on William Morgan five years earlier.[6] A "hood-wink" and "cable tow" were items used in Masonic initiations, which included many of the features of modern-day hazing that served to bind brothers with the secret of shared distressing experiences.[7] The hood-wink was a blindfold that initiates were forced to wear during the secret ceremony until the moment of illumination of the Masonic truths.[8] A cable tow referred to both the metaphorical tie to the Masonic brotherhood as well as a literal rope used in a ritual called "The Living Arch" in which new initiates were tied together and pulled through an arch of Masonic brothers.[9] Passions against Masons ran high in Vermont, and Wait was apprehensive enough to worry about returning to New England. The anti-Mason movement paralleled the rise of populism in Jackson's America as well as the escalation of religious fervor.[10] While it had been sparked by the Morgan affair, the movement came at a time when Americans were questioning elitism and authoritarianism. The Masons' "secrecy, secularism, [and] cosmopolitanism" were antithetical to emerging egalitarian thought.[11] The perceived cover-up of the Morgan affair by powerful Masons had only confirmed the rising concern that members of this secret society considered themselves above the law.[12] In addition to its elitist reputation, the organization's "un-Protestant idolatry prompted evangelical pietists to denounce Masonry as an infidel competitor for men's souls."[13]

Sally confirmed this when she arrived in Brandon after a stop in Bridport, Vermont to visit her brother Jonathan's family. It did not take long for Sally to learn of the political divisions that were tearing families—including hers—apart. The anti-Mason fever made her think an unthinkable thought: that she was glad she and Samuel had not moved back to the region after all, since it would have been impossible for him to "have taken any ground on which [he] could have avoided censure."[14] Nearly all of their reliable friends and family had denounced Masonry, including Elder Sawyer, the Olins (including Achsah's father Henry Olin, a longtime politician and the current lieutenant governor of Vermont), and even most of the stalwart and influential Conants. Sally's cousin John A. Conant had recently been elected to the state legislature on the anti-Mason ticket, which must have caused friction in the family since his father, Sally's uncle John Conant, stood firm as the only pro-Mason holdout in the family. Even that town patriarch had been toppled from his political perch: Uncle John lost his seat as postmaster after seventeen years in the powerful position, which he had held since the year of Sally's conversion.[15] That must have seemed like a lifetime ago, given the impossibility of such an upset of the traditional power structure back then.

It's interesting that Samuel remained steadfast to his Masonic vows, since a renunciation of his oaths would have qualified him to preach in his New England home. It isn't clear why he decided to hang on to his membership when so many others abandoned theirs. New York's Masonic membership fell from 450 lodges representing twenty thousand members in 1825 to only eighty-two lodges in 1830.[16] Why did Samuel refuse? It's possible that the reason for suspicions about Masons was the very reason Wait desired membership. Regardless of the turning tide, being a Mason meant power, respectability, and being part of the ascendant class. Being a Mason was a step up from Wait's otherwise modest upbringing.

Other political dynamics were at play in Brandon, most of which reflected the national tensions of the times. In addition to the anti-Masons, Sally wrote with concern about the "Quids, Jacks, doughfaces, and Straddle-the-fences," who were all being censured.[17] This was a time in the Early Republic when political and sectional divides began to proliferate, starting with the anti-Mason movement. There were horse-trading politicians—presumably the Quids who relied on quid pro quo—and people who refused to take a stand, like "Straddle-the-fences." A "jack" was one of the stigmatized names the fervent anti-Masons used for people who were "neither a Mason nor an anti, but a peaceable citizen attending to his own business and politics," according to a writer at the *Boston Masonic Mirror*.[18] A "doughface" was a derogatory term reserved for Northern sympathizers of slaveholding Southerners that became popular after the 1820 Missouri Compromise.[19] According to Joanne Freeman, it carried with it a particular sting.[20] That Sally was using these terms indicates both the level of antagonism among Vermonters and the political savvy she had developed in her time away from home.

Political thought was not the only thing changing in Sally's hometown. Members of the Merriam family were responding to the pulls of economic change and westward expansion. When Sally had her tearful conversion in 1813, the Merriam family was more or less intact on the family farm a little north of town on what is now Route 7. Sally and Lydia were the only daughters in a houseful of boys. Her two older brothers Jonathan and Isaac had left home but remained nearby, helping to support the family. When Jonathan and Lydia both married in quick succession in the early 1820s, Sally's mother measured their success in the amount of butter and cheese the wives produced, writing that Lydia had "made $60 of the butter when we were there, I think must have $100 by this time beside a fine parcel of cheese."[21] By the early 1830s, their mother would become just as likely to measure her family's accomplishments by the number of candidates brought to baptism in Brandon or the churches her children led.[22]

The Merriam children were moving away, responding to calls to ministry, education, or industry. In the summer of 1830, when Sally returned home, most of her siblings were either gone or contemplating new opportunities. Isaac and Mary were in Deerfield, New Hampshire, another stop in a long string of towns to which her oldest brother was called to preach. Jonathan and Achsah were in nearby Bridport but would soon move on to Passumpsic, Vermont and later Springfield, Illinois. Abel was living with Jonathan and Achsah teaching at a small school in Bridport, but it would not be long before the promise of new opportunity pulled him to Arlington, New York to work in a woolen factory and store.[23] Later he tried to jump-start a business to revolutionize the lumber trade using a new contraption called a circular saw.[24] Charles Rollin Merriam would soon move to Lansingburgh, New York to work in the oilcloth factory of Deborah Ball Powers, a relative of Isaac's wife Mary Powers and Lydia's husband Jacob Powers.[25] Deborah's husband had died in a varnish explosion in his factory in 1829, and Charles Rollin was apparently sent to help keep the family business afloat, until the fumes from the factory made him ill.[26] Mylon had "left the maternal roof" in 1827 and was living with a Mr. Knowles, later moving to Bridport and then Maine for schooling.[27] As members of the dislocated generation of the Early Republic, the Merriam children's "young adulthood had become an unavoidable process of continual self-construction, which at times amounted to a kind of vagabondage, moving from place to place and pursuit to pursuit."[28] The one sibling who continued to anchor Sally to Brandon was her only sister Lydia, who was caring for their widowed mother. Tragically, Lydia's life was nearing an early end.

When Sally arrived in Brandon from New Bern in the summer of 1830, she found Lydia suffering from consumption. She was "reduced almost to a skeleton," and her doctors thought "her case very doubtful."[29] In September, Sally considered leaving Brandon to visit Samuel's family in Tinmouth, Vermont earlier than planned because she worried "the noise of my children added to those of the family, will be a great injury to sister Lydia."[30] She did not travel, however, because her older brother Isaac and his wife Mary were due to arrive in a few weeks. She decided that she would spend the winter in Tinmouth with the Wait clan.[31] Sally was despondent about Lydia's state, writing that it had "cast a gloom on everything around me."[32] By October, Lydia's death seemed imminent; on the nineteenth of that month, Lydia "closed her eyes on all earthly scenes and entered the world of spirits."[33] The state of Lydia's soul at the time of her passing was of utmost importance to Sally as her father's had been to Sally's mother. Sally took care to relate these important details in her letter to Samuel, writing that Lydia's "exit was peaceful and happy. I saw her sink into the arms of death but she feared not its icy grasp. She said, 'through Christ I have gained the victory over the king of Terrors.'"[34] Sally wrote several pages outlining the details of Lydia's hallowed passing, taking time to emphasize the peaceful scene like her mother had done upon her father's death. According to Sally, at one point, Lydia "inquired, 'can this be death? Tis soft as downy pillows are,'" citing a phrase from an Isaac Watts hymn.[35] Samuel was moved by Sally's description, writing that "the account of Sister L.'s death affected me much." He regretted not having yet written her husband Jacob Powers, but with all his backcountry traveling, he had been "so situated as to make it all but perfectly impossible." When Samuel was on the road correspondence was sporadic and unreliable, because his appointments were "at considerable distances from each other. . . . No person can tell till he tries it, how difficult it is to write letters in my situation."[36] Sally's letters had difficulty catching up to him as well, his travels forcing her to anticipate his schedule and make her best guess at what town he would be in on any given day. In fact, his letter commenting on Lydia's death was in reply to a letter Sally had written two-and-a-half months earlier.

The frequent separation and infrequent communication were wearing on the little family. By this time, Samuel and Sally had lived together only about seven years of their thirteen-year marriage. Samuel was concerned about his distance from them, telling Sally to "kiss the dear children for me a thousand times. I pray God that no evil may befall them or you."[37] Sally missed Samuel tremendously. For all her missionary dreams and his wanderings, she wrote that all she really wanted was for God to "preserve your life and health amidst all your wanderings and to bring us all together again, around our own fireside, and our own family altar." She worried that her children were growing up without a father. They missed their "Pa." Shortly after Sally arrived in Brandon, she wrote about her son William Carey and his older sister Ann Eliza: "W.C. begins to say a few words. Ask him where his Papa is and he will reply, 'gone.' A. E. says tell Pa I want to see him and to kiss him. Tell him he must come here in the stage, and I will give him some of Grandma's very sweet apples."[38] Sally continued about Ann Eliza, "She very often dreams about you and wakes me to tell her dream."[39]

During Sally and Samuel's earliest partings, while she may have pined for her husband, she had the comfort that their separation was guided by their shared duty to God. Understanding that concept as an adult Baptist was one thing; explaining it to two tiny children was another. Despite the couple's concerns, Samuel felt "never better satisfied" that he was "in the path of duty."[40] At the same time, he did wonder what it might be like to give up the pull of duty and take an easier path. He was still vacillating about their long-term investment in North Carolina. His current one-year engagement with the North Carolina Baptist Convention would expire in late spring 1831, and he wondered if New England or North Carolina would trumpet their final call. "I have been thinking seriously what I ought to do after next June. . . . I really want to be convinced that it is my duty to return to [New England]—I have sometimes half resolved that . . . I will return and get me a little farm and manage that, preaching as a door might be opened to me."[41] In the next line, however, duty returned to his conscience. "But then, I have now got hold of the plough, and I sometimes fear to look back. I do not believe I could, in any other way have done half so much for the cause of truth, as in the course I have taken."[42] To remind Sally of the progress he had made in the morally desolate Carolina backwoods, Samuel needed only to total up saved souls. He had baptized five people in Anson County alone—four whites and one "black girl," as well as "two blacks in Duplin County" some months earlier. He could only consider returning north if he had a "clear conscience," but how "to leave such a large field where labours are so much wanted?" Samuel felt a strong call to duty in North Carolina despite the pull toward the North, writing, "O, how I want to be within visiting distance of my dear parents and all our family friends. But North Carolina for distance, is nothing to Burmah."[43]

Despite his wavering pen, Samuel's mind seemed made up. But he had to convince Sally that their path was part of a grander purpose, one that called the faithful to make sacrifices to spread the word about salvation. To seal his proposal, Samuel reminded Sally about the inspiration that Ann

Hasseltine Judson had provided her for so long. Comparing North Carolina to Burma brought to mind the sacrifices Sally would have made had they chosen to follow in the Judsons' path. This was not the first time Samuel used the Burma missionaries to put their own trials in perspective. In an 1822 letter, Samuel commented on the first leg of Ann's medical hiatus from Burma, "When you come to read the account of Mrs. Judson's tour, you will think that our separation is a fool to it."[44]

The sentiment of sacrifice may have seemed simple in theory, but it was difficult in practice, especially when there were young children involved. Samuel's thoughts often went to Sally and their "dear babes." He worried that Ann Eliza would forget him and reminded Sally to tell her to "mind her ma—learn to read pretty well before I come—and pray every day." And with William Carey so young, he knew he could not "understand a word I write. . . . How I want to see the little fellow with his cap on, making tracks in the snow."[45] Samuel Wait wrote these words on January 11, 1831 from Anson County, North Carolina, about fifty miles east of Charlotte. What Samuel did not know when he wrote this letter—what he could not have known—was that William Carey, his one-and-a-half-year-old son, was dead.

Four months would pass before Samuel would read the details of his son's death. His early January letter filled with ruminations about the couple's future wended its way to a grieving mother, while Sally's letter, fastened with black sealing wax to indicate the mournful news, tried to catch up to Samuel as he moved from town to town. In May, back in Brandon, Sally penned the painful particulars.[46] As she had planned, Sally traveled with her children a few days before Christmas to Tinmouth, Vermont, where Samuel's father and brothers lived. Tinmouth was less a town than a collection of farms set among the picturesque rolling hills of western Vermont. The closest town was Middletown Springs, the site of the Baptist church where preacher Silvanus Haynes had mentored Samuel in his early years. On December 29, William Carey had been at play, although he seemed to be coming down with a "hard cold." Sally sent for a doctor when his symptoms grew worse and a fever developed; still, she was not particularly alarmed. The attending physician gave the child an emetic, possibly the commonly used tartrate to cause vomiting, which "operated favorably and greatly relieved him." However, the following night, "his respiration became very much oppressed and towards morning his voice entirely failed him." The family again sent for the doctor while they desperately tried to "relieve his lungs, to no effect." His respiration became more labored, and all the while "the little creature was sensible of his sufferings to the last."[47] Sally described the heartbreaking scene at the end, when her son "raised himself in the cradle and desired to be taken into my arms." Sally took William Carey into her lap, holding and rocking the struggling child. Within minutes "his breath suddenly stopped—he gasped twice and expired." Powerless to save her dying baby, Sally "watched the return of another sigh—his lungs had ceased to heave and his spirit had fled from its clayey tenement forever."[48] William Carey died in her arms at half past eleven.[49]

Losing a child in any way, under any circumstances, is a catastrophic event. Having it happen without a spouse or close family nearby must be the most hollow and helpless feeling imaginable. Although Sally was with some of Samuel's family members, neither of the couple was particularly close to them. Other than Samuel's favorite sister Betsey and his young brother Hiram, his family rarely wrote. Upon William Carey's death, members of Sally's family sent immediate condolences, but none were able to travel to Tinmouth to share her grief. Her mother was stranded in Brandon with her former son-in-law Jacob Powers, who was recovering from an illness. "We feel sorry it is not in our power to visit you in this time of your affliction," Jacob wrote. Sally's mother added at the bottom of his letter, "Were it possible for me to be with you . . . it would be highly gratifying to me."[50] Her brother Abel sent regrets from nearby Washington County, New York that he could not come. Charles Rollin wrote on behalf of Jonathan and Achsah, offering their sorrow from Bridport, Vermont. Sally's niece Mary Powers sent sympathies from her parents Isaac and Mary in Deerfield. Sally must have felt isolated, even though Samuel's concerned family surrounded her. Her loneliness was deepened by her separation from Samuel, the one person who could share her pain in a profoundly familiar way. Sally wrote, "Oh, my love, what a moment was for his poor mother . . . far, far from him who alone could feel the full weight of the anguish, which like the rushing of a mighty torrent suddenly overwhelmed her soul."[51]

A funeral was held in Joseph Wait's farmhouse, where Elder Reynolds preached from the Old Testament story of Elisha raising the Shunammite's son in 2 Kings 4:18–26, "Is it well with thee? Is it well with thy husband? Is it well with the child? And she answered, it is well."[52] The stoic sentiment of the funeral sermon was in keeping with the steadfast Calvinist tradition that events were part of God's plan. In a time when babies were taken from families all too often, mothers cautioned each other not to become too attached to their little ones. When Ann Eliza was born, Sally's cousin Cynthia reminded Sally not to place strong affections on the child. "Be careful, in an unexpected moment it may be wrested from you," she wrote. The truly faithful worried that a jealous God would take away the object of one's love if they placed it above Him. "Our idols are most sure to be taken from us," Cynthia had warned.[53] Religious tracts were filled with poems designed to soothe people, such as "A dying infant to a weeping Mother," in which the deceased infant reassures its grieving mother:

> Cease thy weeping, then, be still,
> And learn thy God to trust;
> Bow to his sovereign will,
> And own him just.[54]

Samuel chose a similar sentiment for the stone to mark William Carey's grave. "Sleep on, dear babe, and take thy rest; God call'd thee home, he knew 'twas best."[55] Regardless of the teachings of the faith, the grief was very real for both mother and father. Just as Sally had recounted the details of her experience with their son's death, Samuel later described to Sally in a letter how he felt when he read the news.[56]

He had been traveling in the backcountry in the early part of 1831, making his way toward Rogers' Crossroads Meeting House in Wake County, North Carolina to attend the first annual meeting of the Baptist State Convention. That morning, as he was traveling to the meeting, Wait was "thinking how happy I should be" to "have both of our dear little ones in my arms." Samuel was imagining "how well my little boy could talk" when he exited the hall after John Armstrong's opening sermon. When he was given a letter with a black seal, Wait's hands "trembled while [he] broke it." Knowing the seal signified a family member's death, his first thoughts went to his mother or father, or possibly a sibling. He did not "at that moment think of either of our dear children."[57] His grief was deep. "O, my dear son! . . . I cannot write. . . . O! how I want to see the spot where his precious remains lie."[58] Despite receiving the "heavy tidings," Samuel continued on with the convention meetings. Ironically, just a few days after Samuel received word about his son's death, the convention voted to extend his employment for another year, through August 1832.[59] Samuel "begged them to look around and see if some one could not be obtained. . . . My feelings were much of the time so low that I could not think of being a wanderer any longer."[60]

In the end, Samuel capitulated to the call and "in a word, consented to engage again as the Agent of the Convention." His heart was "in the field at work." The call was strong and the pay was good. "What could I do?" he wrote Sally. "I almost wished I had never seen North Carolina."[61] Samuel asked Sally a final time to make the state their home. He hoped to "go back west of Raleigh perhaps 150 miles and take you and Ann Eliza along with me as far as you can go."[62] He assured her that "many friends as kind as can be, have thrown open their doors for you." He promised to trade in his small sulky for a more suitable gig or carriage so that the family of three could travel together more comfortably. "I can easily procure you a happy and healthy home," he wrote.[63] Sally's reply reveals the depth of her grief about separating from the place of her past. As much as she knew God and duty were calling, the comfort of her old life in New England pulled at her heart. She wrote to her husband on May 16, "You have sadly disappointed both your friends and mine, I am myself a little disappointed. When I think of taking so long a journey alone and the difficulties I must encounter on the way, my courage almost fails me."[64]

Everything was different. Politics had polarized the people around her, and friends and family had died or scattered. In reality, there was little left to keep Sally in Brandon, Vermont. Her home was with Samuel and Ann Eliza, wherever that might be. Within a few weeks, perhaps with the piety and courage of Ann Hasseltine Judson fixed in her mind, she began the three-week trip south. From there, she, Samuel, and her little girl would begin their journey across the state, eventually to a permanent home in Wake Forest, North Carolina.

EPILOGUE

Sally never went to Burma. North Carolina seemed far enough from home. For the next few years, the family bumped along the back roads of the state, relying on strangers to house and feed them most nights. It is likely that Sally and Ann Eliza stayed with friends once they got as far as Wake Forest later that summer, as Samuel had suggested. But from letters and later accounts, it appears they still rode beside him from time to time. As Ann Eliza recalled it to John Brewer for a memoir he wrote about Wait:

> Imagine a covered jersey wagon of good size—a seat across the middle accommodated father and mother; while in front at the mother's feet . . . sat their little daughter, about four years old when this work commenced. In front of the father's feet was a good-sized lunch basket. Along with the basket was a large bottle which was often filled with milk for the comfort of the travelers; sometimes the milk was churned to butter. Behind the middle seat there was room for three trunks of pretty good size. This conveyance was the home of the little family— all the home they had—for two or three years, as they zigzagged back and forth from the mountains to the seaboard.[1]

While Samuel was raising money for the convention, he and other leaders developed a plan to overcome the state's "darkness, ignorance, and bigotry" by emphasizing education as well as missions. Following the Triennial's 1817 playbook, they decided to start an institute for the "proper training of our young brethren designed of God for the ministry."[2] Not everyone in the state was supportive. The Kehukee Association's Joshua Lawrence described the planned institute as being more perilous than the Spanish Inquisition. Paschal quotes Elder Lawrence as saying the "'school priests,' are ready to rob the poor, drain the coffers of the rich, and are the most dangerous robbers and murderers and ever ready to cut throats."[3]

Despite the opposition, the Waits continued their travels along the backroads to raise money and accumulate supplies for the planned school. Samuel later wrote about Sally's "valuable assistance" in gathering objects from the ladies along the way. "If a lady could not furnish a bed, she could probably spare a towel," he wrote.[4] Not much is known about Sally's experience during these three years of intermittent travel, since few letters from this period exist in the archives. However, family lore paints some possible, albeit sentimentalized, details. A 1950s-era handwritten remembrance by Sally's great-great-granddaughter Elizabeth Barnette describes "Mrs. Wait and the little one" (meaning Ann Eliza) as warmly welcomed guests, the former winning "people over by her sweet, soft voice, as she sang old, familiar hymns."[5] These memories also mention that Sally would often draw portraits of her hosts, adorn their hats, or sew clothes for their children as gifts when she visited.

In 1834 Samuel and Sally settled in North Carolina, outside of Raleigh, to establish the Wake Forest Manual Labor Institute, named for a recently vacated plantation.[6] The location of their mission field was finally determined. Sally would not become a famous missionary in a far-flung place, but the wife of a college administrator, supporting her husband and the institution while raising Ann Eliza, her only surviving child. It was a far cry from Burma, but the decision, nearly twenty years in the making, was as significant for Sally Wait as Ann Judson's had been to her.

During the college's first year, Samuel was its only teacher, and Sally assisted her husband by caring for the students and the property with the help of enslaved servants. She seems to have become a matriarch to the students, providing regalia and conducting ceremonies for significant events. In July 1835, when the first literary societies were dedicated, it's possible that Sally sewed the banners for the Philomathesian Society, named from the Greek word meaning "love of learning," and the Euzelian Society, meaning "zeal for good."[7] According to a student who attended the solemn ceremony, at the appointed time Sally stepped onto the small balcony of the former plantation house that served as the school administrative building. The students doffed their hats as Sally presented the society banners and commended the members to "act nobly; and become [Wake Forest's] pride and its glory."[8]

Samuel led the college as president from 1839 until 1845.[9] For much of that time, he was out on the road raising money for the cause and recruiting students to the school.[10] That left Sally at home caring for their home and later a boarding house and farm while Samuel continued his nomadic lifestyle. Historian Andrew Canady concludes, "He liked traveling, preaching, mingling with socially prominent and wealthy Baptists, and was an able fundraiser."[11] As able as he was, the college was constantly trying to get out from under debt associated with constructing and running the school, so much so that Wait and other trustees personally signed themselves to the notes.[12] In 1844, pressured by his personal $2,000 debt to the school, Wait resigned his presidency, which allowed him to "go out on an agency for himself, raising money for his part of the debt."[13] After retirement until his death in 1867, he held various positions as a minister, head of the Oxford (NC) Female Academy, and member of the Wake Forest College board of trustees.[14] None of these activities weighed on him as much as the pressures of keeping a young college afloat had—he wrote to his parents of his relief to be "entirely free from all the responsibility" he had filled.[15] Of most importance to Samuel was the small farm he was finally able to "amuse" himself with, an idea he had entertained since his days in New England. A few years before his retirement, the college transferred $692 in land to the Waits in lieu of overdue salary.[16] Within a few years the Waits named their farm "Elmwood," where they grew mulberry trees, crops, and livestock.[17]

While it may have been Samuel's dream to own a farm, it was Sally who was often left in charge to mind the animals, the land, and the enslaved workers. Samuel's travels and his stint as president of Oxford Female Academy some twenty-five miles away meant Sally once again had her hands full seeing to the family business while Samuel pursued his ambitions. While there were times that she joined Samuel in Oxford, she remained rooted in Wake Forest until her death in 1876.

Evidence during the Wake Forest years indicates that the further entrenched in the South the Waits became, the more engrained slavery became to their way of life. When the Waits left New Bern, Sally had returned North while Samuel traveled the state. It's probable the enslaved girl and young woman from the 1830 census were turned back to their enslaver at that time. When the Waits arrived in Wake Forest to start the institute, they hired local enslaved workers to help serve the students and run the institute's farm. In 1839, when the institute transitioned to a college and began selling plots of land to develop the town, the Waits became slaveholders themselves, purchasing two African American females named Dicey and Mary.[18] It's likely that Dicey and Mary (or Helen as she seemed to be called) were purchased in order to help run a boarding house that the Waits began operating once their new house was built. In addition to these two women, the Waits hired black men to tend to the farm, from time to time hiring them out to the college to sweep and gather firewood for students.[19] Dicey and Helen and other hired enslaved workers were referred to often in letters, usually in fond albeit paternalistic terms.

Sally gives us some idea about her attitudes about participating in the system of slavery in a letter to her daughter Ann Eliza. Writing about her grandchildren, she wrote, "Mary, and Sammy and Carey, and Sallie and that each of their descendants . . . should be a seed to serve God. Oh! Shall we all meet in Heaven at last! You and your children, and our Servants,

Bristor and Dicey, Hellen, and Harriet, and Ranson!"[20] It is reasonable to surmise they considered enslavement to be one of the "afflictions" black slaves experienced, which was part of God's plan for ultimate redemption. Treating them well and saving their souls for eternity became a justification for slaveholding.[21] Despite Sally's family's deep concerns about slavery, this transplanted New Englander seems to have fully acculturated into the slave economy.

This continued when several members of the Merriam family eventually migrated south to join the Waits in North Carolina. First was her brother Charles Rollin Merriam, who worked for Wake Forest College as the steward, which would have included supervising enslaved workers. Judging by the timing, it was his ill health that brought him south; the family hoped getting him away from the fumes in the oil cloth factory where he worked would bring him back to health. Unfortunately he died at the age of twenty-seven shortly after moving south, where he is buried in the Wake Forest Cemetery.[22] Achsah and Jonathan Merriam Jr., who had decried "slavery, slavery" in their letters, enrolled their son Jonathan as a student at Wake Forest, although he later returned to Illinois to serve as a captain in the Union army during the Civil War.[23]

Sally's opinionated brother Isaac, who had been the most vocal opponent to their move, provides the most ironic twist in the family's North-South narrative. Isaac's daughter Mary Powers Merriam married John Brown White, who became the third president of Wake Forest College.[24] They had five enslaved workers in their home in 1850, when Isaac became a fundraising agent for Wake Forest College.[25] Isaac and his wife Mary lived with their daughter and her husband, presumably being served by their enslaved workers.[26] One wonders how Isaac squared his need for employment in 1850 with his outspoken condemnations of his sister and brother-in-law's way of life some twenty years earlier.

Sally and Samuel's daughter Ann Eliza Wait made her life in North Carolina, marrying John Marchant Brewer, a Wake Forest College student from a slaveholding family in Virginia.[27] They had ten children, lived in the town of Wake Forest, and enslaved multiple workers. Family remembrances suggest that Sally was active in the education of her grandchildren. As her great-great-granddaughter Elizabeth Barnette recalled, her own grandmother Sarah Merriam Brewer "described vividly for me the interesting experiences arranged for the Brewer children. . . . Her daily repetition of Joshua 24:15, 'as for me and my house, we will serve the Lord' bore fruit in later years."[28]

These are facts that the documents tell us. The records reveal the larger forces at play, which—combined with Sally's personal circumstances—called her to the South. But the narrative is incomplete. Even with the many personal letters and documents, there is a part of this story we may never know. Documents do not report intimate conversations, private arguments, or whispered concerns. They only include the events and opinions that Sally and her family were willing to commit to paper and then organize and preserve. For many questions we can only speculate an answer.

For instance, how did Sally square her objections to slavery with the fact that she and Samuel ultimately became slaveholders themselves? How did her family members rationalize their own migration to the South after being so opposed to Sally's move? How did she feel about ending up as a college administrator's wife in comparison to her earlier dreams of becoming a missionary? Through a contemporary lens, being the wife of a college president sounds prestigious, yet in the years before the Civil War, Wake Forest's survival was frequently in doubt.[29] She was certainly held in esteem on account of her position and past brushes with celebrity, but considering Sally's concern with class, did she find her status satisfactory? She had achieved what she longed for in 1830, to "bring us all together again, around our own fireside, and our own family altar."[30] Was that enough to satisfy her pious ambitions? Attending to the farm, the boarding house, her grandchildren, and the college was a far cry from saving souls in the jungles of Burma. While educating young men for the ministry would serve the larger goal of spreading the gospel, it was several steps removed from personally witnessing the emotional conversions that she and her family members had tallied and reported in New England the decade prior. The early years of the institute included annual revivals where a few dozen students "indulged the hope that they had passed from death into life," but there is no indication that Sally was present at these events.[31] In the end, how did she measure her contribution to God's work? The time and context of her life decisions may give us some insight to that question. When the Waits weighed their move to North Carolina, the South was a promising place for both Samuel and Sally Wait to make a mark on the world, a mission field open for pursuit of their shared ambitions. The ultimate reasons for Sally's journey south were complex and interconnected.

Most of Sally's life decisions were rooted in the emotional conversion she and countless others experienced during a period of intense religious revival in America. Set against the backdrop of social and political turmoil, Sally's awakening was a reaction to both the universal call for moral rectitude and her personal call for salvation. As the first decades of the nineteenth century unfolded, ministers preached to spiritual seekers with increasing urgency, pointing to natural disasters, war, and epidemics as evidence that the end times were approaching. Sally had heard these warnings at church and read about them in religious tracts, but it was her personal experience with death, particularly the passing of her young friend Nabby Farrington, that sparked her own conversion. Once awakened, the larger Baptist narrative influenced Sally to aspire to a life of missions, role modeled by women like Ann Hasseltine Judson. Judson's romantic and virtuous story inspired thousands of women to pursue a life of Christian purpose, at least within the confines of early nineteenth-century life.

Sally married a minister who shared her aspirations just as a new dimension to the modern missionary movement emerged. As the Baptists' second Triennial Convention approached in 1817, the demand for formally educated ministers and missionaries grew. After all, Adoniram Judson's first task in Burma had been to translate the Bible into the native language. Undertakings such as these required learned men to populate the mission field. Columbian College would have a ripple effect on higher education, providing educated foot soldiers to become leaders at Baptist institutions throughout America, including Wake Forest College.

Samuel Wait's decision to attend Columbian College provided opportunities for him, but the choice exposed the limitations that persisted for women like Sally Wait. Sally's ambitions bumped against the reality that in nineteenth-century America, the needs of men came first and the opportunities for them took precedent. Intertwined with this dynamic were the dramatic changes in the American economy that compelled younger generations to seek opportunity away from the family farm. As a national market economy emerged, new work and career opportunities offered young men a way to leave the farm behind.[32] These factors prevented Sally from joining Samuel at Columbian College initially, causing a setback to her own aspirations. Like many women of her day, Sally had to support her husband's professional ambitions, setting aside her desire to improve intellectually while her brothers and husband pursued their studies. Embracing the emphasis on American manufacturing that political leaders were encouraging, Sally's entrepreneurial venture into bonnet making provided some relief to their finances until Samuel's salary allowed Sally to join him in the South. It was here that the Waits first encountered a society visibly rooted in slavery at a time when the national debate on abolition was approaching full crescendo.

By the time the Waits answered the final call to North Carolina, family dynamics had significantly changed the prospects for their future. Following larger economic trends, the Merriam family farm had broken up after their father's death. Sally's brothers dispersed to other towns to preach, teach, study, or enter industry. Sally's sister Lydia, her strongest anchor to Vermont, died. While Sally's mother was still in Brandon, there was hope that one of the other siblings would make a place for her outside the untenable situation of living in her former son-in-law's care. A few years later, Mother Merriam tried to muster up the courage to move south to join Sally, but she made it only as far as Salem, Massachusetts before turning back, deciding to wait for "further openings from Providence." Her choice to stay in New England away from her only surviving daughter was a difficult one, and she wrote that she had "never never" been in "such a state of suspense."[33] She would live out her life moving from one son to another, dying in 1839 in Otsego County, New York, where Sally's younger brother Mylon led a church.

The shifting political forces as 1830 dawned also affected the family's choice of home. The anti-Mason movement was in full swing in Vermont, and with Samuel unwilling to renounce his oath, his potential to fill a pulpit narrowed. The political tide in the South had a strong influence as well. On one hand, the increasing fears of slave rebellions provided fodder for Sally's family to decry their relocation to the South. On the other, this unrest created additional motivation for the Waits to defeat the growing conservative anti-mission and anti-education movements and bring religion to both blacks and whites in the state. Of course, in addition to economic and political change, there were personal ambitions at play. Evangelical leaders like the Waits saw an opportunity to shape the growth of the Early American Republic. To Northern Baptists, the South was a mission field. Despite Sally's and her family's moral objections to slavery, the opportunity to start the Baptist State Convention and an institute of learning was a call too high to refuse.

In the family's collection of Wait memorabilia, one object stands out: a nineteenth-century Chinese "wedding basket." Approximately seven by four inches and nine inches tall, the sides of the oval basket are constructed with miniscule bamboo rods, the top woven in a tight pattern of herringboned willow. The container is stacked in three units: the bottom and center sections would have held food (although the center unit has lost its divider), and the domed top protected the items inside. The bottom of the basket includes a yellowed and fraying label marked, "Mrs. S. Wait Oxford Female College from Mrs. Yates." Historically used to bring food to a wedding couple in China, such an item would have been a popular keepsake for foreign visitors to bring home to friends and family. That must have been what Eliza Moring Yates had in mind when she brought it back from China as a gift for Sarah Merriam Wait when she returned to North Carolina.

Soon after the Baptists split into north and south conventions over slavery, Wake Forest had readied a young graduate named Matthew Tyson Yates for a foreign mission to China. After commencement in 1846, Yates married Eliza Moring from Chatham County, and soon-to-be Wake Forest President John B. White raised the money for their overseas passage.[34] This was a proud moment for the Waits and their fledgling college. More than thirty years after the Judsons sailed to Burma, a small Southern institution was sending its own missionaries to the Far East. Archives don't record the details of the Yates' departure, but we can assume Sally arranged a suitable farewell for the young couple.

The Chinese basket, almost two hundred years old, is in nearly perfect condition. Other than a small hole in the woven willow on the cover's dome and the missing section divider, the piece has stood the test of time, indicating the family's reverence for the item. Six generations of women have handed this basket down to the next, acknowledging the importance that Sally Merriam Wait placed on this slender object.

To a contemporary observer, this object conjures up unanswerable questions. Where did it sit in Sally's Wake Forest home? Would it have held a place of importance in the family parlor? Or did she keep it in a more private place, perhaps atop her bedroom dresser? When she saw it, was she filled with pride that she and Samuel had sent the Yates off to China to fulfill God's will? Or did her heart drop every time she glimpsed it from the corner of her eye, a reminder that she never traveled to such a faraway land to do God's work? Did it remind her of the pious ambition she wasn't quite able to fulfill? Or did it reinforce her resolve that the conquerable unconverted were waiting to be saved, not only in the jungles of South Asia, but in a forest called Wake?

The answers to these and other questions are unknowable, and they reveal more about the questioner than the subject. We search for meaning in the few surviving fragments of a person's life, reading significance into objects and words that represent only a fraction of the whole. The preservation of these fragile items certainly infers a venerated narrative that Sally's descendants have shared from generation to generation. How Sally Wait herself measured her response to God's call, we will never know.

NOTES

Introduction

1. "Died," *Rutland Herald*, Published as Rutland Vermont Herald, April 7, 1813.
2. "Died."
3. Sally Merriam, "Sally Merriam Journal" (1817), 104, Samuel and Sarah Wait Papers, Z. Smith Reynolds Library Special Collections and Archives, Wake Forest Univ., Winston-Salem, NC.
4. William A. Finney, "A Poem Written by William A. Finney April 4, 1813, on the Occasion of the Death of Abigail Farrington," April 4, 1813, Samuel and Sarah Wait Papers.
5. Sally Merriam, "Sally Merriam Journal," 54, Samuel and Sarah Wait Papers.
6. "The Second Book of Records of the Church of Christ of the Baptist Order In the Township of Brandon, State of Vermont May 26th Ad 1791," June 12, 1813 (Private Collection, 1791–1820). Brandon Baptist Church archives consist of record books, ledgers, official notices, and other documents that remain in the church's collection in Brandon, Vermont. The text in John Conant's hand reads, "Went forward in Baptism after being fellowhip [*sic*] by the Church as Christian Sally Merriam, Sister Brooks and Abigail Avery, and were joined to the church."
7. Merriam, "Sally Merriam Journal," 55.
8. J. M. Opal, *Beyond the Farm: National Ambitions in Rural America* (Philadelphia: Univ. of Pennsylvania Press, 2008) viii.
9. Opal, *Beyond the Farm*, 15.
10. Ashley Moreshead, "The Seed of the Missionary Spirit: Foreign Missions, Print Culture, and the Evangelical Identity in the Early American Republic," (PhD diss., Univ. of Delaware, 2015), 12.

One. AWAKENING

1. Merriam, "Sally Merriam Journal," 104.
2. Merriam, "Sally Merriam Journal," 105.
3. Bill Leonard, *A Sense of the Heart: Christian Religious Experience in the United States* (Nashville: Abingdon Press, 2014), 105.
4. Abby Maria Hemenway and Carrie Elizabeth Hemenway Page, *The Vermont Historical Gazetteer: A Magazine, Embracing a History of Each Town, Civil, Ecclesiastical, Biographical and Military* (Claremont, NH: Claremont Manufacturing Company, 1877), 435.
5. Leon S. Gay, *Brandon, Vermont: A History of the Town* (Brandon: Town of Brandon, 1961), 74.
6. Abby Maria Hemenway, *The History of Rutland County, Vermont: Civil, Ecclesiastical, Biographical and Military* (White River Paper Company, 1882), 454.

7. Hemenway, *The History of Rutland County*, 454.

8. H. P. Smith and W. S. Rann, eds., *History of Rutland County Vermont* (Syracuse: D. Mason & Co., 1886), 21.

9. Hemenway, *The History of Rutland County*, 64.

10. Gordon S. Wood, *Empire of Liberty: A History of the Early Republic, 1789–1815*, reprint ed. (Oxford: Oxford Univ. Press, 2011), 706.

11. 1810 US Census, "Rutland, Vermont Population Schedule," Film 0218669, Roll 65, page 161, image 00108, Family History Library, 1810. The census reports fifteen people, all white, living in the Jonathan Merriam house in 1810. At the time, there were seven people in Sally's immediate family—her parents and four living siblings. The remainder of the household may have been a collection of hired workers. However, because the manufacturing inventory includes two linen wheels and two spinning wheels, it is possible that a related family may have been living with them on a temporary basis. Sally does not mention another family in her journal of 1815–17, and the 1820 census inexplicably omits the Jonathan Merriam household altogether.

12. Sarah Conant Merriam to Sarah Merriam Wait, December 19, 1819, Samuel and Sarah Wait Papers. In letters, punctuation has been added for clarification and minor spelling irregularities have been corrected.

13. Hemenway, *The History of Rutland County*, 164.

14. Hemenway, 435–36.

15. "Died," *Rutland Herald*, Published as *Rutland Vermont Herald*, April 7, 1813, 3.

16. Hemenway and Page, *The Vermont Historical Gazetteer*, 484.

17. Hemenway and Page, 415.

18. Zadock Thompson, *History of Vermont, Natural, Civil and Statistical, in Three Parts, with an Appendix. 1853* (Burlington: self-published, 1853), 209.

19. "Third Book of Records of the Church of Christ of the Baptist Order In Brandon, State of Vermont May 27 1796" (Private Collection, 1791–1820).

20. Vermont Baptist Association, *Minutes of the Vermont Baptist Association, Held in Brandon, October . . . 1814 With Their Circular and Corresponding Letter*, Early American Imprints, second series, no. 30789 (Rutland: Printed by Fay & Davison, 1814), 8, http://opac.newsbank.com/select/shaw/30789.

21. Merriam, "Sally Merriam Journal," 1.

22. William Leigh Pierce, *The Year: A Poem, in Three Cantoes* (Published by David Longworth, At the Shakspeare-Gallery [*sic*], 1813).

23. "Died," *Evening Post*, December 28, 1814.

24. Merriam, "Sally Merriam Journal," 55.

25. Merriam, 55.

26. Catherine A. Brekus, *Sarah Osborn's World: The Rise of Evangelical Christianity in Early America, New Directions in Narrative History* (New Haven: Yale Univ. Press, 2013).

27. Samuel Hopkins and Sarah Osborn, *Memoirs of the Life of Mrs. Sarah Osborn* (Worcester, MS: Leonard Worcester, 1799), 221.

28. Harriet Newell, *Memoir of Mrs. Harriet Newell, Wife of the Rev. Samuel Newell, Missionary to India, 1793–1812* (New York: American Tract Society, 1813), 4.

29. Merriam, "Sally Merriam Journal," 12.

30. Merriam, "Sally Merriam Journal," 13.

31. Merriam, "Sally Merriam Journal," 14.

32. Moreshead, "'Beyond All Ambitious Motives' Missionary Memoirs and the Cultivation of Early American Evangelical Heroines," *Journal of the Early Republic* 38, no. 1 (Spring 2018): 37.

33. Curtis W. Freeman, James Wm. Jr. McClendon, and C. Rosalee Velloso da Silva, *Baptist Roots: A Reader in the Theology of a Christian People* (Valley Forge: Judson Press, 1999), 150.

34. Moreshead, "'Beyond All Ambitious Motives,'" 61.

35. Bill (Bill J.) Leonard, "'Wild and Romantic in the Extreme': Ann Hasseltine Judson, (Her Husband), and a Duty to Go to the 'Distant and Benighted Heathen,'" *American Baptist Quarterly* 32, no. 1 (2013): 81.

36. Moreshead, "'Beyond All Ambitious Motives,'" 39.

37. Charles I. Foster, *An Errand of Mercy: The Evangelical United Front 1790–1837* (Chapel Hill: The Univ. of North Carolina Press, 1960), 64.

38. For more information on missions during this period, see Conroy-Kurtz, *Christian Imperialism: Converting the World in the Early American Republic* (Ithaca, NY: Cornell Univ. Press, 2018).

39. Massachusetts Baptist Missionary Society, *The Massachusetts Baptist Missionary Magazine*, 4 vols. (Boston: Manning & Loring, 1803). As an example, the May 1813 issue featured letters from Mrs. Judson and Mrs. Newell, a "Copy of a Letter from a young Woman in Hamden County, to her Mother, giving an account of her religious exercises," and memoirs of Miss Mary Eaton, Mrs. Holt, and Mrs. Mercy Lovell.

Two. BECOMING

1. Jonathan Merriam Jr. and Sarah Conant Merriam to Samuel Wait and Sarah Merriam Wait, July 26, 1818, Samuel and Sarah Wait Papers.

2. "Blank Books," *Rutland Herald*, Published as *Rutland Vermont Herald*, July 30, 1816.

3. Mary Kelley, "'Pen and Ink Communion': Evangelical Reading and Writing in Antebellum America," *The New England Quarterly* 84, no. 4 (2011): 571.

4. Kenneth A. Lockridge, *On the Sources of Patriarchal Rage: The Commonplace Books of William Byrd and Thomas Jefferson and the Gendering of Power in the Eighteenth Century* (New York: New York Univ. Press, c. 1992), 3.

5. Joan Jacobs Brumberg, *Mission for Life: The Story of the Family of Adoniram Judson* (New York: New York Univ. Press, 1984). 30.

6. Kelley, "'Pen and Ink Communion,'" 571.

7. Vermont Baptist Association, *Minutes of the Vermont Baptist Association, Held at . . . Monkton, October . . . 1812 with the Circular and Corresponding Letter* (Rutland: Printed by W. Fay, 1812), 6. The notice included helpful guidance to identify the

banished minister. "N.B. Considering the great probability that his name, rather than his heart, will be changed—He is a man of refined talents, rather draws his words, somewhat corpulent, very round shouldered, and his neck projects from his body, almost in a horizontal direction."

8. Vermont Baptist Association, *Minutes of the Vermont Baptist Association, Held in Brandon, October . . . 1814.*

9. Sally Merriam, "Sally Merriam's Essay Book" (1816), Merriam Family Papers, 3–5. The Merriam Family Papers consist of Sally Merriam's essay or commonplace book, a collection of 1844 letters, and other documents. These remain in the author's collection in Winston-Salem, NC.

10. Merriam, "Sally Merriam's Essay Book," 6–8.

11. Kelley, "'Pen and Ink Communion,'" 557.

12. Merriam, "Sally Merriam's Essay Book," 12–17.

13. Jonathan Edwards, *The Religious Affections*, reprint ed. (Mineola, New York: Dover Publications, 2013) 120.

14. Edwards, *The Religious Affections*, 308–9.

15. Sarah Merriam Wait to Samuel Wait, December 2, 1821, Samuel and Sarah Wait Papers. Sally wrote, "In the summer I read 'Edwards on religious affections' and 'Thornton Abbey' both excellent books."

16. Matt Johnson, "Sarah Waits Journal," email, April 2, 2019.

17. Merriam, "Sally Merriam Journal," 1.

18. Samuel and Sarah Wait Papers. A note from the provenance file at the Z. Smith Reynolds Library indicates that when a Wait descendent donated a large collection in 1993, he mentioned having discarded a 55-gallon drum of documents because of water damage. However, we know that certain documents were preserved for specific individuals in the Wait Brewer family line. For instance, a cache of letters specific to Ann Eliza Wait's engagement to John Brewer and Sally's commonplace remain in one descendant family line.

19. Laurel Thatcher Ulrich, *A Midwife's Tale: The Life of Martha Ballard, Based on Her Diary, 1785–1812*, 1st ed. (New York: Knopf, 1990), 8.

20. Suzanne L. Bunkers and Cynthia Anne Huff, *Inscribing the Daily: Critical Essays on Women's Diaries* (Amherst: Univ. of Massachusetts Press, 1996), 28.

21. Thomas Baldwin, *Heirs of Grace: A Sermon, Delivered at Charlestown, September 26, 1813, Occasioned by the Death of Mrs. Abigail Collier, Consort of the Rev. William Collier, Pastor of the Baptist Church in Said Town* (printed by Manning), accessed August 7, 2017, http://archive.org/details/heirsofgracesermoobald.

22. Brekus, *Sarah Osborn's World*, 17.

23. Merriam, "Sally Merriam Journal," 52.

24. Baldwin, *Heirs of Grace*, 31–32.

25. Merriam, "Sally Merriam's Essay Book," 23.

26. *The Christian Visitant . . .* 1, issue 25 (Albany, New York: H. C. Southwick, 1815), 189.

Three. COURTING

1. Sally Merriam, "Sally Merriam Journal" (1817), 87, Samuel and Sarah Wait Papers.

2. Leonard I. Sweet, *The Minister's Wife: Her Role in Nineteenth-Century American Evangelicalism*, 1st ed. (Philadelphia: Temple Univ. Press, 1983), 8.

3. Moreshead, "The Seed of the Missionary Spirit," 245.

4. Merriam, "Sally Merriam Journal," 80.

5. Merriam, 86.

6. Merriam, 2.

7. Silvanus Haynes to Samuel Wait, July 13, 1815, Samuel and Sarah Wait Papers. The document reads, "Middletown July 13 1815 Know all mean by those presents, that the bearer hereof, Br. Samuel Waite, is a member in good standing in the Baptist C[hurch]. Of Christ in this place, & from hearing the exercises of his mind, & from a little opportunity that we have had, are indeed to hope that God has bestowed upon him a public gift that may be useful in Zion; & he had the approbation of this ch[urc]h in improving his gift wherever God in his providence shall open the door. May the Lord uphold him by this grace, & resolve him happily instrumental of much good. Signed by the order & on behalf of the ch[urc]h. Silvanus Haynes Paster."

8. John B. Brewer, *North Carolina Baptist Historical Papers, Life of Samuel Wait, D.D.*, vol. 1 (Henderson: North Carolina Baptist Historical Society, 1896).

9. Opal, *Beyond the Farm*, 27.

10. Opal, 27.

11. Washington Zera Wait to Sarah Merriam Wait, October 21, 1867, Samuel and Sarah Wait Papers.

12. Newell, *Memoir of Mrs. Harriet Newell*, 10.

13. Massachusetts Baptist Missionary Society, *The Massachusetts Baptist Missionary Magazine*, 203.

14. Merriam, "Sally Merriam Journal," 20.

15. Merriam, 20.

16. Nicole Eustace, "'The Cornerstone of a Copious Work': Love and Power in Eighteenth-Century Courtship," *Journal of Social History* 34, no. 3 (2001): 529.

17. Silvanus Haynes to Samuel Wait, Samuel and Sarah Wait Papers, December 26, 1815. The letter reads in part, "Know all mean by those presents, that the bearer hereof, Br. Samuel Waite, is a member in good standing in the Baptist Ch[urc]h. Of Christ in this place, & from hearing the exercises of his mind, & from little opportunity that we have had, are indeed to hope that God has bestowed upon him a public gift that may be useful in Zion; & he had the approbation of this ch[urc]h in improving his gift wherever God in his providence shall open the door."

18. Ulrich, *A Midwife's Tale*, 138.

19. Merriam, "Sally Merriam Journal," 22.

20. Newell, *Memoir of Mrs. Harriet Newell*, 11–12.

21. Merriam, "Sally Merriam Journal," 21.

22. James D. Knowles, *Memoir of Mrs. Ann H. Judson, Late Missionary to Burmah: Including a History of the American Baptist Mission in the Burman Empire*, 5th ed. (Boston: Lincoln & Edmands, 1832), 42.

23. Knowles, *Memoir of Mrs. Ann H. Judson*, 44.

24. Sarah Merriam Wait to Samuel Wait, June 16, 1822, Samuel and Sarah Wait Papers.

25. *The Christian Visitant . . .* 1, issue 25: 198.

26. Merriam, "Sally Merriam Journal," 25.

27. Merriam, "Sally Merriam Journal," 21.

28. Jan Lewis, "The Republican Wife: Virtue and Seduction in the Early Republic," *The William and Mary Quarterly* 44, no. 4 (1987): 689–721.

29. Merriam, "Sally Merriam Journal," 57.

30. Merriam, 60.

31. Rachel Walker, "'The Day Which Will Fix My Future Destiny': Courtship, Marriage, and the Companionate Ideal in Early Republican America," *History Matters* (May 2010), 96.

32. Betsy Fisher to Sarah Merriam Wait, May 6, 1816, Sally and Samuel Wait Papers.

33. Timothy Kenslea, *The Sedgwicks in Love: Courtship, Engagement, and Marriage in the Early Republic*, 1st ed., 1st printing ed. (Boston: Northeastern, 2006), 112.

34. Merriam, "Sally Merriam Journal," 59.

35. Hemenway and Page, *The Vermont Historical Gazetteer*, 32.

36. Merriam, "Sally Merriam Journal," 72.

37. Elijah Hewins to Samuel Wait, December 9, 1816, Sally and Samuel Wait Papers. The document reads in part, "Dear Brother The Baptist Church of Christ in Sharon at a meeting the 9th of December 1816 for the purpose of inviting some person to preach among them came to the following result they voted to give you an invitation to preach with them for one year and to give you 200 dollars if you should think it your Duty to Labor among us."

38. Merriam, "Sally Merriam Journal," 72.

39. Ellen K. Rothman, *Hands and Hearts: A History of Courtship in America* (New York: Basic Books, Inc., 1984), 32.

40. Merriam, "Sally Merriam Journal," 77.

41. Walker, "The Day Which Will Fix My Future Destiny," 86.

42. Merriam, "Sally Merriam Journal," 79.

43. Merriam, 30.

44. Thomas Gisborne, *An Enquiry Into the Duties of the Female Sex* (London: Printed by A. Strahan for T. Cadell and W. Davies, 1801), 360.

45. Merriam, "Sally Merriam Journal," 79.

46. Thomas H. Luxon, *Single Imperfection: Milton, Marriage and Friendship* (Pittsburgh: Duquesne, 2005), 124.

47. Walker, "The Day Which Will Fix My Future Destiny," 96.

48. Opal, *Beyond the Farm*, 33.

49. Opal, 33.

50. Merriam, "Sally Merriam Journal," 80.

51. Merriam, 81.

52. Merriam, 85.

53. Eustace, "The Cornerstone of a Copious Work," 529.

54. Merriam, "Sally Merriam Journal," 85.

55. Merriam, 85.

56. Merriam, 86.

57. Rothman, *Hands and Hearts*, 80.

58. Merriam, "Sally Merriam Journal," 91.

59. Merriam, 87.

60. Kenslea, *The Sedgwicks in Love*, 120.

61. Merriam, "Sally Merriam Journal," 95.

62. Merriam, 114.

63. Merriam, 122.

64. "Third Book of Records of the Church of Christ of the Baptist Order In Brandon, State of Vermont May 27 1796," December 31, 1818.

65. Cynthia Merriam to Wait, January 3, 1819, Samuel and Sarah Wait Papers.

66. Merriam to Wait.

67. Lydia Merriam to Wait, April 14, 1819, Samuel and Sarah Wait Papers.

68. Merriam, "Sally Merriam Journal," 124.

69. Merriam, 52.

Four. SETTLING

1. Sarah Conant Merriam to Sarah Merriam Wait, March 28, 1820, Samuel and Sarah Wait Papers, Z. Smith Reynolds Library Special Collections and Archives, Wake Forest Univ., Winston-Salem, NC, USA.

2. Samuel Wait and Isaac Merriam to Sarah Merriam Wait, May 19, 1820, Samuel and Sarah Wait Papers.

3. Thomas Gisborne, *An Enquiry*, 360.

4. Jonathan Allen, *A Sermon Delivered . . . on the Occasion of Two Young Ladies Being about to Embark as the Wives of Rev. Messieurs Judson and Newell, Going Missionaries to India* (Haverhill, MA: W. B. & H. G. Allen, 1812), 19–20.

5. Jonathan Merriam Sr. and Sarah Conant Merriam to Sarah Merriam Wait and Samuel Wait, July 26, 1818, Samuel and Sarah Wait Papers. Emphasis added.

6. Sarah Merriam Wait to Samuel Wait, April 14, 1822, Samuel and Sarah Wait Papers.

7. John Conant to Samuel Wait, June 23, 1820, Samuel and Sarah Wait Papers.

8. "The Second Book of Records of the Church of Christ of the Baptist Order In the Township of Brandon, State of Vermont May 26th Ad 1791" (Private Collection, 1791–1820), 3.

9. Lydia Merriam and Mary Powers Merriam to Sarah Merriam Wait, September 25, 1818, Samuel and Sarah Wait Papers.

10. Samuel Wait to Sarah Merriam Wait, August 31, 1820, Samuel and Sarah Wait Papers. In this and following citations, the emphasis is in the original text.

11. Jonathan Merriam Sr. and Sarah Conant Merriam to Sarah Merriam Wait and Samuel Wait, July 26, 1818, Samuel and Sarah Wait Papers.

12. Bill Leonard, *Baptist Ways: A History* (Valley Forge: Judson Press, 2003), 176.

13. Nathan O. Hatch, *The Democratization of American Christianity* (New Haven: Yale Univ. Press, 1989), 17–18.

14. Betsy Fisher to Sarah Merriam Wait, May 6, 1816, Sally and Samuel Wait Papers.

15. Merriam, "Sally Merriam Journal," 48.

16. Elijah Hewins to Samuel Wait, December 9, 1816, Samuel and Sarah Wait Papers.

17. Sharon Baptist Church Ordination, June 3, 1818, Samuel and Sarah Wait Papers. The ordination reads, "It is hereby certified that, at an Ecclesiastical Council convened in Sharon, at request of the Baptist Church Brother Samuel Waite a member of said church, after due examination, and full satisfaction being obtained, was regularly Ordained, as Pastor of, and over said Church, agreeably to the usages of the Baptist Churches. Joseph Grafton, Modr, Wm. Gammell, Scribe."

18. Elijah Hewins to Samuel Wait, March 26, 1821, Samuel and Sarah Wait Papers.

19. Jeremiah Gould, *Annals of Sharon, Massachusetts, 1830* 1 (Boston: Sharon Historical Society, 1904), 16.

20. Samuel Wait to Sarah Merriam Wait, August 31, 1820, Samuel and Sarah Wait Papers.

21. Abiel Fisher to Samuel Wait, July 29, 1820, Samuel and Sarah Wait Papers.

22. Fisher to Wait.

23. Moreshead, "The Seed of the Missionary Spirit," 33.

24. "Proceedings of the General Convention of the Baptist Denomination in the United States, at Their First Triennial Meeting, Held in Philadelphia from the 7th to the 14th of May, 1817" (Philadelphia, 1817), 131.

25. Donald M. Scott, *From Office to Profession: The New England Ministry, 1750–1850* (Philadelphia: Univ. of Pennsylvania Press, 1978), 63.

26. Moreshead, "The Seed of the Missionary Spirit," 72.

27. Samuel W. Lynd, *Memoir of the Rev. William Staughton, D.D.* (Boston: Lincoln & Edmands, 1834), 19.

28. Roger Hayden, "William Staughton: Baptist Educator and Missionary Advocate," *Foundations* 10, no. 1 (January 1967): 22.

29. Hayden, "William Staughton," 20.

30. Laurel Thatcher Ulrich, "Runaway Wives, 1830–1860," *Journal of Mormon History* 42, no. 2 (April 2016): 8.

31. Lynd, *Memoir of the Rev. William Staughton*, 27.

32. Lynd, 29.

33. William Staughton to William Rogers, April 1795, The William Staughton Collection, Univ. Archives, Special Collections Research Center, Gelman Library, The George Washington Univ.

34. Rev. David Spencer, *The Early Baptists of Philadelphia* (Philadelphia: William Syckelmoore, 1877), 164.

35. Spencer, *The Early Baptists*, 176.

36. Lynd, *Memoir of the Rev. William Staughton*, 74.

37. "National Archives and Records Administration (NARA); Washington, D.C.; Indexes to Naturalization Petitions to the U.S. Circuit and District Court for the Eastern District of Pennsylvania," 1795–1951 (M1248); Microfilm Serial: M1248; Microfilm Roll: 7.

38. Spencer, *The Early Baptists*, 178.

39. John M. Bryan, *Robert Mills: America's First Architect* (Princeton Architectural Press, 2001), 81.

40. David Benedict, *A General History of the Baptist Denomination in America, and Other Parts of the World* I (Boston: Lincoln & Edmands, 1813), 592.

41. Spencer, *The Early Baptists*, 165.

42. George Partridge, *History of the Town of Bellingham, 1719–1919* (Bellingham, MA: Town of Bellingham, 1919), 115.

43. James Barnett Taylor, *Memoir of Rev. Luther Rice, One of the First American Missionaries to the East* (Baltimore: Armstrong and Berry, 1840), 136.

44. Taylor, *Memoir of Rev. Luther Rice*, 179.

45. Lydia Merriam and Mary Merriam to Sally Merriam Wait, September 26, 1818, Samuel and Sarah Wait Papers.

46. H. Leon McBeth et al., *No Longer Ignored: A Collection of Articles on Baptist Women* (Baptist History and Heritage Society, 2007), 93.

47. Samuel Whitcomb, July 16, 1818 Journal Entry, Samuel Whitcomb Papers, 1818–1879, Massachusetts Historical Society, Boston, MA.

48. Taylor, "Thoughts on Missions," Franklin County, TN, 1819, 6.

49. Elmer Louis Kayser, *Bricks without Straw: The Evolution of George Washington University.* (New York: Appleton-Century-Crofts, 1970), 59

50. Kayser, "Bricks without Straw," 65.

51. Samuel Wait to Sarah Merriam Wait, May 13, 1826, Samuel and Sarah Wait Papers.

52. Sarah Conant Merriam to Sarah Merriam Wait, December 19, 1819, Samuel and Sarah Wait Papers.

53. Elijah Hewins to Samuel Wait, December 9, 1816, Samuel and Sarah Wait Papers.

54. Joyce Appleby, *Inheriting the Revolution: The First Generation of Americans*, new ed. (Cambridge, MA: Belknap Press, 2001), 52.

55. Appleby, *Inheriting the Revolution*, 87.

56. Isaac Merriam to Samuel Wait, February 3, 1820, Samuel and Sarah Wait Papers. This letter is misdated 1819; notice of its receipt on the exterior in Samuel's hand reads 1820. Isaac writes, "You ask if I am obligated to refund the expense of my board &c. Ans[wer] yes if God in his provident opens the way, by this I mean moral obligation, I am under no other."

57. Thomas S. Wermuth, "New York Farmers and the Market Revolution:

Economic Behavior in the Mid-Hudson Valley, 1780–1830," *Journal of Social History* 32, no. 1 (Autumn, 1998): 182–83.

58. Sarah Conant Merriam and Jonathan Merriam Jr. to Samuel Wait and Sarah Merriam Wait, June 14, 1819, Samuel and Sarah Wait Papers.

59. Opal, *Beyond the Farm*, 26.

60. Scott, *From Office to Profession*, 39.

61. Opal, *Beyond the Farm*, 152.

62. Lydia Merriam to Sarah Merriam Wait, April 21, 1819, Samuel and Sarah Wait Papers.

63. Sarah Conant Merriam and Jonathan Merriam Jr. to Sarah Merriam Wait, June 14, 1819, Samuel and Sarah Wait Papers.

64. Sarah Conant Merriam to Sarah Merriam Wait, April 21, 1818, Samuel and Sarah Wait Papers.

65. Ulrich, *A Midwife's Tale*, 140.

66. Sarah Conant Merriam to Sarah Merriam Wait, June 14, 1819, Samuel and Sarah Wait Papers.

67. Lydia Merriam and Sarah Conant Merriam to Sarah Merriam Wait, April 14, 1819, Samuel and Sarah Wait Papers. Sarah Conant Merriam writes, "I think it possible we may be disappointed unless Jonathan comes home and takes the care of the business while we are gone it will be very difficult for us to leave the farm as it will be about the time to put in winter grain."

68. Sarah Merriam Wait to Samuel Wait, July 23, 1820, Samuel and Sarah Wait Papers.

69. Moreshead, "The Seed of the Missionary Spirit," 110.

70. Isaac Merriam to Samuel Wait, February 2, 1820, Samuel and Sarah Wait Papers.

71. Sarah Merriam Wait to Samuel Wait, June 4, 1820, Samuel and Sarah Wait Papers.

72. Isaac Merriam to Samuel Wait, February 2, 1820, Samuel and Sarah Wait Papers.

73. Merriam to Wait.

74. Sarah Merriam Wait to Samuel Wait, April 24, 1820, Samuel and Sarah Wait Papers.

75. Sarah Merriam Wait to Samuel Wait, March 31, 1822, Samuel and Sarah Wait Papers. After tutoring her for a year, the student sent a handmade needle case as a present to Sally. Sally wrote to Samuel, "I received yours of the 2nd Inst. and the present from Mary Anna Longstreth."

76. Sarah Merriam Wait to Samuel Wait, April 24, 1820, Samuel and Sarah Wait Papers.

77. Sarah Merriam Wait to Jonathan Merriam Jr., April 20, 1820, Samuel and Sarah Wait Papers.

Five. STRIVING

1. Sarah Conant Merriam to Sarah Merriam Wait, March 28, 1820, Samuel and Sarah Wait Papers.

2. Sarah Merriam Wait to Samuel Wait, June 4, 1820, Samuel and Sarah Wait Papers.

3. Sarah Merriam Wait to Samuel Wait, July 23, 1820, Samuel and Sarah Wait Papers.

4. Sarah Merriam Wait to Samuel Wait, October 26, 1820, Samuel and Sarah Wait Papers.

5. Sarah Merriam Wait to Samuel Wait, April 24, 1820, Samuel and Sarah Wait Papers.

6. Sarah Merriam Wait to Samuel Wait, June 4, 1820, Samuel and Sarah Wait Papers.

7. Sarah Merriam Wait to Samuel Wait, April 14, 1822, Samuel and Sarah Wait Papers.

8. Sarah Merriam Wait to Samuel Wait, August 24, 1820, Samuel and Sarah Wait Papers.

9. Ulrich, *A Midwife's Tale,* 212–17.

10. Mary Palmer Tyler, *Grandmother Tyler's Book: The Recollections of Mary Palmer Tyler (Mrs. Royall Tyler) 1775–1866* (G. P. Putnam, 1925), 298.

11. Tyler, *Grandmother Tyler's Book,* 238.

12. Kayser, "Bricks without Straw," 5.

13. Samuel Wait to Sarah Merriam Wait, July 29, 1820, Samuel and Sarah Wait Papers.

14. Samuel Wait to Sarah Merriam Wait, March 14, 1821, Samuel and Sarah Wait Papers.

15. Sarah Merriam Wait to Samuel Wait, June 4, 1820, Samuel and Sarah Wait Papers.

16. Wait to Wait.

17. Brandon, Vt., School District No. 1, Record Book, March 30, 1813, (Vermont Historical Society Library, Barre, Vermont, 1811-1849), MS 974.31 B734.

18. Jean S. Straub, "Benjamin Rush's Views on Women's Education," *Pennsylvania History: A Journal of Mid-Atlantic Studies* 34, no. 2 (1967): 154.

19. Gordon S. Wood, *Empire of Liberty: A History of the Early Republic, 1789–1815,* reprint ed. (Oxford: Oxford Univ. Press, 2011), 473–74.

20. Lydia Merriam to Sarah Merriam Wait, September 25, 1818, Samuel and Sarah Wait Papers.

21. Appleby, *Inheriting the Revolution,* 105; Sarah Merriam to Samuel Wait, Samuel and Sarah Wait Papers, September 25, 1818.

22. Sarah Merriam Wait to Samuel Wait, June 4, 1820, Samuel and Sarah Wait Papers.

23. Moreshead, "The Seed of the Missionary Spirit," 41.

24. Samuel Wait to Sarah Merriam Wait, April 5, 1821, Samuel and Sarah Wait Papers.

25. Wait to Wait.

26. Myron F. Wehtje, "Charles Willson Peale and His Temple," *Pennsylvania History: A Journal of Mid-Atlantic Studies* 36, no. 2 (April 1969): 162.

27. Wehtje, "Charles Willson Peale," 169–71.

28. Lillian Miller et al., eds., *The Selected Papers of Charles Willson Peale and His Family: Volume 5 The Autobiography of Charles Willson Peale* (New Haven: Yale Univ. Press, 2000), 58.

29. Samuel Wait to Sarah Merriam Wait, August 31, 1821, Samuel and Sarah Wait Papers. About the Peale Museum, Samuel wrote to Sally, "We expect to commence our attendance at the Museum with the Dr. for the purpose of knowledge of natural history next Tuesday morning—price 1.00 each and attend as many times as we please."

30. Lynd, *Memoir of the Rev. William Staughton*, 184.

31. Miller et al., *The Selected Papers of Charles Willson Peale and His Family*, 7.

32. Tyler, *Grandmother Tyler's Book*, 16.

33. Sarah Merriam Wait to Samuel Wait, July 3, 1820, Samuel and Sarah Wait Papers.

34. Mrs. (Jane Haldimand) Marcet et al., *Conversations on Natural Philosophy, in Which the Elements of That Science Are Familiarly Explained, and Adapted to the Comprehension of Young Pupils* (Philadelphia: published and sold by J.Y. Humphreys; Thomas Town, Printer, 1820).

35. Appleby, *Inheriting the Revolution*, 153.

36. Samuel Wait and Jonathan Merriam to Sarah Merriam Wait and Mary Merriam, May 19, 1820, Samuel and Sarah Wait Papers.

37. Wait and Merriam to Wait and Merriam.

38. Samuel Wait to Sarah Merriam Wait, July 29, 1820, Samuel and Sarah Wait Papers.

39. Wait to Wait.

40. Sarah Merriam Wait to Samuel Wait, August 24, 1820, Samuel and Sarah Wait Papers.

41. Wait to Wait.

42. Sarah Merriam Wait to Samuel Wait, December 21, 1821, Samuel and Sarah Wait Papers.

43. Sarah Merriam Wait to Samuel Wait, June 4, 1820, Samuel and Sarah Wait Papers.

44. J. David Lehman, "'The Most Disastrous and Never-to-Be-Forgotten Year': The Panic of 1819 in Philadelphia," *Pennsylvania Legacies* 11, no. 1 (2011): 11.

45. Lehman, "'The Most Disastrous and Never-to-Be-Forgotten Year,'" 11.

46. Laurel Thatcher Ulrich, *The Age of Homespun: Objects and Stories in the Creation of an American Myth*, 1st ed. (New York: Alfred A. Knopf, 2001), 157.

47. Ulrich, *The Age of Homespun*, 332.

48. Ulrich, 196.

49. Wood, *Empire of Liberty*, 703.

50. Sarah Merriam Wait to Samuel Wait, May 12, 1821, Samuel and Sarah Wait Papers.

51. Melissa Sirick, "Sophia Woodhouse's Grass Bonnets," *Connecticut Explored*, March 30, 2016, https://www.ctexplored.org/sophia-woodhouses-grass-bonnets/.

52. Gould, *Annals of Sharon, Massachusetts, 1830*, 1: 20.

53. Mary D. Wade, "Industries in Sharon." *Sharon, Massachusetts—A History* (Boston: Blue Mustang Press, 2005), 128.

54. Sarah Merriam Wait to Samuel Wait, June 4, 1820, Samuel and Sarah Wait Papers.

55. Sarah Merriam Wait to Samuel Wait, July 19, 1821, Samuel and Sarah Wait Papers.

56. Wait to Wait, July 7, 1821.

57. Sirick, "Sophia Woodhouse's Grass Bonnets."

58. Sarah Merriam Wait to Samuel Wait, October 7, 1821, Samuel and Sarah Wait Papers.

59. Wait to Wait.

60. Wermuth, "New York Farmers," 191.

61. David Jaffee, *A New Nation of Goods: The Material Culture of Early America* (Philadelphia: Univ. of Pennsylvania Press, 2010), 200.

62. Moreshead, "The Seed of the Missionary Spirit," 4.

63. Moreshead, 4.

64. Charles Sellars, *The Market Revolution: Jacksonian America 1815–1846* (New York: Oxford Univ. Press, 1991), 230.

65. Samuel Wait to Sarah Merriam Wait, January 17, 1822, Samuel and Sarah Wait Papers.

66. Sarah Merriam Wait to Samuel Wait, March 31, 1822, Samuel and Sarah Wait Papers.

67. Sarah Merriam Wait to Samuel Wait, August 4, 1822, Samuel and Sarah Wait Papers.

68. Sarah Merriam Wait to Samuel Wait, December 21, 1821, Samuel and Sarah Wait Papers.

69. Sarah Merriam Wait to Samuel Wait, August 4, 1822, Samuel and Sarah Wait Papers.

70. Sarah Merriam Wait to Samuel Wait, October 7, 1822, Samuel and Sarah Wait Papers.

71. James Sterling Young, *The Washington Community, 1800–1828* (ACLS Humanities E-Book, 2008), 216–17.

72. Sarah Merriam Wait to Samuel Wait, July 19, 1822, Samuel and Sarah Wait Papers.

73. Sarah Miriam Peale to Sarah Merriam Wait, February 19, 1823, Samuel and Sarah Wait Papers.

74. Sarah Merriam Wait to Samuel Wait, October 27, 1822, Samuel and Sarah Wait Papers.

75. Sarah Merriam Wait to Samuel Wait, October 7, 1821, Samuel and Sarah Wait Papers.

76. Sarah Merriam Wait to Samuel Wait, December 21, 1821, Samuel and Sarah Wait Papers.

77. Sarah Merriam Wait to Samuel Wait, July 19, 1822, Samuel and Sarah Wait Papers. Sally reported to Samuel, "We have just finished our fine bonnet. It is No. 76."

78. Sarah Merriam Wait to Samuel Wait, March 31, 1822, Samuel and Sarah Wait Papers.

79. Sarah Merriam Wait to Samuel Wait, October 27, 1822, Samuel and Sarah Wait Papers.

Six. LOVING

1. Megan Marshall, *The Peabody Sisters: Three Women Who Ignited American Romanticism* (New York: Houghton Mifflin Harcourt, 2005), 280. The author makes the point that Sophia Peabody, an approximate contemporary of Sally Wait (and later wife of Nathaniel Hawthorne) was "well aware of the tradition of circulating highly prized women's journals and letters among female friends and relatives over decades."

2. Samuel Wait to Sarah Merriam Wait, September 30, 1820, Samuel and Sarah Wait Papers.

3. Sarah Merriam Wait to Samuel Wait, October 26, 1820, Samuel and Sarah Wait Papers.

4. Samuel Wait to Sarah Merriam Wait, April 5, 1821, Samuel and Sarah Wait Papers.

5. John B. Brewer, *North Carolina Baptist Historical Papers, Life of Samuel Wait, D.D.* 1 (Henderson: North Carolina Baptist Historical Society, 1896), 16–17.

6. Samuel Wait to Sarah Merriam Wait, April 8, 1821, Samuel and Sarah Wait Papers.

7. Sarah Merriam Wait to Samuel Wait, August 24, 1820, Samuel and Sarah Wait Papers.

8. Sarah Merriam Wait to Samuel Wait, December 21, 1821, Samuel and Sarah Wait Papers.

9. Wait to Wait.

10. Wait to Wait.

11. Sarah Merriam Wait to Samuel Wait, July 23, 1820, Samuel and Sarah Wait Papers.

12. Richard B. Kielbowicz, "A History of Mail Classification and Its Underlying Policies and Purposes" (Postal Regulatory Commission, July 17, 1995), 11, Prepared for the Postal Rate Commission's Mail Reclassification Proceeding, MC95–1.

13. Samuel Wait to Sarah Merriam Wait, October 26, 1820, Samuel and Sarah Wait Papers.

14. Sarah Merriam Wait to Samuel Wait, May 19, 1822, Samuel and Sarah Wait Papers.

15. Sarah Merriam Wait to Samuel Wait, July 3, 1820, Samuel and Sarah Wait Papers.

16. Samuel Wait to Sarah Merriam Wait, November 21, 1820, Samuel and Sarah Wait Papers.

17. Sarah Merriam Wait to Samuel Wait, July 3, 1820, Samuel and Sarah Wait Papers.

18. "Washington, Adams and Jefferson, Raphaelle Peale," *Poulson's American Daily Advertiser*, December 5, 1804, SQN: 104740DBCA256AA2, NewsBank/Readex, Database: America's Historical Newspapers.

19. Samuel Wait to Sarah Merriam Wait, July 5, 1821, Samuel and Sarah Wait Papers.

20. Samuel Wait to Sarah Merriam Wait, July 23, 1820, Samuel and Sarah Wait Papers.

21. Miller et al., *The Selected Papers of Charles Willson Peale and His Family*, 94–95.

22. Samuel Wait to Sarah Merriam Wait, March 14, 1821, Samuel and Sarah Wait Papers. Samuel mentions in his letter that "Mr. Ward has now left us to return no more. . . . His last visit to the Inst[itute], was very gratifying."

23. Samuel Wait to Sarah Merriam Wait, April 11, 1821, Samuel and Sarah Wait Papers.

24. "Founders Online: Thomas Jefferson to Burgess Allison, 20 October 1813," accessed July 4, 2018, http://founders.archives.gov/documents/Jefferson /03–06–02–0441.

25. Miller et al., *The Selected Papers of Charles Willson Peale and His Family*, 63n.

26. "Jefferson Portrait by Raphaelle Peale (Silhouette)," accessed July 4, 2018, https://www.monticello.org/site/research-and-collections/jefferson-portrait -raphaelle-peale-silhouette.

27. Samuel Wait to Sarah Merriam Wait, September 3, 1821, Samuel and Sarah Wait Papers.

28. Sarah Merriam Wait to Samuel Wait, August 24, 1820, Samuel and Sarah Wait Papers.

29. Sarah Merriam Wait to Samuel Wait, October 26, 1820, Samuel and Sarah Wait Papers.

30. Samuel Wait to Sarah Merriam Wait, March 27, 1821, Samuel and Sarah Wait Papers.

31. Sarah Merriam Wait to Samuel Wait, July 23, 1820, Samuel and Sarah Wait Papers.

32. Sarah Merriam Wait to Samuel Wait, March 24, 1822, Samuel and Sarah Wait Papers.

33. Samuel Wait to Sarah Merriam Wait, April 21, 1821, Samuel and Sarah Wait Papers.

34. Samuel Wait to Sarah Merriam Wait, April 11, 1821, Samuel and Sarah Wait Papers.

35. Sarah Merriam Wait to Samuel Wait, June 17, 1821, Samuel and Sarah Wait Papers.

36. Wait to Wait.

37. Wait to Wait.

38. Sarah Merriam Wait to Samuel Wait, May 19, 1822, Samuel and Sarah Wait Papers.

39. Wait to Wait.

Seven. MOVING

1. Jack Larkin, *The Reshaping of Everyday Life: 1790–1840*, reprint ed. (New York: Harper Perennial, 1989), 223.

2. Sarah Merriam Wait to Samuel Wait, October 27, 1822, Samuel and Sarah Wait Papers.

3. Wait to Wait.

4. James D. Knowles, *Memoir of Mrs. Ann H. Judson, Late Missionary to Burmah: Including a History of the American Baptist Mission in the Burman Empire*, 5th ed. (Boston: Lincoln & Edmands, 1832), 241.

5. Knowles, *Memoir of Mrs. Ann H. Judson*, 245.

6. Sarah Merriam Wait to Aunt Conant, December 1822, Samuel and Sarah Wait Papers.

7. Wait to Aunt Conant. The letter is not dated, but the content of the letter indicates Sally wrote it shortly after meeting Ann Judson. The recipient is presumably the wife or sister of John Conant.

8. Wait to Aunt Conant.

9. Sarah Merriam Wait to Samuel Wait, April 14, 1822, Samuel and Sarah Wait Papers.

10. Samuel Wait to Sarah Merriam Wait, October 23, 1822, Samuel and Sarah Wait Papers.

11. James Sterling Young, *The Washington Community, 1800–1828*, 24.

12. Young, *The Washington Community*, 41.

13. Young, 45.

14. E. Howett, *Selections from Letters Written during a Tour through the United States, in the Summer and Autumn of 1819*, 1820.

15. Young, *The Washington Community*, 42.

16. Howett, *Selections from Letters*.

17. Samuel Wait to Sarah Merriam Wait, September 3, 1821, Samuel and Sarah Wait Papers.

18. Howett, *Selections from Letters*, 50.

19. Young, *The Washington Community*, 92.

20. Samuel Wait to Sarah Merriam Wait, October 23, 1822, Samuel and Sarah Wait Papers.

21. Samuel Wait to Sarah Merriam Wait, March 31, 1822, Samuel and Sarah Wait Papers.

22. Kayser, "Bricks without Straw," 28.

23. Samuel Wait to Sarah Merriam Wait, January 8, 1822, Samuel and Sarah Wait Papers.

24. Samuel Wait to Sarah Merriam Wait, January 17, 1822, Samuel and Sarah Wait Papers.

25. *GWU Bulletin*, 1822, 26, http://archive.org/details/gwu_bulletin_1822_v2.

26. Samuel W. Lynd, *Memoir of the Rev. William Staughton, D.D.* (Boston: Lincoln & Edmands, 1834), 248.

27. Lynd, *Memoir of the Rev. William Staughton*, 20.

28. *GWU Bulletin*, 1822, 30, http://archive.org/details/gwu_bulletin_1822_v2.

29. Jonathan Elliot, *Historical Sketches of the Ten Miles Square Forming the District of Columbia: With a Picture of Washington, Describing Objects of General Interest Or Curiosity at the Metropolis of the Union . . .* (Washington, DC: J. Elliot Jr., 1830), 238.

30. William Staughton to Samuel Wait, October 25, 1826, Samuel and Sarah Wait Papers.

31. Joanne B. Freeman, *The Field of Blood: Violence in Congress and the Road to Civil War*, 1st ed. (New York: Farrar, Straus and Giroux, 2018), 54.

32. Thomas A. Apel, *Feverish Bodies, Enlightened Minds: Science and the Yellow Fever Controversy in the Early American Republic* (Stanford: Stanford Univ. Press, 2016), 94.

33. Samuel Wait to Sarah Merriam Wait, August 31, 1820, Samuel and Sarah Wait Papers. Samuel writes, "The people in the city complain some of the Board of Health for not publishing correct statements of the cases of the malignant fever."

34. Samuel Wait to Sarah Merriam Wait, September 3, 1821, Samuel and Sarah Wait Papers.

35. *The Latter Day Luminary*, vol. II (Philadelphia: Printed for the Board, 1821), 129. After the report from the committee, the convention elected its officers and thirty managers. Forty-two were from Northern states, twelve from Southern states, and two from the West.

36. Scott, *From Office to Profession*, 51.

37. *The Latter Day Luminary*, 127.

38. "Washington's Lost Gift," *New York Times*, December 26, 1897, Part Two Page 11.

39. Sarah Merriam Wait to Samuel Wait, February 8, 1822, Samuel and Sarah Wait Papers.

40. Sarah Merriam Wait to Samuel Wait, February 17, 1822, Samuel and Sarah Wait Papers.

41. *GWU Bulletin*, 8.

42. Elliot, *Historical Sketches*, 235.

43. Samuel Wait to Sarah Merriam Wait, June 13, 1822, Samuel and Sarah Wait Papers.

44. Samuel Wait to Sarah Merriam Wait, March 14, 1821, Samuel and Sarah Wait Papers.

45. Samuel Wait to Sarah Merriam Wait, April 5, 1821, Samuel and Sarah Wait Papers.

46. Samuel Wait to Sarah Merriam Wait, January 17, 1822, Samuel and Sarah Wait Papers

47. Irah Chase to Samuel Wait, August 27, 1834, Samuel and Sarah Wait Papers.

48. Sarah Merriam Wait to Samuel Wait, July 2, 1826, Samuel and Sarah Wait Papers. Sally writes, "Give my respects to Dr. Sewall [*sic*] and thank him for me as well as yourself for his kindness during our residence on College Hill."

49. Thomas Sewell, *An Address Delivered Before the Washington City Temperance Society, November 15, 1830* (Washington, DC: The Society, 1830).

50. Gordon Harris, "The Body Snatcher of Chebacco Parish," *Historic Ipswich* (blog), March 19, 2014, https://historicipswich.org/2014/03/18/the-body-snatcher-of-chebacco-parish/.

51. Harris, "The Body Snatcher."

52. Suzanne M. Shultz, *Body Snatching: The Robbing of Graves for the Education of Physicians in Early Nineteenth Century America* (McFarland, 2005), 52.

53. Judah Delano, *Washington Directory, Showing the Name, Occupation, and Residence of Each Head of Family and Person in Business, The Names of the Members of Congress, and Where They Board, Together with Other Useful Information* (Washington, DC: William Duncan, Twelfth Street West, 1822), 90.

54. Harriet Savage Chase to Sarah Merriam Wait, July 24, 1824, Samuel and Sarah Wait Papers.

55. 1820 US Census, "New Hanover, North Carolina Population Schedule," NARA Roll M33_84, page 236, image 240, accessed February 9, 2019, http://ancestry.com.

56. Freeman, *The Field of Blood*, 54.

57. *GWU Bulletin*, 22.

58. 1830 US Census, "Washington Ward 1, Washington, District of Columbia Population Schedule," Film 0006699, Series M19, Roll 14, page 129, Family History Library, accessed March 20, 2019.

59. "Anthony Holmead, I (1724–1802)—Find A Grave . . . ," accessed December 24, 2018, https://www.findagrave.com/memorial/142593714/anthony-holmead.

60. Irah Chase to Samuel Wait, March 20, 1826, Samuel and Sarah Wait Papers.

61. Freeman, *The Field of Blood*, 54.

62. Freeman, 56.

63. Freeman, 56.

64. Sarah Merriam Wait to Samuel Wait, August 9, 1824, Samuel and Sarah Wait Papers. Regarding the "ghost," Mr. Anderson had apparently seen a vision on the steps of College Hill some nights before and was sure it was an apparition of Wait, who was away. In Sally's words, "The story of your apparition being seen on the College steps is proved to be a mistake. Mr. Thresher told me the other evening that he was himself the ghost—that he heard the screaming, and saw the waving

of the towels—that he walked up the steps turned and looked &.C. but that he had on neither coat or gown. I have not yet told Mr. Anderson his mistake and he continues confidently to affirm that he saw you."

65. Harriet Savage Chase to Sarah Merriam Wait, n.d., Samuel and Sarah Wait Papers. While there is no date on the letter, it is circa March 1826, as Harriet expresses her sympathy on the recent news of Sally's father's death.

66. Samuel Wait to Sarah Merriam Wait, May 28, 1821, Samuel and Sarah Wait Papers.

67. Lucille Warfield Wilkinson, "Early Baptists in Washington, D. C.," *Records of the Columbia Historical Society, Washington, D.C.* 29/30 (1928): 233.

68. Wilkinson, "Early Baptists," 254.

69. Samuel Wait to Jonathan Merriam Jr., February 17, 1826, Samuel and Sarah Wait Papers.

70. Seth Rockman and Cathy Matson, *Scraping By: Wage Labor, Slavery, and Survival in Early Baltimore*, 1st ed. (Baltimore: The Johns Hopkins Univ. Press, 2009), 105.

71. Jesse Torrey and Wendell Phillips, *A Portraiture of Domestic Slavery, in the United States: With Reflections on the Practicability of Restoring the Moral Rights of the Slave, without Impairing the Legal Privileges of the Possessor; and a Project of a Colonial Asylum for Free Persons of Colour: Including Memoirs of Facts on the Interior Traffic in Slaves, and on Kidnapping. Illustrated with Engravings.* (Philadelphia: self-published; John Bioren, printer, 1817), 64.

72. John Davis, "Eastman Johnson's Negro Life at the South and Urban Slavery in Washington, D.C.," *The Art Bulletin* 80, no. 1 (1998): 71.

73. Rockman and Matson, *Scraping By*, 239.

74. E. S. Abdy, *Journal of a Residence and Tour in the United States of North America, from April, 1833, to October, 1834, Vol. II* (London: J. Murray, 1835), 96.

Eight. FUSSING

1. Andrew Rothwell, *The History of the Baptist Institutions of Washington City* (Washington, DC: W. Ballantyne, 1867), 31.

2. Rothwell, *The History of the Baptist Institutions,* 30–31.

3. Lynd, *Memoir of the Rev. William Staughton,* 176.

4. James Barnett Taylor, *Memoir of Rev. Luther Rice, One of the First American Missionaries to the East* (Baltimore: Armstrong and Berry, 1840), 56.

5. Taylor, *Memoir of Rev. Luther Rice,* 11.

6. Taylor, 37.

7. Gardiner Spring, *Memoirs of The Rev. Samuel J. Mills, Late Missionary to the South Western Section of the United States, and Agent of the American Colonization Society, Deputed to Explore the Coast of Africa* (New York: New-York Evangelical Missionary Society, 1820), 11.

8. Knowles, *Memoir of Mrs. Ann H. Judson,* 68–83.

9. J. Clément, *Memoir of Adoniram Judson: Being a Sketch of His Life and Missionary Labors* (Auburn; Buffalo: Miller, Orton & Mulligan, 1854), 59.

10. Samuel Wait to Sarah Merriam Wait, January 8, 1822, Samuel and Sarah Wait Papers.

11. Sarah Merriam Wait to Samuel Wait, February 8, 1822, Samuel and Sarah Wait Papers.

12. Knowles, *Memoir of Mrs. Ann H. Judson*, 230.

13. *The Latter Day Luminary*, vol. IV (Washington City: John S. Meehan, 1823), 177.

14. Achsah Olin to Sarah Merriam Wait, February 15, 1823, Samuel and Sarah Wait Papers.

15. Cynthia Conant Merriam to Sarah Merriam Wait, April 16, 1823, Samuel and Sarah Wait Papers.

16. Betsey Wait Burrington and Harry Burrington to Sarah Merriam Wait and Samuel Wait, May 19, 1823, Samuel and Sarah Wait Papers.

17. Sarah Conant Merriam to Sarah Merriam Wait, March 30, 1823, Samuel and Sarah Wait Papers.

18. Merriam to Wait.

19. Isaac Merriam and Mary Powers Merriam to Samuel Wait and Sarah Merriam Wait, July 15, 1823, Samuel and Sarah Wait Papers.

20. Sarah Merriam Wait to Samuel Wait, February 8, 1822, Samuel and Sarah Wait Papers.

21. Abel Merriam to Samuel Wait, February 8, 1824, Samuel and Sarah Wait Papers. In his letter to his brother-in-law Samuel, Abel Merriam conveys several questions from the still convalescing Jonathan Merriam, who is now with the family in Brandon, including, "Does Sally board with the Doctor or Prof. Woods?"

22. Sarah Conant Merriam, Charles Rollin Merriam, and Jonathan Merriam Sr. to Samuel Wait and Sarah Merriam Wait, October 28, 1823, Samuel and Sarah Wait Papers.

23. Merriam, Merriam, and Merriam Sr. to Wait and Wait.

24. Lydia Merriam Powers to Sarah Merriam Wait, April 21, 1824, Samuel and Sarah Wait Papers.

25. Powers to Wait.

26. Sally Merriam, "Sally Merriam Journal," 1, Samuel and Sarah Wait Papers.

27. Merriam, 16.

28. Merriam, 52.

29. John Calvin Stockbridge and Baron Stow, *The Model Pastor: A Memoir of the Life and Correspondence of Rev. Baron Stow, Late Pastor of the Rowe Street Baptist Church, Boston* (Boston: Lee and Shepard; New York: Lee, Shepard and Dillingham, 1871), 38.

30. Stockbridge and Stow, *The Model Pastor*, 36.

31. Charles Harcourt Ainslie Forbes-Lindsay, *Washington, the City and the Seat of Government* (Philadelphia: J. C. Winston Company, 1908), 327.

32. Sarah Vowell, *Lafayette in the Somewhat United States*, 1st ed. (New York: Riverhead Books, 2015), 3.

33. John F. Watson and Willis P. Hazard, *Annals of Philadelphia and Pennsylvania in the Olden Time; Being a Collection of Memoirs, Anecdotes, and Incidents of the City and*

Its Inhabitants and of the Earliest Settlements of the Island That Is Part of Pennsylvania, vol. 3 (Edwin S. Stuart, 1899), 331.

34. Kayser, "Bricks without Straw," 52.

35. Kayser., 52.

36. Stockbridge and Stow, *The Model Pastor*, 43.

37. Lynd, *Memoir of the Rev. William Staughton*, 230.

38. *The Latter Day Luminary A New Series*, vol. V (Washington City: John S. Meehan, 1824), 22–23.

39. Oral tradition through several lines of Wait descendants refers to two pieces of furniture as "Lafayette tables," suggesting the Lafayette reception became family lore. If Sally was not present at the reception, according to family legend, at least her tables were.

Nine. CRUMBLING

1. Kayser, "Bricks without Straw," 57.

2. Harriet Savage Chase to Sarah Merriam Wait, June 11, 1824, Samuel and Sarah Wait Papers.

3. Jonathan Merriam Sr. and Sarah Conant Merriam to Samuel Wait and Sarah Merriam Wait, June 4, 1824, Samuel and Sarah Wait Papers. Sally's father writes, "I feel sorry to find by the Star that Congress is not likely to grant any assistance to the College."

4. Irah Chase to Samuel Wait, June 25, 1826, Samuel and Sarah Wait Papers.

5. William Ruggles to Elon Galusha, October 16, 1826, MS 2132/002–008–1:11, Ruggles Collection, The George Washington Univ.

6. Samuel Wait to Sarah Merriam Wait, December 25, 1826, Samuel and Sarah Wait Papers.

7. Harriet Savage Chase to Sarah Merriam Wait, July 24, 1824, Samuel and Sarah Wait Papers.

8. Isaac Merriam to Samuel Wait and Sarah Merriam Wait, August 9, 1824, Samuel and Sarah Wait Papers.

9. Kayser, "Bricks without Straw," 58.

10. Sarah Merriam Wait to Samuel Wait, August 9, 1824, Samuel and Sarah Wait Papers. Sally writes, "Here I sit all alone by our little table in the entry while I scribble. . . . Yesterday we had no worship in the chapel, and I was here all day—partly because I wished to write, and partly because I feel more at home here, than in the College."

11. Samuel Wait to Sarah Merriam Wait, August 20, 1824, Samuel and Sarah Wait Papers.

12. Samuel Wait to Sarah Merriam Wait, August 28, 1824, Samuel and Sarah Wait Papers.

13. Kayser, "Bricks without Straw," 66.

14. Isaac Merriam to Samuel Wait and Sarah Merriam Wait, October 25, 1824, Samuel and Sarah Wait Papers.

15. Kayser, "Bricks without Straw," 57.

16. Harriet Reynolds to Samuel Wait, March 25, 1825, Samuel and Sarah Wait Papers.

17. Lydia Merriam Powers to Sarah Merriam Wait, August 12, 1825, Samuel and Sarah Wait Papers.

18. Sarah Merriam Wait to Samuel Wait, May 19, 1822, Samuel and Sarah Wait Papers.

19. Sarah Merriam Wait to Samuel Wait, October 8, 1822, Samuel and Sarah Wait Papers.

20. Sarah Merriam Wait to Samuel Wait, March 31, 1822, Samuel and Sarah Wait Papers.

21. Samuel Wait to Sarah Merriam Wait, August 16, 1822, Samuel and Sarah Wait Papers.

22. Sarah Merriam Wait to Samuel Wait, August 25, 1822, Samuel and Sarah Wait Papers.

23. Wait to Wait.

24. Jonathan Merriam Jr. and Achsah Merriam to Samuel Wait and Sarah Merriam Wait, December 25, 1825, Samuel and Sarah Wait Papers.

25. Merriam Jr. and Merriam to Wait and Wait.

26. Isaac Merriam to Samuel Wait, February 27, 1826, Samuel and Sarah Wait Papers.

27. Merriam to Wait.

28. Merriam to Wait.

29. Merriam to Wait.

30. Irah Chase to Samuel Wait, March 20, 1826, Samuel and Sarah Wait Papers. Chase writes, "Thank you, dear brother, for the suggestions you have made in relation to the college. The facts you have stated, and the view you have exhibited, are important. They increase my curiosity."

31. Sarah Merriam Wait to Ann Eliza Wait Brewer, February 1, 1846, Merriam Family Papers.

32. Samuel Wait to Jonathan Merriam Jr., February 17, 1826, Samuel and Sarah Wait Papers.

33. Wait to Merriam Jr.

34. Wait to Merriam Jr.

35. Wait to Merriam Jr.

36. John Conant to Samuel Wait, March 26, 1826, Samuel and Sarah Wait Papers.

37. James D. Knowles, *Memoir of Mrs. Ann H. Judson, Late Missionary to Burmah: Including a History of the American Baptist Mission in the Burman Empire*, 5th ed. (London: Wright and Cramp, 1829), 271.

38. Jonathan Merriam Sr., "The Farewell Address of Deacon J Merriam Dictated to Sarah Conant Merriam," Samuel and Sarah Wait Papers.

Ten. SEEKING

1. George Rogers Howell, *Bi-Centennial History of Albany: History of the County of Albany, N.Y., from 1609 to 1886* (W. W. Munsell & Company, 1886), 488.

2. David Lear Buckman, *Old Steamboat Days on the Hudson River: Tables and Reminiscences of the Stirring Times That Followed the Introduction of Steam Navigation* (New York: Grafton Press, c. 1907), 19.

3. Howell, *Bi-Centennial History of Albany,* 488.

4. Sarah Merriam Wait and Ann Eliza Wait to Samuel Wait, May 22, 1826, Samuel and Sarah Wait Papers, Z. Smith Reynolds Library Special Collections and Archives, Wake Forest Univ., Winston-Salem, NC, USA.

5. Isaac Merriam to Samuel Wait, February 27, 1826, Samuel and Sarah Wait Papers.

6. *Proceedings of the Fifth Triennial Meeting of the Baptist General Convention* (Boston: Lincoln & Edmands, 1826), 18.

7. *Proceedings of the Fifth Triennial,* 18.

8. *Proceedings of the Fifth Triennial,* 42.

9. Samuel Wait to Sarah Merriam Wait, May 13, 1826, Samuel and Sarah Wait Papers.

10. Sarah Merriam Wait and Ann Eliza Wait to Samuel Wait, May 22, 1826, Samuel and Sarah Wait Papers.

11. Sarah Merriam Wait to Samuel Wait, June 11, 1826, Samuel and Sarah Wait Papers.

12. Wait to Wait.

13. Wait to Wait.

14. Sarah Merriam Wait to Samuel Wait, June 11, 1826, Samuel and Sarah Wait Papers.

15. Wait to Wait.

16. "Sarah Merriam Deed to Sally M. Wait," August 16, 1827, Samuel and Sarah Wait Papers.

17. Sarah Merriam Wait to Samuel Wait, February 6, 1827, Samuel and Sarah Wait Papers.

18. William Staughton et al. to Samuel Wait, August 7, 1826, Samuel and Sarah Wait Papers.

19. William Ruggles to Samuel Wait, October 6, 1826, MS 2132/002–008–1:11, Ruggles Collection, The George Washington Univ.

20. Samuel Wait to Sarah Merriam Wait, September 19, 1826, Samuel and Sarah Wait Papers.

21. Samuel Wait to Ann Eliza Wait and Sarah Merriam Wait, October 7, 1826, Samuel and Sarah Wait Papers.

22. Steven C. Bullock, *Revolutionary Brotherhood: Freemasonry and the Transformation of the American Social Order, 1730–1840,* 2nd ed. (Omohundro Institute and The Univ. of North Carolina Press, 1998), 278.

23. Bullock, *Revolutionary Brotherhood*, 17.

24. Ronald P. Formisano and Kathleen Smith Kutolowiski, "Antimasonry and Masonry: The Genesis of Protest, 1826–1827," *American Quarterly* 29, no. 2 (Summer 1977): 148.

25. Kehukee Baptist Association et al., *Minutes of the Kehukee Baptist Association [Serial]* (Halifax, NC: Printed by Abraham Hodge), 5.

26. Samuel Wait to Ann Eliza Wait and Sarah Merriam Wait, November 1, 1826, Samuel and Sarah Wait Papers.

27. Samuel Wait to William Ruggles, October 6, 1826, Ruggles Collection.

28. Samuel Wait, "Samuel Wait Diary New Bern, NC," February 14, 1827, Samuel and Sarah Wait Papers.

29. William Staughton to Samuel Wait, October 25, 1826, Samuel and Sarah Wait Papers.

30. William Ruggles to Samuel Wait, November 17, 1826, Samuel and Sarah Wait Papers.

31. Sarah Merriam Wait to Samuel Wait, January 21, 1827.

32. Wait to Wait.

33. Wait to Wait.

34. Wait to Wait.

35. Sarah Merriam Wait to Samuel Wait, February 6, 1827, Samuel and Sarah Wait Papers.

36. Wait to Wait.

37. Isaac Merriam to Sarah Merriam Wait and Samuel Wait, October 25, 1824, Samuel and Sarah Wait Papers. Isaac wrote, "Jacob went to Brandon with us has agreed to move there to take the place in the stead of Jon[atha]n, has $700.00 that he will put in."

38. Scott, *From Office to Profession*, 78.

39. Charles Rollin Merriam to Sarah Merriam Wait, October 6, 1833, Samuel and Sarah Wait Papers.

40. Sarah Merriam Wait to Samuel Wait, February 6, 1827, Samuel and Sarah Wait Papers.

41. Wait to Wait.

42. John Bruce Brewer, "John Bruce Brewer 1927 Address" (1927), Merriam Family Papers. Brewer, the oldest son of Ann Eliza Wait Brewer and John Marchant Brewer, was a bit of an anomaly. An educator himself, having run several female academies, and ending his service as president of Chowan College, Brewer had personally known every president of Wake Forest, beginning with his grandfather Samuel Wait. In his remarks, Brewer delivered his opinions on the succession of presidents, beginning with the legend of the carriage accident.

43. Samuel Wait to Sarah Merriam Wait, March 9, 1827, Samuel and Sarah Wait Papers.

44. Jonathan Merriam Jr. to Samuel Wait, February 12, 1827, Samuel and Sarah Wait Papers.

45. J. W. Sawyer to Samuel Wait, June 26, 1827, Samuel and Sarah Wait Papers.

46. Harriet Reynolds to Samuel Wait, March 25, 1825, Samuel and Sarah Wait Papers.

47. Leavitt Hewins to Samuel Wait, February 15, 1827, Samuel and Sarah Wait Papers.

48. Sarah Conant Merriam to Samuel Wait and Sarah Merriam Wait, February 22, 1828, Samuel and Sarah Wait Papers.

49. Abiel Fisher to Samuel Wait, July 29, 1820, Samuel and Sarah Wait Papers.

50. Catherine W. Bishir, *Crafting Lives: African American Artisans in New Bern, North Carolina, 1770–1900* (Chapel Hill: UNC Press Books, 2013), 9.

51. Kehukee Baptist Association et al., *Minutes of the Kehukee Baptist Association*, 4.

52. Samuel Wait to Sarah Merriam Wait, March 9, 1827, Samuel and Sarah Wait Papers.

53. Wait to Wait.

54. Kehukee Baptist Association et al., *Minutes of the Kehukee Baptist Association*, 4.

55. *Minute Book No. 3 of St. John's Lodge No. 3*, n.d., https://library.digitalnc.org /cdm/compoundobject/collection/ncmemory/id/248444/rec/4.

56. "New Bern First Baptist Church (New Bern, NC) Records," 340. Handcock is spelled "Hancock" in some records.

57. Col. John D. Whitford and Howard Rawls, *The Home Story of a Walking Stick: The Early History of the "Biblical Recorder" and Baptist Church at New Bern, N.C.* (Raleigh: North Carolina State Archives, 1965), 30.

58. Whitford and Rawls, *The Home Story of a Walking Stick*, 48.

59. Bill Hand, *A Walking Guide to North Carolina's Historic New Bern* (Charleston: The History Press, 2007), 30.

60. James Riggs to Samuel Wait, August 10, 1827, Samuel and Sarah Wait Papers.

61. "New Bern First Baptist Church (New Bern, NC) Records," 340.

62. "New Bern First Baptist Church (New Bern, NC) Records," 340.

63. Samuel Wait, "Samuel Wait Diary New Bern, NC," March 24, 1827, Samuel and Sarah Wait Papers.

64. Lynd, *Memoir of the Rev. William Staughton*, 271.

65. Lynd, 184.

66. Lynd, 285.

67. Samuel Wait, "Samuel Wait Diary New Bern, NC," March 25, 1827, Samuel and Sarah Wait Papers.

68. Samuel Wait to Sarah Merriam Wait and Ann Eliza Wait, June 11, 1827, Samuel and Sarah Wait Papers.

69. Samuel Wait, "Samuel Wait Diary New Bern, NC," June 16, 1827, Samuel and Sarah Wait Papers.

70. Bishir, *Crafting Lives*, 24.

71. Samuel Wait to Sarah Merriam Wait, March 9, 1827, Samuel and Sarah Wait Papers.

72. Irah Chase to Samuel Wait, March 26, 1827, Samuel and Sarah Wait Papers.

73. Chase to Wait.

74. Chase to Wait.

75. Samuel Wait to Sarah Merriam Wait, March 9, 1827, Samuel and Sarah Wait Papers.

76. Wait to Wait.

77. Wait to Wait.

78. Wait to Wait.

79. Samuel Wait to Sarah Merriam Wait, April 30, 1827, Samuel and Sarah Wait Papers.

80. Bishir, *Crafting Lives*, 24.

81. Sarah Merriam Wait and Ann Eliza Wait to Samuel Wait, April 15, 1827, Samuel and Sarah Wait Papers.

82. Bishir, *Crafting Lives*, 10.

83. Whitford and Rawls, *The Home Story of a Walking Stick*, 112.

84. Bishir, *Crafting Lives*, 9.

85. David S. Cecelski, *The Waterman's Song: Slavery and Freedom in Maritime North Carolina*, new ed. (Chapel Hill: The Univ. of North Carolina Press, 2001), xi.

86. Rockman and Matson, *Scraping By*, 7.

87. Bishir, *Crafting Lives*, 70.

88. Bishir, 70.

89. Bishir, 70.

90. John Murphy Smith and L. C. (Lachlan Cumming) Vass, *The History of First Presbyterian Church of New Bern, North Carolina, 1886–1987* (New Bern: Griffin & Tilghman Printers, 1988), 136, http://archive.org/details/historyoffirstprsmit.

91. Smith and Vass, *The History of First Presbyterian Church*, 3.

92. Smith and Vass, 136.

93. Bishir, *Crafting Lives*, 38.

94. Samuel Wait to Sarah Merriam Wait and Ann Eliza Wait, June 11, 1827, Samuel and Sarah Wait Papers.

95. Sarah Merriam Wait and Ann Eliza Wait to Samuel Wait, April 15, 1827, Samuel and Sarah Wait Papers.

96. Sarah Merriam Wait to Leavitt Hewins, March 30, 1830, Samuel and Sarah Wait Papers.

97. Sarah Merriam Wait and Ann Eliza Wait to Samuel Wait, April 15, 1827.

98. Isaac Merriam and Mary Powers Merriam to Samuel Wait and Sarah Merriam Wait, April 20, 1828, Samuel and Sarah Wait Papers.

99. Jonathan Merriam Jr. and Achsah Merriam to Samuel Wait and Sarah Merriam Wait, May 7, 1834, Samuel and Sarah Wait Papers.

Eleven. RECKONING

1. Samuel Wait, "Samuel Wait Diary New Bern, NC," June 18, 1827, Samuel and Sarah Wait Papers.

2. Samuel Wait, "Samuel Wait Diary New Bern, NC," July 11, 1827, Samuel and Sarah Wait Papers.

3. Whitford and Rawls, *The Home Story of a Walking Stick*, 193. "During the ministerial service of the Rev. Dr. Samuel Wait for the Baptists at New Bern, his family occupied the home where the church was born. Mr. Clark having changed his residence."

4. Whitford and Rawls, 72.

5. Samuel Wait to John Armstrong, February 12, 1831, Samuel and Sarah Wait Papers.

6. Bishir, *Crafting Lives*, 39.

7. Samuel Wait to Robert Semple, April 2, 1828, Samuel and Sarah Wait Papers.

8. "YOUNG LADIES' ACADEMY," *Newbern Spectator and Literary Journal* I, no. 7 (September 20, 1828): sec. 2.

9. James Riggs to Samuel Wait, August 10, 1827, Samuel and Sarah Wait Papers.

10. Riggs to Wait.

11. Riggs to Wait.

12. Appleby, *Inheriting the Revolution*, 142.

13. Sarah Conant Merriam and Jonathan Merriam Sr. to Sarah Merriam Wait and Samuel Wait, February 2, 1823, Samuel and Sarah Wait Papers.

14. Sarah Conant Merriam, Charles Rollin Merriam, and Jonathan Merriam Sr. to Samuel Wait and Sarah Merriam Wait, October 28, 1823, Samuel and Sarah Wait Papers.

15. Abel Merriam and Sarah Conant Merriam to Sarah Merriam Wait, August 24, 1828, Samuel and Sarah Wait Papers.

16. Rockman and Matson, *Scraping By*, 103.

17. Sarah Conant Merriam to Sarah Merriam Wait, February 22, 1826, Samuel and Sarah Wait Papers.

18. Jonathan Merriam Sr. and Sarah Conant Merriam to Samuel Wait and Sarah Merriam Wait, May 22, 1828, Samuel and Sarah Wait Papers.

19. Sarah Conant Merriam to Samuel Wait and Sarah Merriam Wait, July 19, 1829, Samuel and Sarah Wait Papers.

20. Sarah Conant Merriam to Samuel Wait and Sarah Merriam Wait, November 10, 1829, Samuel and Sarah Wait Papers.

21. 1830 US Census, "New Bern, Craven, North Carolina Population Schedule," Film 0018085, Series M19, Roll 119, page 120, image 00108.

22. 1830 US Census, "New Bern, Craven, North Carolina Population Schedule," Film 0018085, Series M19, Roll 119, page 134.

23. Rockman and Matson, *Scraping By*, 8.

24. Bishir, *Crafting Lives*, 56.

25. Samuel Wait, "Samuel Wait Diary New Bern, NC," May 7 and June 13, 1827, Samuel and Sarah Wait Papers.

26. Samuel Wait to William Ruggles, June 19, 1830, MS 2132/002–008–1:11, Ruggles Collection, The George Washington Univ.

27. Edna Avery Cook, *"In the Beginning—Baptists"!: History of the First Baptist Church, New Bern, North Carolina, 1809–1984* (New Bern: 1984), 20.

28. Bishir, *Crafting Lives*, 26.

29. Samuel Wait to William Ruggles, June 19, 1830, MS 2132/002–008–1:11, Ruggles Collection, The George Washington Univ.

30. Samuel Wait to Howard Malcom, August 3, 1830, Samuel and Sarah Wait Papers.

31. Wait to Ruggles, June 19, 1830, Ruggles Collection.

32. R. B. Howell to Samuel Wait, June 17, 1830, Samuel and Sarah Wait Papers.

33. Wait to Ruggles, Ruggles Collection.

34. Cynthia Lynn Lyerly, *Methodism and the Southern Mind, 1770–1810*, 1st ed. (New York: Oxford Univ. Press, 2006), 55.

35. Bishir, *Crafting Lives*, 21.

36. Samuel Wait to Sarah Merriam Wait, April 30, 1827, Samuel and Sarah Wait Papers.

37. "New Bern First Baptist Church (New Bern, NC) Records," 349.

38. Lyerly, *Methodism and the Southern Mind*, 56.

39. Samuel Wait to Sarah Merriam Wait, April 30, 1827, Samuel and Sarah Wait Papers.

40. Lyerly, *Methodism and the Southern Mind*, 5.

41. Samuel Wait, "Samuel Wait Diary New Bern, NC," June 9, 1827, Samuel and Sarah Wait Papers.

42. Washington Zera Wait to Samuel Wait, January 8, 1844, Samuel and Sarah Wait Papers.

43. Wait to Wait.

44. Wait to Wait.

45. Bishir, *Crafting Lives*, 49.

46. Judah Delano, *Washington Directory, Showing the Name, Occupation, and Residence of Each Head of Family and Person in Business, The Names of the Members of Congress, and Where They Board, Together with Other Useful Information* (Washington, DC: William Duncan, Twelfth Street West, 1822), 133.

47. Foster, *An Errand of Mercy*, 200.

48. Foster, 200.

49. Jean Fagan Yellin, *Harriet Jacobs: A Life* (New York: Civitas Books, 2005), 52.

50. "Seeking Abraham: A Report of Furman University's Office of the Provost and Task Force on Slavery and Justice" (Greenville: Furman Univ., 2018), 24.

51. Charles Edward Morris, "Panic and Reprisal: Reaction in North Carolina to the Nat Turner Insurrection" (North Carolina State Univ., 1979), 40.

52. Yellin, *Harriet Jacobs*, 35.

53. Cecelski, *The Waterman's Song*, 53.

54. "27 Nov 1830, Page 1—Newbern Spectator at Newspapers.Com," North Carolina Collection, accessed January 17, 2019.

55. Bishir, *Crafting Lives*, 86.

56. Sarah Conant Merriam to Sarah Merriam Wait, April 25, 1830, Samuel and Sarah Wait Papers.

57. Merriam to Wait.

58. Sarah Conant Merriam to Sarah Merriam Wait and Samuel Wait, November 26, 1831, Samuel and Sarah Wait Papers.

59. Merriam to Wait and Wait.

60. Merriam to Wait and Wait.

61. Daniel Sharp, "Review: Counsels and Cautions The Substance of an Address Read before the Conference of Baptist Ministers in Massachusetts, at Their Annual Meeting in Boston, May 27, 1835," *American Baptist Magazine* (November 1835): 35.

62. Lyerly, *Methodism and the Southern Mind*, 59.

63. Charles F. Irons, *The Origins of Proslavery in Christianity* (Chapel Hill: UNC Press Books, 2008), 135.

64. Samuel Wait to Sarah Merriam Wait, October 5, 1830, Samuel and Sarah Wait Papers.

65. Wait to Wait.

66. Brother Kendall to Samuel Wait, October 14, 1833, Samuel and Sarah Wait Papers.

67. "Freeman, Ralf | NCpedia," accessed January 17, 2019, https://www.ncpedia.org/biography/freeman-ralf.

68. Samuel Wait to William Ruggles, June 19, 1830, Ruggles Collection.

69. Scott, *From Office to Profession*, 88.

70. Samuel Wait to William Ruggles, June 19, 1830, Ruggles Collection.

71. Sarah Merriam Wait to Leavitt Hewins, March 30, 1830, Samuel and Sarah Wait Papers.

72. Wait to Hewins.

73. Wait to Hewins.

74. Wait to Hewins.

75. Wait to Hewins.

76. Sarah Merriam Wait to Samuel Wait, August 16, 1830, Samuel and Sarah Wait Papers.

77. Wait to Wait.

78. Wait to Wait.

Twelve. CHOOSING HOME

1. Sarah Merriam Wait to Samuel Wait, October 24, 1830, Samuel and Sarah Wait Papers, Z. Smith Reynolds Library Special Collections and Archives, Wake Forest Univ., Winston-Salem, NC, USA.

2. Sarah Conant Merriam to Sarah Merriam Wait and Samuel Wait, Samuel and Sarah Wait Papers, November 26, 1831.

3. Isaac Merriam to Samuel Wait, June 11, 1830, Samuel and Sarah Wait Papers.

4. Bullock, *Revolutionary Brotherhood*, 290.

5. Jonathan Merriam Jr. to Samuel Wait, April 11, 1831, Samuel and Sarah Wait Papers.

6. Bullock, *Revolutionary Brotherhood*, 281.

7. Bullock, 17.

8. Bullock, 16.

9. Bullock, 271.

10. Formisano and Kutolowiski, "Antimasonry and Masonry," 142.

11. Formisano and Kutolowiski, 142.

12. Formisano and Kutolowiski, 142.

13. Formisano and Kutolowiski, 143.

14. Sarah Merriam Wait to Samuel Wait, September 9, 1830, Samuel and Sarah Wait Papers.

15. Abby Maria Hemenway, *The History of Rutland County, Vermont: Civil, Ecclesiastical, Biographical and Military* (White River Paper Company, 1882), 494.

16. Formisano and Kutolowiski, "Antimasonry and Masonry," 144.

17. Sarah Merriam Wait to Samuel Wait, September 9, 1830, Samuel and Sarah Wait Papers.

18. "To the Editor of the People's Advocate," *Boston Masonic Mirror* (Boston: Moore and Sevey, 1830–1834), 315.

19. Joanne B. Freeman, *The Field of Blood: Violence in Congress and the Road to Civil War*, 1st ed. (New York: Farrar, Straus and Giroux, 2018), 63.

20. Freeman, *The Field of Blood*, 64.

21. Sarah Conant Merriam, Charles Rollin Merriam, and Jonathan Merriam Sr. to Samuel Wait and Sarah Merriam Wait, October 28, 1823, Samuel and Sarah Wait Papers.

22. Sarah Conant Merriam to Sarah Merriam Wait, June 30, 1833, Samuel and Sarah Wait Papers.

23. Abel Merriam to Charles Rollin Merriam, July 12, 1835, Samuel and Sarah Wait Papers.

24. Abel Merriam to Charles Rollin Merriam, January 6, 1836, Samuel and Sarah Wait Papers.

25. Charles Rollin Merriam to Sarah Merriam Wait, January 3, 1832, Samuel and Sarah Wait Papers.

26. Sarah Conant Merriam to Samuel Wait and Sarah Merriam Wait, March 11, 1833, Samuel and Sarah Wait Papers. When Charles Rollin returned home after working in the factory, Sally's mother wrote: "He looked like a walking skilliton when he came home with a blue countenance and skin cleaving to the bone . . . working in those paints and spirits of turpentine so much it has great affect on his health he looks ten years older than he did before he went there."

27. Isaac Merriam and Mary Powers Merriam to Samuel Wait and Sarah Merriam Wait, February 8, 1836, Samuel and Sarah Wait Papers.

28. Scott, *From Office to Profession*, 79.

29. Sarah Merriam Wait to Samuel Wait, September 9, 1830, Samuel and Sarah Wait Papers.

30. Wait to Wait.

31. Wait to Wait.

32. Wait to Wait.

33. Sarah Merriam Wait to Samuel Wait, October 24, 1830, Samuel and Sarah Wait Papers.

34. Wait to Wait.

35. Wait to Wait.

36. Samuel Wait to Sarah Merriam Wait, January 11, 1831, Samuel and Sarah Wait Papers.

37. Samuel Wait to Sarah Merriam Wait, August 19, 1830, Samuel and Sarah Wait Papers.

38. Sarah Merriam Wait to Samuel Wait, September 9, 1830, Samuel and Sarah Wait Papers.

39. Wait to Wait.

40. Samuel Wait to Sarah Merriam Wait, October 5, 1830, Samuel and Sarah Wait Papers.

41. Samuel Wait to Sarah Merriam Wait, January 11, 1831, Samuel and Sarah Wait Papers.

42. Wait to Wait.

43. Wait to Wait.

44. Samuel Wait to Sarah Merriam Wait, May 1, 1822, Samuel and Sarah Wait Papers.

45. Samuel Wait to Sarah Merriam Wait, January 11, 1831, Samuel and Sarah Wait Papers.

46. Sarah Merriam Wait to Samuel Wait, May 16, 1831, Samuel and Sarah Wait Papers.

47. Wait to Wait.

48. Wait to Wait.

49. Wait to Wait.

50. Jacob Powers, Sarah Conant Merriam to Sarah Merriam Wait, January 2, 1831, Samuel and Sarah Wait Papers.

51. Sarah Merriam Wait to Samuel Wait, May 16, 1831, Samuel and Sarah Wait Papers.

52. Wait to Wait.

53. Cynthia Conant Merriam to Sarah Merriam Wait, March 19, 1826, Samuel and Sarah Wait Papers.

54. *The Latter Day Luminary*, vol. I (Philadelphia: Printed for the Board, 1818), 216.

55. Samuel Wait to Sarah Merriam Wait, April 21, 1831, Samuel and Sarah Wait Papers.

56. Wait to Wait.

57. Wait to Wait.

58. Wait to Wait.

59. *Proceedings of the First Annual Meeting of the Baptist State Convention of North Carolina, Rogers Cross Road Meeting House, April 15–18, 1831* (New Bern: John I. Pasteur, 1831), 6.

60. Samuel Wait to Sarah Merriam Wait, April 21, 1831, Samuel and Sarah Wait Papers.

61. Wait to Wait. Samuel wrote, "In the Con[vention] they voted me 1 dollar per day, but by private subscription they raised my salary to 500 doll[ars]; Br. Armstrong thinks it will be 550."

62. Wait to Wait.

63. Wait to Wait.

64. Sarah Merriam Wait to Samuel Wait, May 16, 1831, Samuel and Sarah Wait Papers.

Epilogue

1. John B. Brewer, *North Carolina Baptist Historical Papers, Life of Samuel Wait, D.D.* 1 (Henderson: North Carolina Baptist Historical Society, 1896), 16–17.

2. Brewer, *North Carolina Baptist Historical Papers*, 22.

3. George Washington Paschal, *History of Wake Forest College* (Wake Forest: Wake Forest College, 1935), 58.

4. Paschal, *History of Wake Forest College*, 67.

5. Elizabeth Lumpkin Barnette, "Sarah Conant Merriam Wait" (unpublished notes written by Sally Wait's great-great-granddaughter in the author's possession, n.d.), 6.

6. Andrew Canady, *A Place of Its Time: The Origin and History of Wake Forest Institute* (unpublished manuscript in the author's possession, 2019), 1–3.

7. Paschal, *History of Wake Forest College*, 156.

8. Paschal, 151.

9. Paschal, 379.

10. Canady, *The College, the Town, and Samuel Wait*, 9.

11. Canady, 10.

12. Canady, 16.

13. Canady, 17.

14. Paschal, *History of Wake Forest College*, 386.

15. Canady, *The College, the Town, and Samuel Wait*, 18.

16. Canady, 20.

17. Canady, 31–35.

18. Canady, 32. Canady gives a full accounting of the enslaved history of the college and the Waits in his forthcoming history of the college.

19. Canady, 33–35.

20. Sarah Merriam Wait to John Marchant Brewer and Ann Eliza Brewer, October 5, 1856, Samuel and Sarah Wait Papers.

21. Canady, *The College, the Town, and Samuel Wait*, 40–41.

22. Paschal, *History of Wake Forest College*, 119.

23. Paschal, 407; The National Archives at Washington, DC; Record Group Title: Records of the Department of Veterans Affairs, 1773–2007; Record Group Number: 15; Series Title: US, Civil War Pension Index: General Index to Pension Files, 1861–1934; Series Number: T288.

24. Paschal, *History of Wake Forest College*, 123.

25. Paschal, 263.

26. 1850 US Census Slave Schedule, The National Archive in Washington DC; Washington, DC; NARA Microform Publication: M432; Title: Seventh Census Of The United States, 1850; Record Group: Records of the Bureau of the Census; Record Group Number: 29.

27. Paschal, *History of Wake Forest College*, 40.

28. Barnette, "Sarah Conant Merriam Wait," 8.

29. Canady, *The College, the Town, and Samuel Wait*, 1.

30. Sarah Merriam Wait to Samuel Wait, September 9, 1830, Samuel and Sarah Wait Papers.

31. Paschal, *History of Wake Forest College*, 159–65.

32. Moreshead, "The Seed of the Missionary Spirit," 108.

33. Sarah Conant Merriam to Sarah Merriam Wait, November 12, 1833, Samuel and Sarah Wait Papers.

34. Paschal, *History of Wake Forest College*, 404, 422.

BIBLIOGRAPHY

Primary Sources

1810 US Census. "Rutland, Vermont Population Schedule." Film 0218669, Roll 65, page 161, image 00108.

1820 US Census. "New Hanover, North Carolina Population Schedule." NARA Roll M33_84, page 236, image 240.

1830 US Census. "New Bern, Craven, North Carolina Population Schedule." Film 0018085, Series M19, Roll 119, page 133.

———. "New Bern, Craven, North Carolina Population Schedule." Film 0018085, Series M19, Roll 119, page 120, image 00108.

———. "New Bern, Craven, North Carolina Population Schedule." Film 0018085, Series M19, Roll 119, page 134.

———. "Washington Ward 1, Washington, District of Columbia Population Schedule." Film 0006699, Series M19, Roll 14, page 129. Family History Library.

1850 US Census Slave Schedule, The National Archive in Washington DC; Washington, DC; NARA Microform Publication: M432; Title: Seventh Census Of The United States, 1850; Record Group: Records of the Bureau of the Census; Record Group Number: 29.

Abdy, E. S. *Journal of a Residence and Tour in the United States of North America, from April, 1833, to October, 1834, Vol. II.* 3 vols. London: J. Murray, 1835.

Allen, Jonathan. *A Sermon Delivered . . . on the Occasion of Two Young Ladies Being about to Embark as the Wives of Rev. Messieurs Judson and Newell, Going Missionaries to India.* Haverhill, MA: W. B. & H. G. Allen, 1812.

Baldwin, Thomas. *Heirs of Grace: A Sermon, Delivered at Charlestown, September 26, 1813, Occasioned by the Death of Mrs. Abigail Collier, Consort of the Rev. William Collier, Pastor of the Baptist Church in Said Town.* Boston: Manning, 1813.

Benedict, David. *A General History of the Baptist Denomination in America, and Other Parts of the World.* Vol. I. Boston: Lincoln & Edmands, 1813.

"Blank Books." *Rutland Herald,* published as *Rutland Vermont Herald.* July 30, 1816.

"Brandon, VT School District No. 1, Record Book." Vermont Historical Society Library, Barre, Vermont, 1811-1849. MS 974.31 B734.

Brewer, John Bruce. "John Bruce Brewer 1927 Address." 1927. Merriam Family Papers.

The Christian Visitant 1, issue 25. Albany, New York: H.C. Southwick, 1815.

Clément, J. *Memoir of Adoniram Judson: Being a Sketch of His Life and Missionary Labors.* Auburn; Buffalo: Miller, Orton & Mulligan, 1854.

Delano, Judah. *Washington Directory, Showing the Name, Occupation, and Residence of Each Head of Family and Person in Business, The Names of the Members of Congress, and Where They Board, Together with Other Useful Information.* Washington, DC: William Duncan, Twelfth Street West, 1822.

"Died." *Evening Post.* New York: December 28, 1814.

"Died." *Rutland Herald*, published as *Rutland Vermont Herald*. Rutland: April 7, 1813.

Edwards, Jonathan. *The Religious Affections*. Reprint edition. Mineola, New York: Dover Publications, 2013.

Elliot, Jonathan. *Historical Sketches of the Ten Miles Square Forming the District of Columbia: With a Picture of Washington, Describing Objects of General Interest Or Curiosity at the Metropolis of the Union . . .* Washington, DC: J. Elliot Jr., 1830.

"Founders Online: Thomas Jefferson to Burgess Allison, 20 October 1813." Accessed July 4, 2018. http://founders.archives.gov/documents/Jefferson/03-06-02-0441.

Gisborne, Thomas. *An Enquiry Into the Duties of the Female Sex*. London: Printed by A. Strahan for T. Cadell and W. Davies, 1801.

Gould, Jeremiah. *Annals of Sharon, Massachusetts, 1830*. Vol. 1. Boston: Sharon Historical Society, 1904.

GWU Bulletin, 1822. http://archive.org/details/gwu_bulletin_1822_v2.

Hopkins, Samuel, and Sarah Osborn. *Memoirs of the Life of Mrs. Sarah Osborn*. Worcester, Massachusetts: Leonard Worcester, 1799.

Howett, E. *Selections from Letters Written during a Tour through the United States, in the Summer and Autumn of 1819*. 1820.

Kehukee Baptist Association, Abraham Hodge, Thomas Henderson, Strother & Marcom, and Southerner Office. *Minutes of the Kehukee Baptist Association [Serial]*. Halifax, NC: Printed by Abraham Hodge, 1826.

Knowles, James D. *Memoir of Mrs. Ann H. Judson, Late Missionary to Burmah: Including a History of the American Baptist Mission in the Burman Empire*. Fifth edition. London: Wright and Cramp, 1829.

———. *Memoir of Mrs. Ann H. Judson, Late Missionary to Burmah: Including a History of the American Baptist Mission in the Burman Empire*. Fifth edition. Boston: Lincoln & Edmands, 1832.

The Latter Day Luminary. Vol. I. Philadelphia: Printed for the Board, 1818.

The Latter Day Luminary. Vol. II. Philadelphia: Printed for the Board, 1821.

The Latter Day Luminary. Vol. IV. Washington City: John S. Meehan, 1823.

The Latter Day Luminary A New Series. Vol. V. Washington City: John S. Meehan, 1824.

Lynd, Samuel W. *Memoir of the Rev. William Staughton, D.D.* Boston: Lincoln & Edmands, 1834.

Marcet, Mrs. (Jane Haldimand), Charles A. (Charles Atwood) Kofoid, Thomas Town, and J. Y. Humphreys. *Conversations on Natural Philosophy, in Which the Elements of That Science Are Familiarly Explained, and Adapted to the Comprehension of Young Pupils*. Philadelphia: J. Y. Humphreys; Thomas Town, Printer, 1820.

Massachusetts Baptist Missionary Society. *The Massachusetts Baptist Missionary Magazine*. 4 vols. Boston: Manning & Loring, 1803.

Merriam, Sally. "Sally Merriam Journal," 1817. Samuel and Sarah Wait Papers, Z. Smith Reynolds Library Special Collections and Archives, Wake Forest Univ., Winston-Salem, NC, USA.

———. "Sally Merriam's Essay Book," 1816. Merriam Family Papers.

Minute Book No. 3 of St. John's Lodge No. 3. 1807–1849. https://library.digitalnc
.org/cdm/compoundobject/collection/ncmemory/id/248444/rec/4.

"National Archives and Records Administration (NARA); Washington, D.C.;
Indexes to Naturalization Petitions to the U.S. C," 1795–1951.

The National Archives at Washington, DC, Record Group Title: Records of the
Department of Veterans Affairs, 1773–2007, Record Group Number: 15, Series
Title: US, Civil War Pension Index: General Index to Pension Files, 1861–1934,
Series Number: T288.

"New Bern First Baptist Church (New Bern, NC) Records." Winston-Salem, NC,
CRMF689. Z. Smith Reynolds Library Special Collections and Archives, Wake
Forest Univ.

Newbern Spectator, November 27, 1803.

Newell, Harriet. *Memoir of Mrs. Harriet Newell, Wife of the Rev. Samuel Newell,
Missionary to India.* 1793–1812. New York: American Tract Society, 1813.

Pierce, William Leigh. *The Year: A Poem, in Three Cantoes.* Published by David Longworth at the Shakespeare-Gallery, 1813.

Proceedings of the Fifth Triennial Meeting of the Baptist General Convention. Boston:
Lincoln & Edmands, 1826.

*Proceedings of the First Annual Meeting of the Baptist State Convention of North Carolina,
Rogers Cross Road Meeting House, April 15–18, 1831.* New Bern: John I. Pasteur,
1831.

*Proceedings of the General Convention of the Baptist Denomination in the United States, at
Their First Triennial Meeting, Held in Philadelphia from the 7th to the 14th of May,
1817,* Philadelphia, 1817.

Ruggles Collection, MS 2132/002–008–1:11, Ruggles Collection, The George
Washington Univ.

Samuel and Sarah Wait Papers, Z. Smith Reynolds Library Special Collections and
Archives, Wake Forest Univ., Winston-Salem, NC, USA.

"Samuel Wait Diary New Bern, NC." Samuel and Sarah Wait Papers, Z. Smith
Reynolds Library Special Collections and Archives, Wake Forest Univ., Winston-Salem, NC, USA.

Samuel Whitcomb Papers, 1818–1879, Massachusetts Historical Society, Boston, MA.

"The Second Book of Records of the Church of Christ of the Baptist Order In the
Township of Brandon, State of Vermont May 26th AD 1791." Private Collection, Brandon Baptist Church Brandon, Vermont, 1791–1820.

Sewell, Thomas. *An Address Delivered Before the Washington City Temperance Society,
November 15, 1830.* Washington, DC: The Society, 1830.

Sharp, Daniel. "Review: Counsels and Cautions The Substance of an Address Read
before the Conference of Baptist Ministers in Massachusetts, at Their Annual
Meeting in Boston, May 27, 1835." *American Baptist Magazine,* November 1835.

Spring, Gardiner. *Memoirs of The Rev. Samuel J. Mills, Late Missionary to the South
Western Section of the United States, and Agent of the American Colonization Society,
Deputed to Explore the Coast of Africa.* New York: New-York Evangelical Mission-
ary Society, 1820.

State of Vermont. Vermont Vital Records through 1870. Vermont, Vital Records, 1720–1908, New England Historic Genealogical Society, Boston, Massachusetts.

The Staughton Collection, April 1795, Univ. Archives, Special Collections Research Center, Gelman Library, The George Washington Univ.

Taylor, James Barnett. *Memoir of Rev. Luther Rice, One of the First American Missionaries to the East.* Baltimore: Armstrong and Berry, 1840.

Taylor, John. "Thoughts on Missions." Franklin County, TN, 1819. http://baptiststudiesonline.com/wp-content/uploads/2007/02/thoughts-on-missions.pdf.

"Third Book of Records of the Church of Christ of the Baptist Order In Brandon, State of Vermont May 27 1796." Private Collection. Brandon Baptist Church Brandon, Vermont, 1791–1820.

"To the Editor of the People's Advocate," *Boston Masonic Mirror.* Boston: Moore and Sevey, 1830–1834.

Torrey, Jesse, and Wendell Phillips. *A Portraiture of Domestic Slavery, in the United States: With Reflections on the Practicability of Restoring the Moral Rights of the Slave, without Impairing the Legal Privileges of the Possessor; and a Project of a Colonial Asylum for Free Persons of Colour: Including Memoirs of Facts on the Interior Traffic in Slaves, and on Kidnapping. Illustrated with Engravings.* Philadelphia: self-published; John Bioren, Printer, 1817.

Vermont Baptist Association. *Minutes of the Vermont Baptist Association, Held at . . . Monkton, October . . . 1812 with the Circular and Corresponding Letter.* Rutland, VT: Printed by W. Fay, 1812.

Vermont Baptist Association. *Minutes of the Vermont Baptist Association, Held in Brandon, October . . . 1814: With Their Circular and Corresponding Letter.* Early American Imprints. Second Series, No. 30789. Rutland, VT: Printed by Fay & Davison, 1814.

"Washington, Adams and Jefferson, Raphaelle Peale." *Poulson's American Daily Advertiser.* December 5, 1804. SQN: 104740DBCA256AA2.

"Washington's Lost Gift." *New York Times,* December 26, 1897, Part Two Page 11.

"YOUNG LADIES' ACADEMY." *Newbern Spectator and Literary Journal* I, no. 7 (September 20, 1828): sec. 2.

Secondary Sources

"Anthony Holmead, I (1724–1802)—Find A Grave . . ." Accessed December 24, 2018. https://www.findagrave.com/memorial/142593714/anthony-holmead.

Apel, Thomas A. *Feverish Bodies, Enlightened Minds: Science and the Yellow Fever Controversy in the Early American Republic.* Stanford: Stanford Univ. Press, 2016.

Appleby, Joyce. *Inheriting the Revolution: The First Generation of Americans.* New edition. Cambridge, MA: Belknap Press, 2001.

Barnette, Elizabeth Lumpkin. "Sarah Conant Merriam Wait." Unpublished notes written by Sally Wait's great-great-granddaughter in the author's possession, n.d.

Bishir, Catherine W. *Crafting Lives: African American Artisans in New Bern, North Carolina, 1770–1900:* Chapel Hill: UNC Press Books, 2013.

Brekus, Catherine A. *Sarah Osborn's World: The Rise of Evangelical Christianity in Early America, New Directions in Narrative History.* New Haven: Yale Univ. Press, 2013.

Brewer, John B. *North Carolina Baptist Historical Papers, Life of Samuel Wait, D.D.* Vol. 1. Henderson: North Carolina Baptist Historical Society, 1896.

Brumberg, Joan Jacobs. *Mission for Life: The Story of the Family of Adoniram Judson.* New York: New York Univ. Press, 1984.

Bryan, John M. *Robert Mills: America's First Architect.* Princeton: Princeton Architectural Press, 2001.

Buckman, David Lear. *Old Steamboat Days on the Hudson River: Tables and Reminiscences of the Stirring Times That Followed the Introduction of Steam Navigation.* New York: Grafton Press, 1907.

Bullock, Steven C. *Revolutionary Brotherhood: Freemasonry and the Transformation of the American Social Order, 1730–1840.* Second edition. Omohundro Institute and The Univ. of North Carolina Press, 1998.

Bunkers, Suzanne L., and Cynthia Anne Huff. *Inscribing the Daily: Critical Essays on Women's Diaries,* Amherst: Univ. of Massachusetts Press, 1996.

Canady, Andrew. *A Place of Its Time: The Origin and History of Wake Forest Institute.* Unpublished Manuscript in Author's Possession, 2019.

———. *The College, the Town, and Samuel Wait.* Unpublished Manuscript in Author's Possession, 2020.

Cecelski, David S. *The Waterman's Song: Slavery and Freedom in Maritime North Carolina.* New edition. Chapel Hill: The Univ. of North Carolina Press, 2001.

Cook, Edna Avery. *"In the Beginning—Baptists"!: History of the First Baptist Church, New Bern, North Carolina, 1809–1984.* New Bern: 1984.

Davis, John. "Eastman Johnson's Negro Life at the South and Urban Slavery in Washington, D.C." *The Art Bulletin* 80, no. 1 (1998): 67–92.

Eustace, Nicole. "'The Cornerstone of a Copious Work': Love and Power in Eighteenth-Century Courtship." *Journal of Social History* 34, no. 3 (2001): 517–46.

Forbes-Lindsay, Charles Harcourt Ainslie. *Washington, the City and the Seat of Government.* Philadelphia: J. C. Winston Company, 1908.

Freeman, Curtis W., James Wm. Jr. McClendon, and C. Rosalee Velloso da Silva. *Baptist Roots: A Reader in the Theology of a Christian People.* Valley Forge: Judson Press, 1999.

Freeman, Joanne B. *The Field of Blood: Violence in Congress and the Road to Civil War.* First edition. New York: Farrar, Straus and Giroux, 2018.

"Freeman, Ralf | NCpedia." Accessed January 17, 2019. https://www.ncpedia .org/biography/freeman-ralf.

Formisano, Ronald P., and Kathleen Smith Kutolowiski. "Antimasonry and Masonry: The Genesis of Protest, 1826–1827." *American Quarterly* 29, no. 2 (Summer 1977).

Foster, Charles I. *An Errand of Mercy: The Evangelical United Front 1790–1837.* Chapel Hill: The Univ. of North Carolina Press, 1960.

Gay, Leon S. *Brandon, Vermont: A History of the Town.* Brandon: Town of Brandon, 1961.

Hand, Bill. *A Walking Guide to North Carolina's Historic New Bern.* Charleston: The History Press, 2007.

Harris, Gordon. "The Body Snatcher of Chebacco Parish." *Historic Ipswich* (blog), March 19, 2014. https://historicipswich.org/2014/03/18/the-body-snatcher-of-chebacco-parish/.

Hatch, Nathan O. *The Democratization of American Christianity.* New Haven: Yale Univ. Press, 1989.

Hayden, Roger. "William Staughton: Baptist Educator and Missionary Advocate." *Foundations* 10, no. 1 (January 1967): 19–35.

Hemenway, Abby Maria. *The History of Rutland County, Vermont: Civil, Ecclesiastical, Biographical and Military.* White River Paper Company, 1882.

Hemenway, Abby Maria, and Carrie Elizabeth Hemenway Page. *The Vermont Historical Gazetteer: A Magazine, Embracing a History of Each Town, Civil, Ecclesiastical, Biographical and Military.* Claremont: Claremont Manufacturing Company, 1877.

Howell, George Rogers. *Bi-Centennial History of Albany: History of the County of Albany, N.Y., from 1609 to 1886.* New York: W. W. Munsell & Company, 1886.

Irons, Charles F. *The Origins of Proslavery in Christianity.* Chapel Hill: UNC Press Books, 2008.

Jaffee, David. *A New Nation of Goods: The Material Culture of Early America.* Philadelphia: Univ. of Pennsylvania Press, 2010.

"Jefferson Portrait by Raphaelle Peale (Silhouette)." Accessed July 4, 2018. https://www.monticello.org/site/research-and-collections/jefferson-portrait-raphaelle-peale-silhouette.

Johnson, Matt. "Sarah Waits Journal," email, April 2, 2019.

Kayser, Elmer Louis. *Bricks without Straw: The Evolution of George Washington University.* New York: Appleton-Century-Crofts, 1970.

Kelley, Mary. "'Pen and Ink Communion': Evangelical Reading and Writing in Antebellum America." *The New England Quarterly* 84, no. 4 (2011): 555–87.

Kenslea, Timothy. *The Sedgwicks in Love: Courtship, Engagement, and Marriage in the Early Republic.* First edition, first printing edition. Boston: Northeastern, 2006.

Kielbowicz, Richard B. "A History of Mail Classification and Its Underlying Policies and Purposes." Postal Regulatory Commission, July 17, 1995. Prepared for the Postal Rate Commission's Mail Reclassification Proceeding, MC95–1.

Larkin, Jack. *The Reshaping of Everyday Life: 1790–1840.* Reprint edition. New York: Harper Perennial, 1989.

Lehman, J. David. "'The Most Disastrous and Never-to-Be-Forgotten Year': The Panic of 1819 in Philadelphia." *Pennsylvania Legacies* 11, no. 1 (2011): 6–11.

Leonard, Bill. *Baptist Ways: A History.* Valley Forge: Judson Press, 2003.

Leonard, Bill. *A Sense of the Heart: Christian Religious Experience in the United States.* Nashville: Abingdon Press, 2014.

Leonard, Bill (Bill J.). "'Wild and Romantic in the Extreme': Ann Hasseltine Judson, (Her Husband), and a Duty to Go to the 'Distant and Benighted Heathen.'" *American Baptist Quarterly* 32, no. 1 (2013): 74–95.

Lewis, Jan. "The Republican Wife: Virtue and Seduction in the Early Republic." *The William and Mary Quarterly* 44, no. 4 (1987): 689–721.

Lockridge, Kenneth A. *On the Sources of Patriarchal Rage: The Commonplace Books of William Byrd and Thomas Jefferson and the Gendering of Power in the Eighteenth Century.* New York: New York Univ. Press, c. 1992.

Luxon, Thomas H. *Single Imperfection: Milton, Marriage and Friendship.* Pittsburgh: Duquesne, 2005.

Lyerly, Cynthia Lynn. *Methodism and the Southern Mind, 1770–1810.* First edition. New York: Oxford Univ. Press, 2006.

Marshall, Megan. *The Peabody Sisters: Three Women Who Ignited American Romanticism.* New York: Houghton Mifflin Harcourt, 2005.

McBeth, H. Leon, William L. Lumpkin, Carolyn DeArmond Blevins, Norman H. Letsinger, Carolyn Weatherford Crumpler, Helen Emery Falls, Catherine B. Allen, et al. *No Longer Ignored: A Collection of Articles on Baptist Women.* Baptist History and Heritage Society, 2007.

Miller, Lillian, Mr. Sidney Hart, Mr. David C. Ward, Lauren E. Brown, Sara C. Hale, and Leslie K. Reinhardt, eds. *The Selected Papers of Charles Willson Peale and His Family: Volume 5.* New Haven: Yale Univ. Press, 2000.

Moreshead, Ashley. "'Beyond All Ambitious Motives' Missionary Memoirs and the Cultivation of Early American Evangelical Heroines." *Journal of the Early Republic* 38, no. 1 (Spring 2018).

———. "The Seed of the Missionary Spirit: Foreign Missions, Print Culture, and the Evangelical Identity in the Early American Republic." PhD diss., Univ. of Delaware, 2015. http://udspace.udel.edu/handle/19716/17172.

Morris, Charles Edward. "Panic and Reprisal: Reaction in North Carolina to the Nat Turner Insurrection." North Carolina State Univ., 1979.

Opal, J. M. *Beyond the Farm: National Ambitions in Rural America.* Philadelphia: Univ. of Pennsylvania Press, 2008.

Partridge, George. *History of the Town of Bellingham, 1719–1919.* Bellingham, MA: Town of Bellingham, 1919.

Paschal, George Washington. *History of Wake Forest College.* Wake Forest: Wake Forest College, 1935.

Rockman, Seth, and Cathy Matson. *Scraping By: Wage Labor, Slavery, and Survival in Early Baltimore.* First edition. Baltimore: The Johns Hopkins Univ. Press, 2009.

Rothman, Ellen K. *Hands and Hearts: A History of Courtship in America.* New York: Basic Books, Inc., 1984.

Rothwell, Andrew. *The History of the Baptist Institutions of Washington City.* Washington, DC: W. Ballantyne, 1867.

Scott, Donald M. *From Office to Profession: The New England Ministry, 1750–1850.* Philadelphia: Univ. of Pennsylvania Press, 1978.

"Seeking Abraham: A Report of Furman University's Office of the Provost and Task Force on Slavery and Justice." Greenville: Furman Univ., 2018.

Sellars, Charles. *The Market Revolution: Jacksonian America 1815–1846.* New York: Oxford Univ. Press, 1991.

Shultz, Suzanne M. *Body Snatching: The Robbing of Graves for the Education of Physicians in Early Nineteenth Century America.* McFarland, 2005.

Sirick, Melissa. "Sophia Woodhouse's Grass Bonnets." *Connecticut Explored,* March 30, 2016. https://www.ctexplored.org/sophia-woodhouses-grass -bonnets/.

Smith, H. P., and W. S. Rann, eds. *History of Rutland County Vermont.* Syracuse: D. Mason & Co., 1886.

Smith, John Murphy, and L. C. (Lachlan Cumming) Vass. *The History of First Presbyterian Church of New Bern, North Carolina, 1886–1987.* New Bern: Griffin & Tilghman Printers, 1988.

Spencer, Rev. David. *The Early Baptists of Philadelphia.* Philadelphia: William Syckelmoore, 1877.

Stockbridge, John Calvin, and Baron Stow. *The Model Pastor: A Memoir of the Life and Correspondence of Rev. Baron Stow, Late Pastor of the Rowe Street Baptist Church, Boston.* Boston: Lee and Shepard; New York: Lee, Shepard and Dillingham, 1871.

Straub, Jean S. "Benjamin Rush's Views of Women's Education." *Pennsylvania History: A Journal of Mid-Atlantic Studies* 34, no. 2 (1967): 147–57.

Sweet, Leonard I. *The Minister's Wife: Her Role in Nineteenth-Century American Evangelicalism.* First edition. Philadelphia: Temple Univ. Press, 1983.

Thompson, Zadock. *History of Vermont, Natural, Civil and Statistical, in Three Parts, with an Appendix. 1853.* Burlington: self-published, 1853.

Tyler, Mary Palmer. *Grandmother Tyler's Book: The Recollections of Mary Palmer Tyler (Mrs. Royall Tyler) 1775–1866.* G. P. Putnam, 1925.

Ulrich, Laurel Thatcher. *A Midwife's Tale: The Life of Martha Ballard, Based on Her Diary, 1785–1812.* First edition. New York: Knopf, 1990.

——. "Runaway Wives, 1830–1860." *Journal of Mormon History* 42, no. 2 (April 2016).

——. *The Age of Homespun: Objects and Stories in the Creation of an American Myth.* First edition. New York: Alfred A. Knopf, 2001.

Vowell, Sarah. *Lafayette in the Somewhat United States.* First edition. New York: Riverhead Books, 2015.

Wade, Mary D. "Industries in Sharon." *Sharon, Massachusetts—A History.* Boston: Blue Mustang Press, 2005.

Walker, Rachel. "'The Day Which Will Fix My Future Destiny': Courtship, Marriage, and the Companionate Ideal in Early Republican America." *History Matters* (May 2010): 85–112.

Watson, John F., and Hazard, Willis P. *Annals of Philadelphia and Pennsylvania in the Olden Time; Being a Collection of Memoirs, Anecdotes, and Incidents of the City and Its*

Inhabitants and of the Earliest Settlements of the Island That Is Part of Pennsylvania. Vol. 3. 3 vols. Edwin S. Stuart, 1899.

Wehtje, Myron F. "Charles Willson Peale and His Temple." *Pennsylvania History: A Journal of Mid-Atlantic Studies* 36, no. 2 (April 1969): 161–73.

Wermuth, Thomas S. "New York Farmers and the Market Revolution: Economic Behavior in the Mid-Hudson Valley, 1780–1830." *Journal of Social History* 32, no. 1 (Autumn, 1988): 17.

Whitford, John D, Col., and Howard Rawls. *The Home Story of a Walking Stick: The Early History of the "Biblical Recorder" and Baptist Church at New Bern, N.C.* Raleigh: North Carolina State Archives, 1965.

Wilkinson, Lucille Warfield. "Early Baptists in Washington, DC." *Records of the Columbia Historical Society, Washington, DC* (1928): 211–68.

Wood, Gordon S. *Empire of Liberty: A History of the Early Republic, 1789–1815.* Reprint edition. Oxford: Oxford Univ. Press, 2011.

Yellin, Jean Fagan. *Harriet Jacobs: A Life.* New York: Civitas Books, 2005.

Young, James Sterling. *The Washington Community, 1800–1828.* New York and London: Columbia Univ. Press, 1966.

INDEX

Page numbers in **bold** refer to illustrations.